Lecture Notes in Computer Science

Edited by G. Goos, J. Hartmanis, and J. van Leeuwen

Springer
Berlin
Heidelberg
New York
Hong Kong
London
Milan
Paris
Tokyo

Markus Schumacher

Security Engineering
with Patterns

Origins, Theoretical Model, and New Applications

 Springer

Series Editors

Gerhard Goos, Karlsruhe University, Germany
Juris Hartmanis, Cornell University, NY, USA
Jan van Leeuwen, Utrecht University, The Netherlands

Author

Markus Schumacher
Darmstadt University of Technology
Department of Computer Science (@ITO)
IT Transfer Office
Wilhelminenstr. 7
64283 Darmstadt
Germany
E-mail: ms@ito.tu-darmstadt.de

Darmstädter Dissertation, Hochschulkennziffer D17

Cataloging-in-Publication Data applied for

A catalog record for this book is available from the Library of Congress.

Bibliographic information published by Die Deutsche Bibliothek
Die Deutsche Bibliothek lists this publication in the Deutsche Nationalbibliografie;
detailed bibliographic data is available in the Internet at <http://dnb.ddb.de>.

CR Subject Classification (1998): D.2.11, D.2, D.4.6, D.4, K.4.4, K.6.5, C.2.0

ISSN 0302-9743
ISBN 3-540-40731-6 Springer-Verlag Berlin Heidelberg New York

Springer-Verlag Berlin Heidelberg New York
a member of BertelsmannSpringer Science+Business Media GmbH

http://www.springer.de

© Springer-Verlag Berlin Heidelberg 2003
Printed in Germany

Typesetting: Camera-ready by author, data conversion by Boller Mediendesign
Printed on acid-free paper   SPIN: 10930700   06/3142   5 4 3 2 1 0

Foreword

Security comes as a second thought, or even a nice-to-have add-on? At least you can get this impression thinking about *when* security is considered in the development of many devices, systems and applications. Have a look at the evolution of cars. In the first place the purpose of a car was to transport you from one location to another. Having solved this somehow, the engineers started to think about safety – especially because vulnerabilities caused severe problems. Some of the "additional" car features were safety belts, ABS and airbags. At least some car manufacturers have seen these as extra features for a long time. This is where I start to be really puzzled. Security as an extra feature? Is it so irrelevant that we can neglect it?

This would support my initial hypothesis – security comes as an afterthought. Considering modern IT networks, IT systems and IT applications, we can see no difference. The primary goal is to enhance functionality and performance but not to mitigate risk. Security and dependability comes later if at all.

In contrast to traditional engineering domains it is, however, very difficult to add security features seamlessly as a new "module." Adding security afterwards is difficult if not impossible. Ad hoc security solutions usually introduce new, unforeseen problems and you suddenly find yourself in a vicious circle.

Somehow new technologies such as Wireless LAN, Internet Telephony or Instant Messaging seem to follow that way. We can identify severe flaws – both in design and implementation – that inevitably lead to severe vulnerabilities. This can't be the right way. We can't always try to catch up with the wily hacker and think about security *after* an incident has occurred.

Based on our experience in teaching, research and development in the areas of digital watermarking, copyright protection in wide-area video-on-demand, firewalls, security in media gateways, vulnerabilities in Internet Telephony, the Darmstadt Hacker Contest and public key infrastructures, I must emphasize: it is time for a new security paradigm. Security must be a mandatory feature, considered from the very first line on the drawing board. Certainly, there is no (and will never be) 100 percent security. Nevertheless, a user should be able to take security for granted, i.e., it should be possible to operate a system with an acceptable residual risk.

A common counterargument is that such a proactive security approach is too expensive. I don't believe this. Certainly, the development process and the resulting product will be more complex. Certainly, developers have to have a broad knowledge in several engineering domains (including security). In the sense of quality of service, we have to determine whether a system works or not. And only a secure system can work as intended. Thus I think that the initial efforts on behalf of security are more than compensated for, as a proactive approach will stop the repair-service behavior observed today.

Recently a very promising solution toward such a way of engineering security has been developed: *Security Patterns* capture proven solutions for recurring security problems in a structured way. Due to an organized peer-review process the quality of such solutions can be taken for granted. As security patterns are best practices that are codified by security experts and refer to related problems, the user can also be sure to proactively solve the overall problem – not only parts, no longer in a repair-service mode.

Dr. Markus Schumacher is already known as the driving force of and a leading worldwide authority on security patterns. In this book he provides a thorough introduction to security patterns. Due to his profound security knowledge he has been able to establish security patterns as a complementary approach for seamless security engineering. Based on his model for security patterns, security novices are now in a position to understand how experts solve problems and can basically act like them.

Once again: Does security come as a second thought? It shouldn't. However, I cannot answer this question once and for all. Nevertheless, security must and will be mandatory for all modern IT systems. Second-class solutions will always be offered and used. Hence, first-class hackers will carry out successful attacks. The earlier we start to treat security as an equivalent requirement with a high priority, the quicker our know-how and skills with seamless security solutions will evolve. This would considerably reduce the residual risk involved in using IT systems in more and more sensitive environments. I believe that this is a feasible approach. We can have secure systems and we have to do it without patchwork – security patterns are a very important step in this direction.

Darmstadt, June 2003   Ralf Steinmetz

Preface

To improve on the unsatisfactory security level we can observe today, we have to close a gap between the theory and the code of security practice. We also have to close a gap in the security knowledge process and make proven solutions available in a suitable way before an incident occurs. This book is considered as a contribution to this problem.

Abstract

We develop a systematic security improvement approach based on the pattern paradigm. *Security Patterns* can be used especially when the people in charge of security have no security expertise or when security aspects are not considered as primary requirements. The basic idea of patterns is to capture expert knowledge in documents with a particular structure. Basically, they contain proven solutions for recurring problems in a given domain.

Using patterns as a means of improving security, we first examine a set of commonly used security techniques. The result is that a pattern-based security approach features many advantages compared to the other approaches, e.g., side-effects can be considered appropriately and the expertise required to use patterns is rather low. Furthermore, patterns can be found at different levels of abstraction and for different life-cycle phases. Thus, they can also be integrated into the regular engineering process serving as a complement to other security techniques. A requirement when using patterns as a security engineering tool is a thorough understanding of security patterns. Thus, we clarify the key concepts of security patterns, define their semantics as well as their syntax, and show how they can be used. This approach is summarized in the following paragraphs.

We introduce the structure of security patterns and their distinguishing features in comparison to traditional patterns in the software domain. In particular, we conclude that the problem statement of security patterns deals with threats and attacks whereas the solution provides the corresponding countermeasures. We also discuss security-related forces and how they are resolved when a particular pattern is applied. Hereby we see that security always has an impact on other, perhaps contradictory requirements. The solution has to balance such forces according to the code of practice. Based on that, we identify basic approaches for capturing security knowledge with patterns.

Having introduced the meaning of security patterns, we derive a theoretical model for them. Hereby we rely on definitions of key security concepts and relations between them, which builds an extensible security core ontology. Based on the definitions of security patterns and their relations, we are in a position to prove that the application of a security pattern leads to a state of security. Specifying the intuitive and commonsense knowledge, we clarify the internals of the security patterns, i.e., the theoretical model contributes to an intersubjective understanding of security patterns within the community. Furthermore, such a model is an important prerequisite for any kind of tool support. The theoretical model defines the syntax of the security patterns and security pattern systems. With this rather loosely structured meta-information model we are, however, able to make the advantages of security patterns usable.

In order to show the conclusiveness of our approach, we develop a prototype of a security pattern search engine. That way we can present new applications of security patterns, e.g., simulating how potential flaws in the implementation of a pattern affects other patterns, or maintaining a security pattern system. This proof of concept shows that our theoretical model makes patterns useful as a security engineering approach. All applications of security patterns described in the thesis are codified with an ontology and can be used via a Web interface.

Acknowledgements

This book captures the results of the most interesting years of my professional career so far. In particular, working for several years for major IT and software companies within an academic environment was an endeavor with a shaping influence. This is the time to thank those who helped and supported me.

I want to thank my supervisor Prof. Dr.-Ing. Ralf Steinmetz. He supported my decision to work on a Ph.D. and gave me the freedom to choose my environment on my own. His continuous support – in good and especially the critical times – helped me to find my own way. His steady monitoring of my progress was also very appreciated and helpful. I also want to thank Prof. Dr. rer. nat. Claudia Eckert for her willingness to be the second reader of my thesis. She gave me valuable feedback during all stages of this document and gave me confidence that it would succeed eventually.

Furthermore, I express my thanks to Prof. Alejandro Buchmann, Ph.D., for the considerable, valuable advice he gave me. He helped me to always remember the human aspect in many situations. In addition, thanks belong to Prof. Dr.-Ing. Peter Kammerer, one of the founders and "old school" (in the best sense) professors of the IT Transfer Office where I worked. It was always nice to have the backing from such competent and nice people.

The feedback of colleagues and friends was also very appreciated. First of all, I want to thank Dr.-Ing. Utz Roedig for discussing and shaping core ideas of my pattern approach in the context of security for two years. Furthermore, thanks go to Dr.-Ing. Felix Gärtner. The discussions with him were a valuable exchange between the theory (him) and the code of practice (me). He also was the first proofreader of my thesis and gave me motivation for the last mile. I also want to thank Dr.-Ing. Roger Kilian-Kehr who provided feedback on the essential chapters. In addition, the ontology-related meetings with Andreas Faatz were very illuminating. Another thank you to Ralf Ackermann who was the first person to listen to my ideas in Venice.

I had (and have) also a very pleasant time with the guys of the steadily growing security pattern community. Thanks go to Ben Elsinga for giving me the trigger to initiate our thriving movement and for telling countless jokes and riddles at Kloster Irsee. Accordingly, I have to thank Aaldert Hofmann for driving the pattern stuff forward. Last, but not least, I'm happy to have had the chance to work/talk/write with Prof. Eduardo Fernandez, Duane Hybertson and Sasha Romanosky. Generally, I'm glad to have joined the pattern community as far as I know it – everyone should participate in a *PLoP conference at least once in his/her life.

I also won't underestimate the importance of a pleasant working environment. Thus, thanks go to the ITO crew who accompanied me through the last few years: Lars Brückner, Peer Hasselmeyer, Marios Padelis, Jan Steffan and Marco Voss. A joint "thank you" goes to my colleagues at the Database and Distributed Systems Group (DVS) and the Multimedia Communications (KOM) people.

Fundamental support (for the last 30 years) came from my parents. They always gave me the freedom to realize myself. I guess that I owe them the better parts of my personality. Very, very special thanks go to my sister Heike. Besides lowering many educational hurdles for me, she edited the manuscript of this thesis.

I wish to express my biggest gratitude to Anette Mai – my partner and best friend. Thank you for all the love, faith and support you gave me throughout the last decade. I'll never forget this! My family and my friends, both at home and at work, helped me to keep my feet on the ground and to maintain a satisfying life.

Darmstadt, June 2003   Markus Schumacher

Contents

1. Introduction

"If anything can go wrong, it will."

MURPHY'S LAW

"Murphy's law is wrong."

BOB COLWELL

1.1 Motivation

Since the breakthrough of the Internet as virtual backbone for electronic commerce and similar applications, security is recognized as an elementary requirement. Before we step into this book we briefly want to discuss what security in the context of a more and more networked world means and why anyone, not only from the academic world, but also from industries, should pay attention to it.

Commonly used definitions of security can be found in dictionaries. For example the Oxford Advanced Learner's Dictionary defines security as "freedom or protection from danger or worry". A look-up in *WordNet*, a database that allows the user to explore a dictionary on the basis of semantics revealed that security is "the state of being free from danger or injury". Although these are rather general definitions, they cover two important aspects of security that can be adapted to the world of computers:

1. *Danger.* Security is a condition of safety from threats and any threatening event can lead to worry. Neglecting natural threats to computers such as earthquakes or fire, usually accidental and intentional threats to information systems are distinguished. The former means that for example a legitimate user accidently deleted a file. The latter means deliberate actions intended to misuse a computer. Typically such actions are called attacks. Note that if you don't know what threats could be posed against your systems, you perceive false security: not knowing a threat doesn't mean that there is no threat.

M. Schumacher: Security Engineering with Patterns, LNCS 2754, pp. 1-9, 2003.
© Springer-Verlag Berlin Heidelberg 2003

2. *Protection.* Security is achieved by a set of safeguards and countermeasures applied to maintain the condition of being safe from threats. Here we can basically distinguish between actions that prevent, detect or react to threatening events. The overall question is what happens if a specific measure to protect a system will be omitted? In that case you implicitly express that a threat will not lead to worry, i.e. you are going to accept such a risk.

Using these definitions would mean if we have countermeasures against each threat, we would achieve security. The exponential growth of the number of incident shows, however, that we still need quite some time and effort to reach sufficient security levels in the digital world (see figure 1.1 which shows the number of incidents reported to the international CERT/CC [38]).

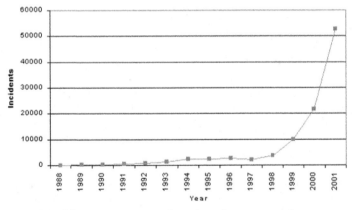

Figure 1.1. CERT/CC statistics: number of incidents reported.

We briefly examine some reasons for this menacing situation in the following. We do this by a comparison of the "traditional" (technical) world and the new digital realm. In the traditional world the threats are well-known, typically we know the likelihood how often they occur, we apply countermeasures and can accept the remaining risk accordingly. For uncertain cases there are insurances which cover the loss in case of a damage. As technicians, engineers and users can rely on hundreds of years of experience, we can rely on traditional technologies. Nevertheless, errors and accidents always occur. In fact such situations are a chance for improvement. Ideally, "traditional" engineers go through a certain learning process: making errors, learning from them, improve the technology and using the better version. In the digital world such a learning process has not yet been established in a sufficient way, especially when we consider the security of today's IT landscape. We discuss this by a brief analysis of two typical examples:

Point-to-Point Tunneling Protocol. The Point-to-Point Tunneling Protocol (PPTP) as specified in RFC 2637 is considered to be secure. During the implementation for the Windows NT platform some basic mistakes were made though [192]. The establishment of an encrypted link requires a shared secret between both Virtual Private Networks (VPN) endpoints. Unfortunately, the chosen shared secret was based on the Windows password scheme which is known to be breakable and insecure. Even worse, this secret was the basis for both authentication and encryption of the tunnel. As a consequence, the overall implementation of PPTP was insecure and the endpoints could be attacked as well.

Melissa Macro Virus & Co. In March 1999, the *Melissa* macro virus within a Microsoft Word document having been distributed via the email program Microsoft Outlook, caused severe damage (about 80 million dollars). The reason was that Microsoft Word was able to (mis)use the e-mail interface of Microsoft Outlook. In March 2000, the *Love Letter* virus caused a damage of 10 billion dollars. This virus used almost the same methods as the first one, i.e. the e-mail functions of Microsoft Outlook could be used to spread all around the world.

Both scenarios have one thing in common: the reason for the vulnerability can be traced back to well-known problems. One should have known that a user-selected password is not a good starting point for a VPN system. Furthermore such a "secret" must not be shared for both authentication and encryption. As this key was initially transmitted in plain-text, the overall implementation was doomed to failure from the very beginning. On the other hand we had the Melissa incident and should have learned. We haven't. Although the newer attacks were more sophisticated in so far as they social-engineered the user (hiding a malicious script as a apparently harmless text file) we could observe several viruses and worms which exploited similar principles of attack since then.

Often, security mechanisms are not installed or turned off because they are too expensive or affect efficiency. Thus, it might be sometimes reasonable to have "insecure" systems. However, this obviously doesn't hold for the above examples. We conclude that there is obviously no mechanism or process established which enables us to learn from errors which are made over and over again (in fact there are many more examples as discussed before). Thus, we understand this book as a step toward such a learning process. We show a way how to capture such knowledge and make it available to both security professionals and novices.

1.2 Problem Statement

As the core of the problem we see two aspects. First, security is less a technical but human problem. Second, security is often considered as an afterthought. We will sketch out these statements in the following.

One of the quotes at the beginning says that Murphy's law is wrong. Related to the digital world this means that security breaches are not necessarily random accidents. Both professionals and novices are in a situation where errors will inevitably occur (as in the traditional world): the IT world is complex, dynamic, intransparent. In such scenarios it is difficult to consider all side-effects and time-dependencies appropriately. Although solutions for well-known problems should be available, many approaches for security improvement seem to be alien concepts to many software practitioners and users: they are not applied in a satisfying way - if at all.

The other part of the problem is that security is not well integrated in regular engineering and work processes. Unfortunately, security becomes often important after an incident, i.e. when it is basically too late. However, security should be considered at the early stages of the life-cycle of any distributed software application or system. Especially during the design of a system it is important to avoid conceptual errors as it is very difficult (and expensive) to fix such problems in a system that has been developed without security in mind.

As a consequence a solution to these problems should strive for an appropriate consideration of the human factor as well as for a better integration of "security engineering" with other (software) engineering domains.

Capturing expert-knowledge and providing proven solutions for recurring problems is the basic idea of software (design) patterns. The pattern paradigm is an established concept in the software community and a frequently used tool in software engineering. Our approach is to apply patterns to security problems as described before. Patterns are an approach to bring expert knowledge to novices making security concepts and techniques less alien. As such they address the human factor. Patterns dedicated to security could also contribute to a better integration of security into the overall life-cycle of a system.

1.3 Solution

In this book we develop an approach for improving security which builds up on an intuitively comprehensive and understandable notion of security. Hereby, the focus is more on prevention rather than the "repair-service" approach we can observe today. The key idea is to apply the the idea of (design) patterns which are an established software development technique in order to improve security. This is illustrated in the following.

Toward Security Engineering with Patterns. In fact, patterns are loosely structured documents which capture the knowledge of domain experts. Thus, they should help to improve the skills of novices which use them. Nevertheless, patterns are useful for both parties: professionals can apply our pattern-based approach for reference purposes and for naming and handling problems more efficiently. As patterns show relations to other patterns, a hierarchy is built which guarantees a sense of complete coverage of the problem space if certain boundary conditions hold. Thus, novices can solve problems in a structured way, without missing side-effects and being sure that no piece of available expert knowledge has been missed. Achieving this we have to examine how we can improve security with patterns efficiently. This means to make the added values of security patterns as discussed above available. In particular, we want to achieve a sufficient level of *assurance* that patterns in fact contribute to an increased security level. Thereby, we have to consider the following questions:

- What are the distinguishing properties of security patterns?
- How can we make use of these properties?
- How can a user benefit from a security approach based on patterns?
- What level of security can be achieved with patterns?

Furthermore, there is a requirement that must be met: the patterns should remain prose and therefore not be touched as a written document. On the one hand it would be too difficult to rewrite and adapt all patterns according to our approach. On the other hand we observed that the community would not accept a strict template for patterns as this would unnecessarily limit the freedom of pattern authors. Thus, our solution is based on a compromise: we map and assign a syntactical and semantical structure to the actual pattern documents. We will show that this is sufficient to overcome the drawbacks of using today's security patterns and to keep the patterns as they are. Namely, there are no sophisticated search and retrieval capabilities for such documents. As a consequence the benefits of security patterns as outlined above cannot be used efficiently. The core contributions of our pattern-based security improvement approach are introduced in the following.

Understanding Security Patterns. We provide *key definitions* of what security patterns are. Hereby, we discuss their origin, how they evolved, introduce the core elements of security patterns and show how they can be found and documented. We also provide some examples to illustrate the idea of security patterns. That way, we describe the *semantics* of security patterns.

Making Security Knowledge accessible. A central part of this book is our theoretical model for security patterns which defines the core concepts and relations of security patterns. This *syntactical model* helps to clarify the properties of security patterns. In particular, the approach of achieving security with patterns can be derived from this. As patterns are distributed all over the world, it is necessary to make them available to users. We can use our model to assign meta-information to these documents (i.e. we don't need to modify the documents themselves) and can make their properties usable.

Representing and Processing Security Patterns. The bridge between human-readable and computer-processable knowledge is realized with a *security core ontology* which contains practicable and intuitively understandable definitions of key security concepts and relations between them.

Security Engineering with Patterns. Accordingly, we can realize a "security pattern search engine" that offers improved search and retrieval capabilities for security patterns. As proof of concept we show several *new applications of security patterns.*

This book follows the pattern paradigm itself as it shows that we don't always need a completely new approach for solving security problems in a convenient way. Instead, it is a worthwhile endeavor to combine, extend and apply proven techniques in a new way.

1.4 Unaddressed Related Issues

Security is related to the more general domain of dependability [144]. Dependability is a quality that describes the trustworthiness of a system. Thereby, security is considered as a sub-characteristic at the same level as availability, reliability and safety. Hereby, availability addresses dependability regarding the readiness for usage, reliability covers dependability with respect to the continuity of a service, and safety is about dependability with respect to the avoidance of catastrophic events. As such there is a natural relation to these domains and there are sometimes fuzzy boundaries [95]: on the one hand safety can require security when authorized access can result in an accident that affects human lives or the environment. On the other hand, security is a part of safety when unauthorized access is perceived as an accident. There are several contributions which deal with security in such an integrated context (see for example [40, 160]). However, a closer consideration of this related areas is out of scope of this book.

Furthermore, we exclude errors which occur during codifying a piece of software. Often, this leads to buffer overflows which are a known phenomenon since the Morris Worm incident. There are several known solutions to this problem (e.g. using additional libraries [13] or source code scanners [232]). The focus of this book is, however, on problems at the architectural and design level.

Besides, we don't provide a proposal for a general, integrated process where security is considered at all life-cycle phases. However, our pattern-based approach would support such a process as security patterns integrate security and system/software engineering.

1.5 Structural Overview

The organization of this book is outlined in the following. Beside the sequential order of the chapters some dependencies between the individual chapters are indicated as dashed arrows in Figure 1.2. Logically, the document consists of three parts which follow the structure of a pattern: we have a context which explains the background, a problem statement and a part which contains the solution.

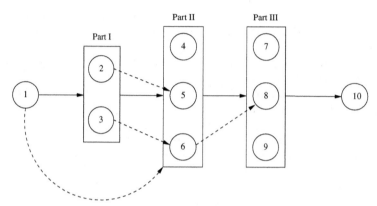

Figure 1.2. Dependencies between chapters.

Part I: Context. The first part of the book provides some background information regarding patterns and ontologies as both paradigms play an important role for the solution provided in this book. If the reader is familiar with patterns or ontologies, the Chapter 2 and 3 can be *skipped*.

- *Chapter 2:* We give an introduction to patterns in software development. First, we briefly discuss how patterns evolved from the domain of urban planning to the world of software. Then we introduce the basic concepts of patterns and describe different kinds of pattern collections. This is important as patterns are usually related to other patterns. After that we describe some approaches for classifying patterns which is required as soon as a certain number of patterns is available. Furthermore, we outline important elements of the community process for writing patterns. In addition we refer to concepts of cognitive psychology in order to show how patterns can be used solving problems.
- *Chapter 3:* Ontologies as used in computer science can be applied to formalize knowledge domains. We show how such an ontology could basically fit into an overall security knowledge process. Then we introduce the core idea of representing knowledge with ontologies. After that we look at the development of ontologies. This includes typical criteria which should be

met during ontology design, several methodologies for the development, and a set of representative representation languages. Finally, we discuss certain tools for such a "knowledge engineering".

Part II: Problem. In the second part we examine the problem statement introduced before in more detail.

- *Chapter 4:* We discuss why security is not only a technical but a human problem. We do this by examining two new application types where basically known errors are repeated in a new domain: we discuss IP Telephony and Instant Messaging. Afterwards, we refer to some general psychological insights which can be transferred to the computing area and explain why security fails today.
- *Chapter 5:* Assuming that "security engineering" is not integrated very well with other engineering domains we compare selected approaches for security improvement. We introduce a simple framework for classifying such "security improvement artifacts". Finally, we can show that a pattern-based approach could generally be applied as a security tool. Based on our framework we can identify the limitations on this matter. Together with the results of the previous Chapter this draws up the requirements for the solution presented in Part III.
- *Chapter 6:* We also discuss a security core ontology that is on the one hand useful to clarify the security terminology we use throughout this document. On the other hand we can use such an ontology in order to formalize security patterns later. The ontology is the result of a collaborative approach to ontology design, i.e. we worked together with a couple of experts in order to improve the definitions iteratively.

Part III: Solution. In part three we present the solution for the problems identified in the chapters before.

- *Chapter 7:* Then we introduce the foundations of security patterns, i.e. what are the distinguishing aspects considering the "traditional" patterns. We describe how security patterns evolved, introduce a template for security patterns, discuss security-related forces and how we are going to organize these patterns. The other part of this Chapter deals with mining security patterns from security information providers as well as security standards.
- *Chapter 8:* The central element of this book is our theoretical model for security patterns which is needed in order to make the added values of security patterns available to its users. We introduce our formalization approach, provide formal definitions of the core elements of security patterns and relations between them. Based on that we can draw up the local criteria "coverage" which says whether a set of security patterns contains countermeasures for all occurring threats and attacks. Then we can prove that such a security pattern system is secure according to our definition.

– *Chapter 9:* Our theoretical model is also a prerequisite for the implementation of a security patterns search engine which should deliver deterministic results. As a proof-of-concept we discuss certain experiments we conducted with this prototype. Our results show that security patterns are in fact a suitable tool for security improvement.

Chapter 10 summarizes and concludes this book. If available, the related work is discussed separately in each chapter. The appendices contain additional background material. In particular, Appendix A presents selected information sources which have been observed while looking for case studies for Chapter 4. Furthermore, some more examples are outlined. We also present selected security patterns together with the corresponding meta-information in Appendix B. Regarding the design of the core security ontology in Chapter 6, we provide the identified competence questions, the results of the two improvement iterations and selected examples of the ontology, rules and queries in Appendix C. The latter should be seen as a complement for the examples provided in Chapter 9. In Appendix D we provide a brief introduction into F-Logic as representation language of the knowledge base and queries which are discussed by examples in Chapter 9. Finally, Appendix E outlines occasions where the author could gather and apply his security expertise.

2. Patterns in Software Development

> I think you have to deal with the
> confused situation that we're
> faced by seizing on the glimpses
> and particles of life, seizing on
> them and holding them and
> trying to make a pattern of
> them. In other words trying to
> put a world back together again
> out of its fragmentary moments.
>
> ARCHIBALD MACLEISH

2.1 Introduction

Patterns are a literary form of a problem-solving discipline that has its roots
in a design movement of the same name in contemporary architecture, literate
programming, and basically the documentation of best practices and lessons
learned. Formally codifying these solutions and their relationships successfully captures the body of knowledge which defines our understanding of best
practices that meet the needs of users in a particular problem domain. The
primary focus is not so much on technology but rather on creating a culture
to document and support sound engineering and design.

Today the pattern approach is applied to different problem domains such
as Human Computer Interaction (HCI) or Teaching and Learning. In the
following we provide a general introduction of basic concepts and terms of
patterns. More detailed essays on patterns were, for instance, written by
Appleton and Lea [12, 146].

The outline of this chapter is as follows: in the next section we outline the
rather young history of software-related patterns. Afterwards, we introduce
basic software pattern concepts in Section 2.3. As patterns typically show
interactions with other patterns, we discuss different kinds of pattern collections in Section 2.4. It is also important to introduce a classification schema
when the number of patterns increases. Major classification approaches are
discussed in Section 2.5. Then we introduce the community's way of writing

M. Schumacher: Security Engineering with Patterns, LNCS 2754, pp. 11-27, 2003.
© Springer-Verlag Berlin Heidelberg 2003

patterns in Section 2.6. As patterns provide solutions to problems we briefly discuss them in the general context of problem solving that is a discipline from the field of psychology in Section 2.7. Finally, we summarize the results of this Section.

2.2 Pattern History

In the following a brief overview of the history of patterns is given. This outline is based on relevant pattern resources such as [35], [54] and [93].

The original idea of patterns was laid down by the architect Christopher Alexander. The key concepts are laid down in his classical books "The Timeless Way of Building" [5] and "A Pattern Language" [6]. In the context of urban planning and building architecture Alexander and his team identified more than 250 patterns that "are ordered, beginning with the very largest, for regions and towns, then working down through neighborhoods, clusters of buildings, buildings rooms and alcoves, ending finally with details of construction." Furthermore, they identified the context-problem-solution structure of patterns, known as the Alexandrian form.

Ward Cunningham and Kent Beck were the first ones that applied the pattern approach to software development. In 1987, they decided to experiment with a couple of their patterns for the design of user interfaces with Smalltalk during a consulting job. Eventually, staff members of their customers could finish a problematical design with this small collection of patterns. As novices they were suddenly enabled to take advantage of Smalltalk's strengths and to avoid common pitfalls. Encouraged by the results of the experiment they presented their work at the ACM Conference OOPSLA [15]. Since then, both of them continued their work and "have written many more patterns" [35].

Shortly after, James O. Coplien published ,,Advanced C++ Programming Styles and Idioms" [49]. Although the term pattern is not used and the C++ concepts are not written in pattern style, this book contains many valuable C++ best practices at a low layer of abstraction. At the same time Peter Coad had a look at patterns and wrote about them in a 1991 issue of his newsletter and in an article in the Communications of the ACM in 1992 [48].

In 1991 and 1992 Bruce Anderson arranged a workshop at OOPSLA where many key figures of the pattern community met together. At this time Erich Gamma, Richard Helm, Ralph Johnson, and John Vlissides, the Gang of Four (GoF) , worked on another compilation of patterns that was being discussed by the growing pattern community.

The Hillside Group being the leading organization of the pattern community started in August 1993 after a mountain retreat in Colorado which was sponsored by Kent Beck and Grady Booch. Erich Gamma's work was picked up as a basis for the future of patterns in the field of software engineering.

Another workshop, this time explicitly dedicated to patterns, was held at OOPSLA'93 and then in April 1994, the Hillside Group met again to plan the first conference on Pattern Languages of Programs (PLoP) . The same year, nearly 80 people came to Monticello, Illinois, to translate these plans into action. The first PLoP proceedings were published in May 1995 [50].

The GoF finished the work on their patterns and published the textbook "Design Patterns - Elements of reusable Object-Oriented Software" [93] which can thoroughly be called the definitive break-through of the pattern idea. Another cornerstone is the book "Pattern Oriented Software Architecture - A System of Patterns" (known as the POSA book) written by leading practitioners in software development.

Beside, the "traditional" PLoP a couple of other pattern-related conferences were established such as EuroPLoP which took place for the first time in 1996. Similarly to PLoP, such conferences offer a series of writer's workshops where authors can improve their patterns. Additionally, there are discussion groups as well as working groups to dedicated pattern topics. Other pinpoints are dedicated pattern issues such as how to write patterns and pattern languages in general.

The increasing number of pattern conferences emerging all around the world indicates that the pattern community grows steadily. In 2001 Hillside Europe was founded "to promote patterns and pattern-related activities in Europe." Certainly this doesn't mark stagnancy but a constant progress of the success story of software patterns.

2.3 Basic Pattern Concepts

Patterns are structured documents that capture proven solutions for recurring problems. The basic idea is to write down best practices and lessons learned from a given problem domain in a systematic way. Christopher Alexander provided the first definition of a pattern and its structure [5, 6]:

"Each pattern describes a problem which occurs over and over again in our environment, and then describes the core of the solution to that problem ... "

"Each pattern is a three-part rule, which expresses a relation between a certain context, a problem, and a solution."

These definitions do already contain the core concepts of the pattern idea. In order to achieve convenience and clarity, Alexander stated that each pattern should have the same structure. This allows a better comprehension, comparison and usage of patterns. According to [153] *Name, Context, Problem, Forces,* and *Solution* are the mandatory elements of a pattern.

Name. Each pattern has a name. The assignment between name and the pattern are determined according to the conventions of the pattern community. Thereby we can say that a pattern becomes a part of the vocabulary of the pattern community. It is important that the name of a pattern is easy to remember and refer to. A good name should be evocative and give an image what the pattern might be about.

Context. The context is a description of the environment before the pattern is applied. It outlines the preconditions under which the problem and its solution appear. Thus the context shows when and where the pattern will work. Furthermore, the importance of the forces is determined by the context. Often the context is introduced with the help of a scenario.

Problem. Within the given context a non-trivial and recurring problem occurs. "Non-trivial" means that only experts know how to solve the problem. "Recurring" means that it is a typical problem in the given context. The problem statement describes the goals and objectives a pattern wants to reach and what is currently not working. The description of the specific problem that needs to be solved should be kept separate from the constraints on the solution.

Forces. The forces define the kinds of trade-offs that must be considered in the presence of the tension or dissonance they create (e.g. usability vs. security). It should be described how they interact and conflict with one another and the goals that should be achieved.

Solution. This section describes a proven solution of the problem. This means that experts usually solve the problem this way. There has to be consensus between experts and the pattern's author that the solution is really a proven solution. It should have successfully worked at least once and a good solution should address the highest priority forces.

The description of the pattern's solution may indicate guidelines to keep in mind as well as pitfalls to avoid when attempting a concrete implementation of the solution. Sometimes possible variants or specializations of the solution are also described.

Typically a problem can have more than one solution, but the most appropriate solution is uniquely determined by the context in which the problem occurs. As put by Harrison "a single pattern should contain one problem, one context, and one solution" [106].

Related Patterns. Usually, patterns don't exist in isolation, i.e. there are relationships to other patterns. For example, there are other solutions to the same problem in a different context, more general or more specific variations of the pattern, and patterns that solve some problems that arise after the application of the pattern (i.e. in the resulting context). Such relationships provide linkage to subsequent patterns of a collection of patterns.

Other elements may be included, if they make the pattern easier to understand or provide better linkage between the pattern in question and related patterns. Typical examples for these optional pattern elements are described in the remainder of this section.

Examples. Concrete examples illustrate the application of the pattern. Visual examples and analogies can be very illuminating, easy-to-understand examples from well-known environments should be preferred. Some authors prefer to use running examples throughout a set of related patterns.

Resulting Context. When the pattern has been applied, the initial environment has changed. The resulting context describes the consequences, postconditions and side-effects of applying the pattern. It can include new problems to solve which provides linkage to subsequent patterns. This can be called the resolution of forces as it describes which forces have been resolved, which ones remain unresolved, and which patterns may now be applicable.

Rationale. The rationale is the justification of the way how and why a pattern solves the problem. The solution component of a pattern may describe the outwardly visible structure and behavior of the pattern but the rationale is what provides insight into the deep structures and key mechanisms that are going on beneath the surface of the system.

Known Uses. Describes known occurrences of the pattern and its application within existing systems. This helps validating a pattern by verifying that it is indeed a proven solution to a recurring problem. Known uses of the pattern can often serve as instructional examples.

Depending on the pattern template different pattern elements are used. Sometimes different names are used for the elements (e.g. motivation instead of context). The basic pattern structure and the mandatory elements can and should, however, be found in all known pattern templates.

2.4 Collections of Patterns

As we already mentioned patterns typically don't exist in isolation. Depending on the relationships between patterns different concepts for collections of patterns are distinguished. Buschmann et al. identified pattern catalogs, pattern systems as well as pattern languages [35]. In the following we briefly show a kind of evolution from pattern catalogs over pattern systems to pattern languages.

Pattern Catalogs. When you start to merge several individual patterns into a bigger collection of patterns, a big challenge will be to find out the relationships between the patterns. It should already be possible to classify the patterns according to certain categories of patterns. Furthermore, you can expect that patterns from different authors use different pattern templates, i.e. you have no uniform structure within the pattern collection. As a consequence, a pattern catalog offers only a minimum amount of structure and organization. If any, it shows only outwardly visible structures and relationships. Thus such a pattern catalog is a more loosely coupled set of patterns.

Pattern Systems. Over time a pattern system evolves from a pattern catalog. A pattern system precisely describes the relationships and shows the interactions between individual patterns. Related patterns are subdivided into groups at multiple levels of granularity. These patterns work together to address more complex problems in a given domain. In contrast to a pattern catalog, there have been efforts to achieve a consistent and uniform structure of the patterns. This increases readability and comparability. Nevertheless the area covered by a pattern system may still be broad, i.e. there is not the one big challenge the patterns address. Although pattern systems contain a sufficient amount of patterns to work with, several gaps may be unfilled in the problem space. A pattern system is a more interwoven and tightly coupled set of patterns than a pattern catalog.

Within this document we also prefer the notion of a pattern system: on the one hand we have security as the overall concern but on the other hand current collections of security patterns are far from being complete. We adopt the POSA definition of a pattern system:

Definition 1 (Pattern System). A pattern system for software architecture is a collection of patterns for software architecture, together with guidelines for their implementation, combination and practical use in software development.

Pattern Languages. Pattern languages are the last stage of the evolution process. They provide some sense of closure, i.e. all patterns and the relations between them should be contained. However, it will remain difficult to prove such a computational completeness (this is why some people prefer to speak of pattern systems). A pattern language contains tightly interwoven patterns and forms a "super pattern". This means that all patterns share a common pre-defined goal and each of them contributes at some level to provide a solution for an overall problem. Thus pattern languages are more robust and comprehensive than pattern systems.

2.5 Pattern Classification Approaches

The more patterns are contained in a collection of patterns the more important is an organization scheme for them. Only with a convenient approach the pattern collection remains being useful, i.e. as a user you are able to find the appropriate pattern for the given problem. In the following, we briefly introduce prominent classification approaches for patterns.

GoF Approach. The Gang of Four classify design patterns by two criteria: purpose and scope [93].

– The criterion *purpose* describes what a pattern actually does. The following purposes are distinguished: *creational patterns* are related to the creation of objects, *structural patterns* are about the composition of classes and objects, and *behavioral patterns* describe the way how classes and objects collaborate and allocate responsibilty.
– The criterion *scope* defines whether a pattern is basically related to classes or to objects. Patterns based on classes deal with rather static aspects of classes and class relationships (e.g. inheritance). Object-based patterns address more dynamic relationships between objects that are determined during runtime. The authors state that most patterns are object-based.

The authors are also aware of the fact that there is more than one way to classify patterns. For example, they suggest to categorize them by the kinds of relationships they have with other patterns. Furhermore, they welcome different views on patterns as this helps understanding, comparing and using them.

POSA Approach. Buschmann et al. defined a set of properties a classification schema should have [35]. The overall premise is to keep such a schema simple being therefore easy to learn and to use. Following this, the schema should be restricted to "only a few classification criteria" and each of them should be related to "natural properties" of the patterns. Meeting these requirements, the POSA classification scheme consists of two criteria:

– *Pattern Categories*
  The patterns are subdivided according to general successive software development activities: definition of the architecture followed by the design followed by the implementation.
    – *Architectural patterns* belong to a high level of the software development process. These patterns are about the "fundamental structural organization schema for software systems." Subsystems, their tasks and their relationships among each other are decribed.
    – *Design patterns* are at a medium level and refine the subsystems or components of a software system as well as the relationships between them. They have no effect on the architecture but they are still independent from specific programming languages.
    – *Idioms* are patterns at the lowest level, i.e. they deal with problems during codifying of a solution. Building on the features of a given programming language idioms contain best practices for the implementation of a design.
  These pattern categories are widely adpoted in the pattern community. However, the POSA authors stress that these guidelines "are not an immutable rule" as exceptions can occur (i.e. a pattern can also be used in different categories).

- *Problem Categories*
  The other criteria are "problem categories that correspond directly to concrete design situations." Each problem category is derived from specific problems of related patterns. Examples are *Access Control*, *Communication*, and *Resource Handling*.

The POSA classification scheme is extensible as new categories can be added if a pattern doesn't fit into an existing one. The authors proved that by integrating the GoF patterns. Compared to the GoF approach, they think that especially problem categories are more helpful looking up a pattern.

The Scalability Model. Mowbray et al. introduced the scalability model for categorizing patterns [32, 158]. They say that "a sense of scale is missing from most design patterns." Thus they present a scalability model that consists of several levels of software architecture that are directly related to the scope of the software:

- The largest scale is at the *global level* that deals with software that operates across the boundaries of several enterprises. As these boundaries are difficult to define, standards and policies play an important role at this level.
- The *enterprise level* contains patterns that can be found in a single organisation. They address multiple systems and (typically distributed) applications. At this level the enterprise has control over its policies and resources and makes decisions for the further development of the organization.
- Typically several integrated applications can be found at the *system level*. Whereas the applications deal with functionality, the systems provide an execution environment, interoperation facilities for applications and resource management procedures.
- The *application level* comprises several frameworks, microarchitectures and objects. At this level the design patterns for an application can be found. The requirements of the user have to be met by the application.

Mowbray et al. also identified primal forces that are most important for each scale. For example, the management of functionality and performance are seen as the most important forces at the application level.

Categorization of Pattern Relations. Several people picked up the idea to classify patterns by their relations. Building on Zimmer's work Noble analyzed the pattern literature and identified a set of three primary pattern relations [246, 165]. Noble distinguihes primary and secondary patterns relations. Whereas secondary relations can be expressed in terms of primary relations, the latter cannot be decomposed any further. The primary relations are *uses*, *refines*, and *conflicts*:

- Almost every set of patterns contains the *uses* relationship that means that a pattern X *uses* a pattern Y and that pattern Y helps pattern X to accomplish something.

- If pattern X *refines* pattern Y, this means that X is "a specialisation of a more general, more simple, or more abstract pattern." It has similar but more special solution and problem sections, as well as the same (or more) forces.
- A pattern X *conflicts* with pattern Y, if both of them "provide mutually exclusive solutions to simlar problems." Often this kind of relationship is not expressed explicitly.

Drawing an analogy to the object-oriented paradigm the *uses* relationship is equivalent to *composition*, whereas the *refines* relationship is equivalent to *inheritance*. The secondary relationships are used less frequently and can be derived from the primary relationships. Some of them are just inverse primary relationships (e.g. *used by* or *refined by*), whereas others are more elaborated (e.g. *variant uses, similarity, combination*, etc.).

The Layer Approach. Fernandez was the first to discuss a classification approach specificly for security. He proposed to decompose collections of patterns according to the Layers pattern described in the POSA book [85, 84, 35]. Such a layer approach helps to "put things in perspective and to emphasize the encompassing nature of security [85]."

Patterns at the highest level (the *meta level*) address application classes. They are followed by the *application layer* that contains the corresponding objects. Below is the *system layer* that provides an execution environment. For example it includes databases and operating systems. Within the *distribution layer* processes and objects are assigned to different nodes. At the lowest layer the *hardware configuration* is addressed, e.g. each node provides one or more CPUs that are interconnected by some kind of (network) protocols. This way high-level security statements can be transformed to lower layers until the "technical" layers are reached that enforce security.

Pedagocial Patterns. Voelter proposed other interesting properties of pedagocial patterns [234]. We think, however, that they can be applied to any kind of patterns. The *time* property describes when a pattern should be applied (e.g. during development, deployment, operation, etc.). The *aspect* property describes "which aspect of the overall problem space does the pattern address". This is equivalent to the concept of problem categories used in the POSA book. The *scope* defines the level of applicability of a pattern, e.g. it can be applied in general, only in academic environments, or in specific domains. Finally, it can be defined to which *domain* a pattern applies. Voelter notes explicitly that multiple values are possible for some categories.

2.6 Writing Patterns

As patterns are best practices, they are not something new. Patterns are found, not invented. On the contrary they are discovered looking at solutions that worked well in the past. Or as put by Alexander: "in order to discover patterns which are alive we must always start with observation" [5]. In this section, we address how to find (or mine) patterns, community processes for assuring the quality of patterns and what should be considered when new patterns are integrated into an existing collection of patterns.

2.6.1 Pattern Mining Approaches

Kerth and Cunningham identified several basic approaches of pattern mining [132]. The following list might not be a complete list of all approaches and it is possible to apply combinations of them to achieve useful results.

Introspective Approach. People analyze systems that they had already built. They try to identify solutions that worked well. By nature, this approach leads to patterns that are limited to individual experiences. Therefore, the author has to take care that other experts also agree that the author's insights are indeed patterns, i.e. they apply the same solutions to a given problem, too.

Artifactual Approach. The pattern's author examines software artifacts. He was not involved in the design and development of a system. The author investigates systems that had been made by different people trying to solve a similar problem. He tries to find the commonalities and to write them down in a more abstract, unified form. Chances are high that this will result in a pattern but as neither the author isn't necessarily the expert nor had the experts the opportunity to look at the resulting pattern, additional refinements of the pattern might be necessary.

Sociological Approach. This approach involves several experts in the problem domain. Different people that built similar systems are asked how they solved particular problems and why this was a good solution. Through interviews the problems in the system and the interactions between developers can be determined. It is possible to get direct feedback on the pattern from the experts themselves. That way, a sound pattern can be expected as a result.

2.6.2 Quality Assurance by Community Processes

It is the major claim of patterns to write up real solutions for recurring problems. However, this can only be guaranteed, if the patterns are published and somehow reviewed by a community of experts. As seen before different pattern mining approaches lead to different levels of "quality" or maturity of the resulting patterns. In the following, we will first discuss what the qualities of a pattern are. After that, we will have a look at processes developed by the pattern community in order to systematically improve both style and content of patterns: *shepherding* and *writer's workshops*. Beside looking at pattern literature, the description of both processes is based on personal experiences of the author participating at various conferences of the PLoP series.

Qualities of Patterns. Lea compiled a set of qualities that patterns should have [146]. If a document written in pattern form exhibits these features, it can really be called a pattern.

- Every pattern is an *encapsulation* of a problem and a solution. The boundaries of a pattern are clear and patterns are to a certain degree self-contained, i.e. the steps of the solution are sound and really do solve the problem.
- A pattern should also be *generative*, i.e. it should help to construct the solution. The application of a pattern changes the initial context and settles the scene for the application of further patterns.
- The application of a pattern leads to *equilibrium*, as the forces are resolved or existing conflicts are at least minimized. There is also evidence that the steps of the solution are "true" and lead to equilibrium (e.g. by convincing examples, empirical data, analysis of failed solutions, etc.).
- A pattern is an *abstraction* of particular "nuggets" of expert knowledge. This is reflected in a rating that can be assigned to a pattern for example in [6]: no asterisk means that there are certain ways of solving the problem, i.e. the solution is more an example and the true invariant of the pattern has not yet been found. One asterisk means that the author believes having made some progress toward finding an invariant pattern. Patterns rated with two asterisks are believed to describe a true invariant.
- Every pattern should be *open* to be extended or parameterized by other patterns. Together they can solve a bigger problem. They should also be so open that they can be implemented in different ways.
- Each pattern contributes to the overall solution. This requires the *composibility* of each pattern. This feature is reflected in the (hierarchical) relationships between patterns.

Although it will be difficult to achieve all of these features during the first writing attempt, a pattern becomes more and more mature over time ("piecemeal growth"). This requires, however, processes for the ongoing improvement of patterns.

Shepherding. A very important process for the improvement is the shepherding which means the guidance of an author by an experienced pattern writer. Harrison described how the quality of a pattern can be improved before the actual peer review process starts [106].

Although shepherding is itself a review process, there is a rather close one-to-one relationship between the pattern's author (the *sheep*) and an experienced pattern writer (the *shepherd*). The overall goal of the shepherding is to help the author to get his work into a real pattern. Ideally the shepherd knows the process itself - either as sheep from own pattern contributions or as shepherd of other authors. Shepherding turned out to be more powerful than regular review processes of scientific work as both sheep and shepherd work together intensively for a longer time and share a common goal: if the contribution is really a pattern, it *must* be published.

In the following, we summarize key concepts of shepherding: an important step is to "establish a productive relationship" between shepherd and sheep. On the one hand the author should be confident that he can count on the shepherd's support. On the other hand the shepherd must take care that he doesn't play the author's role in writing the pattern. Regarding the content of the pattern, the reader should be able to immediately understand the core of the pattern, i.e. both problem and solution must be expressed in a precise way. Accordingly, one works towards a close match between solution and problem. Furthermore, the solution itself must be convenient for both experts and novices. If these and further steps are taken into consideration, the pattern is in good shape and prepared for being reviewed during writer's workshops or other review processes.

Writer's Workshops. A writer's workshops is a structured peer-review process. After shepherding, individual candidates for a contribution to the pattern literature are discussed in a circle of further authors, who are ideally experts on the respective problem domain. The basic idea is to get as much suggestions for the improvment of the contribution as possible. Writer's workshops are the focal point at conferences of the PLoP series. However, they can also be held on other occasions. The participants expect that everyone has read the contribution of each other. A moderator is steering the workshop according to the following schema:

1. Exclusion of the author
   The pattern's author doesn't play an active role during the discussion of the pattern. After reading a paragraph of his work, he becomes a "fly on the wall", i.e. he is not allowed to say anything until he is invited to join the circle again. The participants start the discussion pretending the author would not be present. The idea behind this convention is to let the work of an author speak for itself. The author should not justify anything but see and hear how his contribution is interpeted by readers. That way he can learn what parts do and don't work as intended.
2. Summary
   Then the pattern is summarized by two participants. This helps to get a first hint whether the pattern is written in a comprehensive way and that context, problem and solution are correctly understood by the reader.
3. Positive aspects
   Then the participants talk over the positive aspects of the pattern. On the one hand this includes the style of the pattern, i.e. pattern template, page layout, labeling of problem and solution (e.g. by headings or by bold face), appropriate use of drawings and examples, etc. On the other hand comments regarding the content of the pattern are equally important. The discussion is about why the pattern is indeed a proven solution for a recurring problem. Furthermore the participants have a look on the

resolution of the forces and whether the relationships to other patterns are determined appropriately.

4. Suggestions for improvement

   Afterwards the participants discuss how the given pattern can be improved. In the same way as before both style and content of the pattern are taken into consideration. By that time the author directly benefits from the experience of the participants. For example, they suggest more scenarios where the pattern has been successfully applied, alternative names, in order to improve the association between name and solution, or more precise problem statements in order to make the pattern more time-invariant.

5. Questions

   Finally, the author is invited to join the circle again. Based on notes he took during the workshop, he is allowed to ask questions for clarification in case he didn't understand a particular remark. Again it is important to note that he should not justify anything but listen to the insights of the group in order to improve his contribution.

The author summarizes the discussion from his point of view. He has now enough ideas how to improve his work and he can be sure that the improved document will really be a pattern and can be made accessible to the public. The user of a pattern can also be confident that the pattern doesn't only reflect experience of the author but of a couple of domain and pattern experts.

2.6.3 Integration of Patterns

During the Bird's of Feather session "Merging Pattern Languages" at EuroPLoP 2001 we discussed questions that arise when single patterns and collections of patterns are going to be integrated into a bigger system of patterns [235]. As soon as a significant amount of patterns emerge in a particular domain, it is necessary to merge them in order to make the collection of patterns more useful. A precondition of such a merger is to adopt the patterns during processes known as *refactoring* and *rewriting*:

– Rewriting

  For the sake of readability it is desirable to change both form and level of abstraction of the patterns. This is required as it cannot be expected that patterns from different authors follow the same style conventions.

– Refactoring

  Refactoring goes far beyond rewriting. Refactoring means to change even the content of the pattern, i.e. to reconsider essential parts such as context and forces in order to make the pattern fit into the overall collection of patterns. If one or more patterns are very similar, they can be joined (see Figure 2.1(a)). If they overlap, it is necessary to change the boundaries

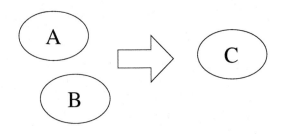

(a) Joining patterns.

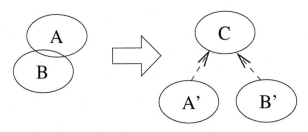

(b) Changing boundaries of patterns.

Figure 2.1. Refactoring of patterns

of the patterns, i.e. adjust context, problem and forces in order to make them complementary. It might even be required to introduce a third, more general pattern that helps to select one of several alternative solutions (i.e. alternative patterns, see Figure 2.1(b)).

Integrating new patterns into a system of patterns doesn't necessarily involve the original authors. However, their work should be acknowledged and referenced accordingly.

2.7 Problem Solving with Patterns

The genuine purpose of patterns is to provide solutions to problems. Thus we are going to have a general look at problem solving as part of cognitive psychology from the viewpoint of patterns. We will show that many concepts and terms of patterns are directly related to these areas.

In terms of information processing a problem consists of three parts: initial state, goal state, and a sequence of operations leading from the initial state to the goal state [162]. The *problem space* consists of a set of nodes where each node represents a state of the problem. The links between nodes represent the operations that lead from one state to another. In the world of patterns such states can be described by the context of each pattern. The application of the pattern is equivalent with carrying out an operation that leads to another state. In fact the application of a pattern changes the context and does therefore lead to another state.

Simon also stressed the importance of distinguishing well-structured and ill-structured problems [217]. Ill-structured problems are characterized by vague descriptions of initial state, goal state, and the set of operations. In such cases it could happen that a solution cannot be found at all. For example an ill-structured problem is "How do I design a house?". Alexander's patterns directly address this particular question. His patterns help to structure this overall problem space and to select the right operations in order to build buildings and towns [6]. In general, patterns are a vehicle to specify well-defined problems and appropriate solutions on different levels of abstraction.

Another important concept of cognitive psychology is the acquisition of know-how and skills. The improvement of cognitive skills is often illustrated by the difference between experts and novices [116]. Briefly said, experts can rely on a large amount of *knowledge* regarding a particular class of problems. Such an *expertise* comprises:

- Sets of rules, schemata, and scripts.
- Heuristic short-cuts in order to determine appropriate solutions.
- Applying both bottom-up and top-down processing.
- Storage of huge amounts of knowledge about facts and actions as well as a broad perspective.
- The ability to apply common or everyday knowledge to technical or specific domains.

Novices become experts by continuous training with feedback (e.g. other experts point out a mistake). It is, however, interesting that experts can demonstrate their expertise but often cannot explain how exactly they solved a problem. Patterns are one way to systematically write down such expert knowledge and to make it available to novices. Applying patterns doesn't transform a novice to an expert immediately. However, he can be sure that he is going to solve a problem the same way an expert would do it. Patterns help to avoid typical pitfalls and to apply proven solutions. Over time, with more and more training, he will become an expert, too.

2.8 Summary

Patterns have their origin in architecture. Christopher Alexander introduced the concept of patterns in order to solve recurring problems during the construction of buildings, towns, etc. Furthermore, he provided practical evidence that the pattern approach actually works. In 1987, the movement of the software pattern community slowly started. The breakthrough came with the publication of the GoF and POSA cornerstones in pattern literature. Since then, patterns are an established approach for software development and can be found in almost all software-related areas.

Having discussed the origins of patterns and how they were adopted by the software community, we introduced the basic concepts of patterns. A pattern is a named piece of information that describes how a problem that occurs over and over again in a particular context is usually solved by domain experts. Furthermore, a pattern resolves high priority forces, i.e. (conflicting) constraints and goals on the solution. Beside these mandatory elements of a pattern, optional elements can be used, if they make the pattern easier to use.

Patterns interact with other patterns, e.g. they require that another pattern has to be applied before. There are pattern collections with different "levels of maturity". A pattern catalog is a rather loosely coupled set of patterns with minimum amount of structure and organization. A pattern system is a more interwoven and tightly coupled set of patterns. However, several gaps may be unfilled in the problem space. Pattern languages are to some degree complete, i.e. all relevant patterns and the relationships between them should be contained. As this is hard to achieve (and to prove) in practice, we prefer the term "pattern system" within this document.

As soon as a significant amount of patterns is identified, it becomes important to classify them. Only then it is possible to efficiently find the "right" pattern. Established classification schemes have been provided by GoF (classification by purpose and scope) and POSA (classification by pattern and problem categories). However, other approaches are known and combinations are useful, as it helps to understand and to apply patterns, if you have different views on them.

After that, we have described important aspects of pattern writing. Pattern mining is the process of identifying proven solutions. Depending on how the author of the pattern has been involved in the software development, the quality of the initial pattern draft varies. To assure that a pattern features the qualities of a pattern (e.g. encapsulation, equilibrium, abstraction, openness, etc.), the community has elaborated certain processes for "quality assurance". One process is the shepherding that is basically the guidance of an author by an experienced pattern writer before the pattern draft is reviewed by more people. They work together for a longer time in order to get the pattern published eventually. Other processes are the writer's workshops which are structured peer-reviews. Other experts discuss the pattern draft and help the author to improve it and to make it a real pattern. As new patterns typically relate somehow to already published work, it is also important to know what to consider when they are integrated into an existing collection of patterns (i.e. joining equivalent patterns or changing the boundaries, if two or more patterns overlap).

Finally, we have shown how patterns relate to problem solving that is a part of cognitive psychology. In fact, important concepts of problem solving directly correspond to the pattern approach: patterns help to avoid ill-structured problems, they capture expertise literally, and they help to make novices act as experts over time.

3. Ontologies

> Most of the Web's content today
> is designed for humans to read,
> not for computer programs to
> manipulate meaningfully.
>
> TIM BERNERS-LEE ET AL.

3.1 Introduction

By systematically learning from errors and the experiences of others, we can continuously improve the overall quality and adapt to the ever changing circumstances of today's networks. This way we can also make the right choices when we face security risks – but much more important – we can invest our resources saved thereby into prevention and security improvement. Today, there is no "strong and institutionalized learning mechanism as for example usual in the flying community" [10]. One reason for this is that security knowledge is spread among information sources of very different kinds. Especially for novices it is difficult to find the "right" information to solve a particular security problem.

A first step towards such a process is therefore to annotate and integrate such information in order to achieve tool support and to overcome the limitations described before. We consider ontologies as a suitable aid for this endeavor: the usage of ontologies for codifying such knowledge (i.e. concepts and relations) and drawing conclusions (i.e. inferencing) helps both to share and to use security information more efficiently. Adopting this approach they are a fundamental prerequisite for automating the security knowledge life cycle.

This chapter is organized as follows: in Section 3.2 we introduce the security knowledge process in order to show why ontologies contribute to solve the dilemma described before. With this big picture in mind we introduce the concept of ontologies in Section 3.3. We describe what ontologies are, why they should be used and how they are generally used in computer science today. After that we step into details of the development of ontologies in Section 3.4. This includes the introduction of design criteria, methodologies,

M. Schumacher: Security Engineering with Patterns, LNCS 2754, pp. 29-44, 2003.

representation languages and tools for the development of ontologies. Finally, we summarize the results of this Chapter in Section 3.5.

3.2 Security Knowledge Process

It seems that in the field of security the same errors are made over and over again [10]. Therefore, the broader context of our research is to understand why security solutions fail and to establish a security learning process, i.e. required security *knowledge* should be available whenever needed.

This requires monitoring many different kinds of security information sources. An overview and evaluation of such information sources was conducted by both Hurler and Goerlach [118, 97]. The effort to capture such knowledge, to process and (re)use it in order to achieve an improvement is, however, very high. Only approaches offering at least semi-automated support can help here.

Our approach is to look for basic components required for such a systematic security improvement process. In the following, we introduce major building blocks based on the notion of a knowledge feedback loop [3, 203].

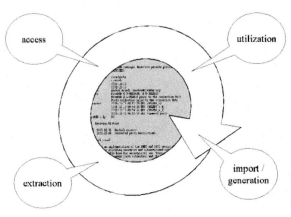

Figure 3.1. Security knowledge process.

Import. The first step is to gather security related information from relevant information sources. External sources could be mailing lists, newsgroups, WWW sites, or more "traditional" knowledge resources in articles and books. Based on the type of information sources, a semi-automated import of raw data is possible [198].

Extraction. The next step is to annotate the imported knowledge making the raw data processable in a meaningful way. Thus, the semantics of the information can be captured. This is the only way to infer relations among different pieces of information. With such a generation of meta-data the gathered information can be made compliant to public (e.g. Common Criteria) or de-facto standards (e.g. CERT terminology) or the internal conventions. That way, the knowledge is normalized according to a given terminology.

Access. The next step is to access the now normalized knowledge. The users can explore the knowledge, can query or search the underlying data sources. They are able to find relevant security information about dedicated topics e.g. known vulnerabilities of Apache Web servers.

Utilization. Finding security information is, however, not sufficient. Depending on the knowledge level of a user, it is possible to present different views, e.g. for novices or experts. Furthermore, an analysis (e.g. with the help of data-mining methodologies [198]) can reveal relations that haven't been obvious before. Similarly it is possible to improve the interlocking with subsequent applications (e.g. a security scanner tool).

Generation. The last step actually closes the feedback-loop. Hereby, the knowledge that was imported and processed in order to improve the security of systems is applied. By using improved systems new raw data is generated. Furthermore, new knowledge is generated, too. Additional internal knowledge can be gathered from internal documentation of knowledge.

Without a defined syntax and semantics of an inquiry there is, however, no way to get such mechanisms for the specific procurement of information implemented. This is possible with special cases such as vulnerability databases but for more general inquiries they are no longer applicable. Thus it is necessary to establish a representation mechanism that can map the relevant concepts and structures of a domain appropriately.

3.3 Knowledge Representation with Ontologies

The notion "ontology" has its origin in the Greek word "ons-ontos" and has the meaning of "being". The greek philosopher Aristotle had already tried to classify different types of being according to a set of predicates. From this, ontology as a "a branch of philosophy dealing with the order and structure of reality" evolved [115]. This scientific discipline is the study of being. Ontology denotes the most general being as "entity". Assuming this all other things of the world are hierarchically ordered.

Computer scientists adopted the ontology concept. They refer to ontology as a conceptual formalization of knowledge domains. Often Gruber's definition of ontology is used in this context [104]:

"An ontology is a formal, explicit specification of a shared conceptualization."

Another definition is provided by Berners-Lee et al. [20]:

"The most typical kind of ontology (for the Web) has a taxonomy
and a set of inference rules."

An ontology models a part of the world. Such a model can be used by
humans *and* computers in order to establish a common "understanding" of
relevant concepts and the relations between them.

Illustrating this we show an excerpt of the Computer Science Department
Ontology compiled by Heflin within the Simple HTML Ontology Extensions
(SHOE) project [109]. In Figure 3.2 we see several concepts such as *Professor*, *Student*, and *University*. Furthermore, we see relations between these
concepts, e.g. a `Professor` *has doctoral degree from* a *University* and *is advisor of* a *Student*. The concepts represent entities within the world of the
computer science department.

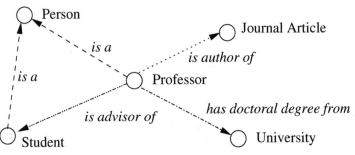

Figure 3.2. Excerpt of an example ontology.

From a syntactical point of view such an ontology represent nothing more
than a set of symbols (i.e. the concepts) and predicates (the relations). However, semantic arises from human interpretation. For example, assume that
someone sees a classroom in a university with an older person - the professor
- standing in front of a group of younger people - the students. As there is a
link between the representation of the visual appearance of the entities acting
and the representation of the verbal form that describe them, he can bring
the situation in the right context, understand it, and can talk to it to other
people. In that sense, an ontology captures semantic, if it is a) syntactically
correct and b) if the concepts and relations which represent a part of the
world match human intuition. Accordingly we use the following definition for
an ontology:

Definition 2 (Ontology). An ontology specifies the conceptualization of a
knowledge domain with a set of commonly agreed concepts, relations between
them, and inference rules.

When the concepts of such an ontology are linked to information sources, ontologies serve as means for structuring information. Adding such meta-information to documents has several advantages [20]. The major benefit is that ontologies enable computers to go beyond the mere layouting of documents (e.g. by Web pages). They capture the semantics of a document and enable computers to process them in a *meaningful* way. Although the computer doesn't really understand the enhanced information, the results are more meaningful for the human user. For example, you can enable a computer to answer questions like "Where has Professor Smith received his Degree?" or "Who is the advisor of the student McGregor?".

Furthermore, some sort of intelligent behavior can be imitated, for instance, when deductive rules are codified (i.e. when a certain condition is satisfied, the conclusion of the rule also holds). Such inference rule can be used to derive facts that are not necessarily contained in the annotated documents.

3.4 Development of Ontologies

There is no standard method for the development of an ontology. The essential job to be done in the beginning is to insert new concepts into an existing taxonomy (that is to say a hierarchy of concepts and sub-concepts). Thereby you can choose a top down approach or a bottom up approach, mostly it is a mixture of both. Thus the process of building up an ontology is necessarily an iteration process. Noy and McGuiness produced an informal guideline for the development of knowledge ontologies [168].

In this section we discuss criteria that should be considered during ontology design. We also present selected methodologies for the development of ontologies. Finally, we introduce selected tools for the development of ontologies as they are an important prerequisite for knowledge management and engineering.

3.4.1 Design Criteria

The following is a brief outline of some characteristic requirements of ontologies based on Gruber's design criteria [105]. Corcho et al. present more detailed information about requirements for the development of ontologies [51].

Clarity. This requirements is to guarantee that the ontology provides the meaning of the defined notions by means of commonly agreed definitions and also disposes of natural language documentation. This should hold for each concept. For example, the concept **Professor** could be documented as "A professor is a teacher at an university".

Coherence. This should guarantee that possible inferences are consistent with the given definitions, i.e. an ontology should be able to provide meaningful answers to human users. This refers both to syntax and semantics, e.g. if you look for a student of a certain professor you don't expect that a query on the ontology returns an animal (that belongs to a different class of concepts). And if the name of a student is returned, you expect that the answer is true.

Extendibility. The monotonic extendibility refers to new (general or specific) concepts. Those should adapt to the ontology without the need to change existing definitions. For example, you could add the sub-concepts of *Person* such as *Secretary* or *Caretaker* to the ontology without changing existing definitions.

Minimal Encoding Bias. The ontology should be independent of its representation, i.e. proprietary language characteristics should not be used to encode the concepts and relations.

Minimal Ontological Commitments. This means that as little assumptions as possible should be made as to the world to be shaped in order to keep the ontology flexible and reusable. Ontological commitments guarantee consistency but not completeness of an ontology.

Talking about the development of ontologies its reusability through a third party should especially be considered, too. A lot of new developments in the field of tools for ontologies and the developments of ontology languages do consider this [43]. These considerations concern conceptual aspects, the representation, and underlying logic calculus (in order to draw conclusions). Therefore the development of ontologies should also look at general requirements that are considered for any mathematical system: consistency, decidability, and completeness. The demand for consistency means that within any set of concepts (and the corresponding relations) of the ontology there should not be an inconsistency. Decidability means that for every set of related concepts within the ontology it must be, by means of the axioms defined in it, possible to decide whether it is true or false. Completeness means that an ontology should cover all semantic inferences of the part of the reality that is modeled[1]. These requirements, already put up by David Hilbert in 1928 [112], can be applied to the development of ontologies, too. A further important point is the correctness, i.e. all inferences contained in the ontology should correctly be reflected in the reality - that is to say in the semantics. It is, however, not trivial - if not impossible at all - to give evidence that these criteria are met. Thus, practitioners of the Semantic Web take this into account consciously in order to be able to achieve a highest possible level of variety [20]. They prefer a fuzzy or ambiguous result instead of having no result at all.

---

[1] This does not refer to the complete reproduction of the reality but to the completeness of inferences.

3.4.2 Methodologies

The establishment of new and also the maintenance and the evaluation of existing ontologies is no trivial job to do. As a consequence various approaches for a structured procedure have been developed. Working with such methodologies increased since 1995. The Cyc methodology, already published in 1990, can be considered as a model. Further known methodologies for the development of ontologies based on the works of Corcho et al. and Jones et al. are presented in the following [51, 127]. Hereby our focus is on methodologies treating the new establishment of ontologies. The selection represents popular methodologies which have a significant user community. Besides, they represent different approaches of developing an ontology. Note that we do not consider proprietary approaches that are not generally applicable.

Cyc Methodology. The classic, being the basis of the Cyc Upper Ontology, proceeds as follows: first knowledge is extracted manually from existing sources of knowledge. Later on, given the existence of a basic ontology, the further extraction of knowledge is continued through the recognition of natural language or automated learning tools. Lenat and Guha provide an in-depth discussion about this methodology [148]. Particularly, they discuss the development of very large ontologies.

Enterprise Model Approach. The approach described by Uschold and King first starts with identifying the purpose of the original ontology [231]. Then the concepts and the relations to one another have to be captured. Moreover, the notions refering to those concepts and relations are identified. Finally the ontology is encoded. At last there is a documentation and an evaluation of the ontology. The latter should prove that the ontology meets its requirements and can be used as intended. Existing ontologies can generally be integrated.

TOVE. Grüninger and Fox look at a formal approach for the development of ontologies [102, 230]. Thereby the possible application scenarios are first identified intuitively. Then a set of so called competence questions is asked to determine the horizon of the ontology. An ontology must basically be in a position to answer these questions. From those the essential concepts are drawn, their properties, their relations to one another and the axioms that are formally depicted in Prolog[2].

KACTUS and CommonKADS. The KACTUS approach is a successor of the popular CommonKADS methodology [197, 18]. The KACTUS methodology is based on an application of a Knowledge Base by means of an abstraction process. The more applications are produced, the more general the ontology becomes, that is to say it departs from a Knowledge Base. In other words

---

[2] Prolog statements can directly be used to represent concepts and relations of an ontology. For example the Prolog fact `color(leaf,green)` represents the statement that the *color* of a *leaf* is *green*. That way, hierarchical relations of concepts and sub-concepts can also be modeled.

the proposal is to first produce a Knowledge Base for a specific application and later, when a new Knowledge Base is needed in a similar field, the first Knowledge Base should be generalized and adopted for both applications. Applying this recursively the ontology would portray the generic knowledge of all applications.

Methondology. Methondology is a methodology that can be applied in different ways [86, 87]. Ontologies can be created as completely new ones, reused as a whole or restructured. It enables the establishment of ontologies on the knowledge level. This includes the identification of a process for developing the ontology. Thereby the main activities are identified first, i.e. evaluation, configuration management, conceptualization, integration, implementation, etc. Moreover a life cycle is determined on the basis of prototypes. In addition, the methodology itself is determined. This includes the steps necessary for the execution of all activities, the techniques used, the output products as well as their evaluation. Methontology is partially supported by the Ontology Development Environment WebODE (see Section 3.4.4).

SENSUS. The SENSUS methodology is a top down method to disincorporate one domain specific ontology from a large ontology [225]. The authors propose to define a lot of relevant "seed terms" of a domain. These terms are manually connected to a general ontology (in this case the SENSUS ontology containing more than 50,000 concepts). The relevant terms are automatically selected and the domain specific ontology is extracted. Thus the algorithm provides a hierarchically structured set of concepts belonging to this partial domain.

On-To-Knowledge. The On-To-Knowledge project applies ontologies on information that is digitally available in order to improve the quality of knowledge management in larger or distributed organizations [196, 220]. The methodology provides guidelines for the implementation of knowledge management concepts and tools and thus helps to make knowledge available rapidly and efficiently. The methodology includes the identification of the aims to be achieved by the knowledge management tools and is based on an analysis of application scenarios and roles the knowledge engineers and others play in organizations. Moreover the architecture of the On-To-Knowledge suite of tools is presented. Every tool is described according to application oriented ontology development. Finally the application of the methodology and its evaluation by means of On-To-Knowledge case studies is explained.

IDEF5. The IDEF5 methodology was drafted with the aim to support the establishment, modification and maintenance of ontologies [131]. As the ontological analysis can necessarily not be completed, one proposes not to proceed with the ontology development according to the pattern of a cookbook. Thus IDEF5 is a general procedure including some basic instructions. These are finding out the purpose, the view and the context of the ontology project, the collection of "raw data" and following that their analysis, the development of a first ontology and in time its refinement and validation. For the establishment of the first ontology one uses a graphical notation that is translated to a language based on KIF in later phases.

Findings. The study of Jones et al. [127] does not try to find the best of the methodologies presented but rather to extract some kind of general methodology from their common ground. Comparing the different approaches that way, they found the following:

- As starting point most of the methodologies choose a task. Proceeding like this is perfectly obvious: knowledge acquisition, evaluation and features of the later ontology become clearer. The question is, however, to what extent the ontology is independent from this task as defined in the general requirements for ontologies (see last section).
- The methodologies presented can be roughly classified in two categories. There are the rather phases-based prototypes and on the other hand the prototypes developing in an evolutionary way. If the purpose and the requirements are clear, the phases-based procedures are more adequate whereas in the other case the evolutionary procedure seems to be more favorable.
- Typically there are two stages during the development, the first one being the production of an informal description of the ontology and the second one the embedding into an ontology language. These two descriptions are an important characteristic because the informal description often directs through the more formal phase. Thus the ontologies often bridge the gap between a running system and the part of the world they are to shape.
- A complete methodology should offer guidelines that help the knowledge engineer choosing various abstraction levels, starting from the structural level of the ontology to smaller modeling details.

Jones et al. conclude that one should not rely on one or two single methodologies [127]. The reason is that the field of the ontology development is still in the developmental stage. Thus they worked out the above mentioned points that are essential in most of the methodologies. This is not very helpful because there is only the possibility left to work freehand according to any methodology and in consideration of the above points.

3.4.3 Ontology Representation Languages

Ontologies can be presented in various ways including natural language, graphical representation, logic-based approaches and many other formalities. Refer to Bibel et al. for a comprehensive survey of basic knowledge representation mechanisms [23]. In the following we look at some approaches that have been accepted for the representation of ontologies. They mainly differ in the way they are suitable to represent knowledge on the one hand and to support mechanisms for inferences on the other hand. We follow the studies of Corcho and Gómez-Pérez who developed a classification framework for ontology representation languages [52].

Ontolingua. Ontolingua is based on the Knowledge Interchange Format (KIF) and combines the first grade knowledge representation paradigms, frame-based and predicate logic. [45, 79]. It enables the representation of concepts, taxonomies of concepts, n-ary relations, functions, axioms, instances and procedures. Ontolingua disposes of a high grade of expressiveness. This does, however, lead to difficulties when establishing mechanisms for the execution of inferences[3]. Moreover Ontolingua is very related to OCML.

OKBC. The Open Knowledge Base Connectivity (OKBC) protocol (formerly known as Generic Frame Protocol (GFP)) defines the access to knowledge bases and should be considered as supplement to language specifications which support knowledge sharing [45]. The GFP knowledge model, being the basis of OKBC, supports an object-centered representation of knowledge and disposes of a lot of representation constructs that can typically be found in frame representation systems. Moreover OKBC defines a complete interaction interface for knowledge bases which can be accessed via the OKBC protocol. In addition, there are procedures to describe complex operations that can be accessed in a knowledge base via the network. Furthermore the OKBC ontology compatible to the protocol was developed for Ontolingua.

OCML. The Operational Conceptual Modeling Language (OCML)is very similar to Ontolingua [66, 157]. It does, however, offer additional components such as the deduction and production rules and operational definitions. By means of OMCL functions, relations, classes, instances and rules can be expressed. There is also a rather strong constraint checker included that can verify type as well as cardinality. Moreover constraints, associations to relations, slots and classes can be verified. OCML has already been used in a series of applications: as support of the knowledge management process, for the development of ontologies, for E-commerce and for knowledge-based systems. OCML can be translated to Ontolingua, RDF and XML-based representations of OCML models. Furthermore it can be used as object language for UPML by means of a plug-in for Protégé. OCML disposes of a big supply of reusable models.

F-Logic. F-Logic (FLogic or Frame Logic, respectively) is a language being based on first-order predicate calculus as well as on frames [133]. It thereby follows the approach to represent syntax and semantics of constructs of a higher order directly. Its aim is to apply the object-oriented paradigm to database programming. Concepts such as objects, inheritance, polymorphic types, query methods, encapsulation are available. The driving force of this procedure is the coping with the so-called impedance mismatch between programming languages for application development and languages for queries

---

[3] Although a theorem-proving tool for KIF terms is available.

of relational databases. The view of ontologies as knowledge bases illustrates the proximity to databases, especially since some development tools for ontologies manage their data internally as relational database. The larger an ontology the more important again become the performance aspects. As many logic calculus and formalisms have to face efficiency problems, a reinforced orientation on the performance of databases has proven to be useful.

LOOM. Originally LOOM was not specifically meant for ontologies [125, 150]. It generally addressed to the development of knowledge bases, expert systems and other intelligent applications. It is a successor of KL-ONE[4] and it is based on description logics and production rules. LOOM integrates the rule-based and the frame-based paradigm. The language enables the representation of concepts, taxonomies, n-ary relations, functions, axioms and production rules. The reasoning takes places by means of automatic classification, verification of consistency, constraint checking, multiple inheritance, non-monotony and other mechanisms. As such LOOM is quite a powerful language.

XOL. The focus of the XML-Based Ontology Exchange Language (XOL) is on the exchange of ontologies between various database systems or knowledge bases, ontology development tools or application programs, respectively [130]. XOL allows to define a subset of OKBC in XML-syntax. Classes, slots and facets can be described but no frames.

SHOE. The approach of the Simple HTML Ontology Extension (SHOE) first was an enhancement of HTML. Thereby machine-readable knowledge was connected to WWW documents or the HTML code, respectively. In the meantime SHOE is also adapted to XML. The objective of SHOE is to provide meaningful information for software agents. The processing of knowledge and search mechanisms should thus be improved. In order to reach that an ontology for the description of valid classifications and their relations to one another is defined. The HTML pages can be enriched with the corresponding annotations in order to describe the contents semantically. According to the SHOE web-site the SHOE project is no longer being actively maintained. The developers work now on projects which use OWL Web Ontology Language and DAML+OIL (both partly based on SHOE).

RDF and RDF Schema. The Resource Description Framework (RDF) provides means for describing and exchanging meta-information about Web resources [29]. RDF is written in a predefined XML syntax. Basically, everything that has an URI counts among the resources. Going beyond information of a typical Web resource (e.g. author, title, copyright, etc.) all things which are identified on the Web can be modeled with RDF. RDF statements consist of three parts: subjects, predicates and objects. Thereby, subject and objects are treated as nodes in a graph whereas the predicate represents a directed

---

[4] KL-ONE is an ancestor of today's languages for knowledge representation.

edge between them. Thus, RDF is suitable to represent ontology concepts and relations. Treating RDF statements as assertions (which can be composed to more complex statements) it is possible to transform RDF graphs into logical statements for inferencing purposes. RDF Schema provides capabilities to specify "classes and properties as part of a vocabulary, and to indicate which classes and properties are expected to be used together" [236]. RDF Schema uses RDF in order to define the type system of RDF.

OIL. As XOL the Ontology Inference Layer (OIL) is planned for the exchange of ontologies [81, 82]. OIL builds up on RDF(S) whereby RDF(S) constructs are used if possible in order to reach a high level of backward compatibility. OIL combines the basics of modeling from frame-based languages with formal semantics and inference by using description logics. The classifier FaCT executes an automatic classification of instances as well as constraint-checking in taxonomies and definitions of OIL concepts.

DAML+OIL. DAML+OIL is the successor of OIL. DAML+OIL "builds on earlier W3C standards such as RDF and RDF Schema, and extends these languages with richer modelling primitives" [19]. It is a semantic markup language for network resources which is the result of various international cooperations for the creation of a standard language for the Semantic Web. DAML+OIL implements the basic elements of frame-based languages and description logic languages. One can depict concepts, taxonomies, binary relations, functions and instances. Newer versions also allow the use of XML Schema data types. The semantics of DAML+OIL is well defined and there exists a set of approaches offering reasoning mechanisms.

MIX. The Meta-data based Integration model for data X-change (MIX) forms the basics for the representation and the integration of data from different sources [26]. The underlying flexible data model especially admits the representation of semi-structured data as well as the explicit enrichment with context information in form of meta data. MIX is based on ontologies whereby the focus is on the data conversion. In addition, tools for the establishment and the monitoring of data wrappers and ontologies were developed for the MIX model. Moreover MIX can be converted to XML.

Findings. The ontology languages presented differ in the specificity of knowledge representation and in their ability for reasoning. In the following we present the results of the very detailed study of Corcho and Gómez-Pérez in a brief version [52]. Moreover we give an evaluation of the languages presented here that were not considered.

- For the exchange of ontologies the XML-oriented languages should be preferred.
- For the modeling of ontologies, requiring a high expressiveness, the rather "traditional" languages are recommended. Only in comparatively simple cases the XML-based languages are an alternative.

– For the execution of the reasoning the XML-based languages are not suited due to missing inference possibilities. Here the traditional languages are to be preferred, too.

We concentrate on the logic-based languages, as we need their ability for inferences in order to improve search and retrieval of specific security patterns and because we want to conduct queries that would otherwise not be possible (see Chapter 8 and 9). These languages offer the basic modeling concepts to define concepts, relations, multiple inheritance and class relations as well as to generate instances. Hereby LOOM is the most powerful language, followed by OCML.

The possibilities to define axioms are a good measure for the expressiveness of a language. Thereby Ontolingua with concepts of the first-order and second-order predicate calculus proves to be the most powerful language. OCML and F-Logic also offer good possibilities here.

In the field of the reasoning Ontolingua proves to be the most powerful language but on the other hand there is no inference mechanism available. LOOM and OCML are not complete in their inference possibilities. Only F-Logic and OIL do offer completeness, the latter has also got (as well LOOM) an automatic classifier. Moreover F-Logic is the only language that explicitly offers exceptions.

Comparing them directly OKBC first drops out of the running as well as Ontolingua which disposes of quite powerful language constructs but the missing of a tool for the execution of inferences considerably reduces its utility. F-Logic , OCML and particularly LOOM do very well. In comparison to LOOM, F-Logic has got an unlimited expressiveness. Especially with logic-based languages, functional limitations are, however, accepted facing a gain of performance. In particular with respect to performance the database-oriented F-Logic has got advantages over LOOM.

3.4.4 Tool Support

From a certain size of the ontology the support of tools is indispensable. In the easiest of cases the tools help the knowledge engineer to model a knowledge domain. By means of tools existing ontologies can, for example, be integrated easier. Help functions are, however, especially useful, too in order to formulate more complex axioms and to execute various tests whether all language characteristics were correctly applied. On the other hand axioms can also be checked on plausibility by means of tools, i.e. when the ontology does not give the reply expected by intuition by the user. In the following we present a choice of known tools: Protégé, WebOnto, OntoSaurus, KADS22, OntoEdit, Ontolingua-Server, and WebODE. This selection is not complete but shows different approaches of tool support. Furthermore, the focus is on tools which have a significant user community and are in fact used to design ontologies.

Protégé. Protégé has got quite a huge user community, as it has already been available for some years and thus belongs to the matured solutions in the field of ontology development. [166, 167]. To be in a position to extent the functionality in a flexible way, a broad range of plug-ins is available or in planning stage, respectively. Thus RDF(S) and XML documents can be handled, for instance, i.e. they can be imported as well as stored. Via the plug-in "Flora" one can also work with F-Logic. The representation paradigm used by Protégé are frames, i.e. its abilities and limitations go together with those of the frame paradigm. Differences between the knowledge models are resolved by declaration via meta classes. According to the developer this, together with OKBC, allows a simple adaption of various knowledge models to Protégé. The editor disposes of a Java-GUI. The central point here is the working on the class hierarchy or taxonomy, respectively. The classes dispose of "template slots" that contain the corresponding properties for instantiation. One can define concrete as well as abstract classes. Multiple inheritance is possible and even classes can be instantiated from a meta class.

WebOnto. WebOnto imports and exports OCML ontologies [64]. The query interface expects requests in OCML [66, 65, 244]. WebOnto is accessible as Java applet online via the WWW browser. An advantage of this approach is the direct access to a large number of already developed ontologies. These can be indicated in the source text and be exported to Ontolingua. WebOnto offers a graphic depiction of the instances contained in the ontology. The depiction can adapt to various needs and views. One can also execute a series of operations such as "Ask, Tell" and "Evaluate". As those are OCML-oriented, corresponding language knowledge is necessary.

OntoSaurus. OntoSaurus also offers a Web interface that can be accessed via a standard Web browser. The ontologies to be accessed that way are implemented in LOOM with OntoSaurus. The main function is the browsing through these ontologies. It is possible to execute deductive queries and to establish ontologies with the declarative mechanisms of the language LOOM. A classifier executes forward-chaining, semantic unification and object-oriented truth maintenance. Ontologies can be verified in a clearly structured way and minor modifications can easily be done. For major ones, a deeper comprehension of LOOM is, however, necessary and those are no longer easy to model.

KADS22. KADS22 is part of the CommonKADS project. With KADS22 knowledge models can be developed by means of the CommonKADS methodology. Thereby the models are specified in the Conceptual Modeling Language (CML) KADS22 is an interactive interface for CML. It also disposes of a graphical interface. Via that interface the following functionality is accessible: Parsing of CML data files, hypertext browsing, generation of a graphical notation, query, creation of a glossary and production of HTML.

K-Infinity. K-Infinity is a suite of tools for the development and the usage of "knowledge networks" [103, 129, 221]. The core component is the Knowledge Builder which is used to create and edit concepts, instances, relations, synonyms, attributes and roles. A mark-up function for the annotation of documents is also integrated. A built-in search function can be used to conduct queries which can be stored, too. The Accelerator is a browser-based user interface that can be used to maintain and extend the knowledge network. The Semantic Matcher helps to weight the relations and to evaluate these by the graph-based visualization of concepts and instances. The K-Infinity Server stores the data consistently and persistently. The overall architecture supports cooperative work in groups. Internally, the knowledge network is represented proprietarily. However, import and export functions via XML, CSV and ODBC are available.

OntoEdit. OntoEdit is a development environment for the establishment of ontologies. Contrary to the Web-based tools, OntoEdit is locally installed on a workstation. The architecture enables enhancements via plug-ins. The conceptional model of the established ontologies can be reproduced in various representation languages. The public domain version offers a small palette of functions whereas the commercial version, storing ontologies in a relational database, offers extended possibilities. Moreover axioms can be formulated and tested by this variant. Ontologies can be established in XML, F-Logic, RDF(S) and DAML+OIL and be edited with a GUI. OntoBroker should be considered as a supplement to OntoEdit. Thereby we talk about an inference and query machine.

Ontolingua-Server. For Ontolingua a server of the same name exists which is accessible via the WWW [141]. The server contains a collection of ontologies that can also be reused or modified for the establishment of new ontologies. This does considerably simplify the ontology development if suitable ontologies are available. Working with the server is done via a Web interface using a standard Web browser. Thus multi-user operation is supported, i.e. cooperative ontology development is possible. The Ontolingua server offers the most extensive import and export possibilities of all the tools mentioned here. Concepts can easily be modeled, multiple inheritance is supported. Apart from a "guided tour" there are, however, no online help functions to Ontolingua so that implementation problems are not always easy to solve.

WebODE. WebODE can also be accessed via a Web interface. The ontologies to be reached via WebODE are internally stored in a relational database. An API is to simplify the integration with other systems and applications. Therefore the WebODE is also named "advanced ontological engineering workbench" [237]. Apart from the WebODE-specific XML-format ontologies can also be imported or exported as RDF(S) and OIL. Editing of ontologies is done via a form- based GUI, in addition supported by the possibility to manage various views. Moreover the following is available: a consistency verification, different kinds of constraints, taxonomies (also multiple inheritance), relations, constants, forms, instances of concepts and references. A flexible design is possible through the different views that can also be freely defined as well as through the definition of different sets of instances which can be exchanged against one another. Working in groups is also possible for ontologies.

3.5 Summary

A systematic way of learning from errors that can lead to security breaches is an important prerequisite for establishing an acceptable security level. This can be achieved by a security knowledge process based on the notion of a feedback loop. Technically, this can only be implemented if we define syntax and semantics of relevant security information.

We consider ontologies as a suitable approach contributing to solve this problem: they help to clarify the structure of knowledge and enable knowledge sharing [43]. In particular, this contributes to close the gap between theoretical security concepts and the code of practice. Both, security experts and novices can work together more efficiently supported by tools which evaluate corresponding meta-information.

Developing a suitable ontology means to follow a set of design criteria which refer to the content and the underlying logic. Looking at methodologies for the development of ontologies we can conclude that there is more than one way to do it right. It is recommendable to combine two or more approaches in order to have different views on a knowledge domain. All methodologies show a set of commonalities: task definition, phase-based or evolutionary improvement, informal description and transformation in an ontology representation language. Considering such languages we have to look at the representation of knowledge and the suitability for reasoning. Concerning the latter the more traditional languages should be preferred rather than XML-based languages.

4. The Human Factor

4.1 Introduction

In this chapter we derive the working hypothesis for the book: human failures are a major reason for security breaches in IT Systems. It seems to be inevitable that human will make errors - especially in such complex situations such as the development of software. Thereby, we follow a two-step approach. Firstly, we examine two selected case studies which have in common that they are both new application domains and that well-known errors are made again. The reasons can be found in failures in all phases of a system's life-cycle (e.g. design, implementation, operation). Secondly, we provide analogies to cognitive psychology in order to clarify the human limitations in characteristic situations. Before we summarize and conclude this chapter, we refer to related work that also focuses on the human factor.

4.2 Case Studies

It is difficult to get in-depth knowledge of what really happened during an attack and what exactly were the reasons for an incident. We assume that the "victims" often don't like to talk too much about security breaches as they might fear a loss of reputation. For the same reason we can expect a high number of incidents that are not reported anyway. Furthermore, we can

M. Schumacher: Security Engineering with Patterns, LNCS 2754, pp. 45-55, 2003.
© Springer-Verlag Berlin Heidelberg 2003

imagine a certain number of undetected security breaches as well as near misses, i.e. something went wrong but an incident actually did not yet occur.

The intention of the discussion of two selected case studies in this section is, however, to provide some typical real-world examples for human failures that led to security breaches. The first example presents results of an examination of IP telephony systems conducted in 2001 [3]. By nature, we are able to present more details being personally involved in the analysis process. The second example shows severe design flaws in technologies that provide Instant Messaging (IM) services. Based on these examples we identify and characterize typical problems that usually occur in new solutions.

4.2.1 Internet/Telephony Integration

The phone network and the Internet are converging. In 2001, IP telephony applications were considered to have a huge economic potential. The phone network is rather hard to attack for the occasional hacker. For example, he needs to understand complex protocols, needs physical access, and must be able to manipulate both voice and control channels. On the contrary the Internet is a publically shared network that can be accessed by anyone. Furthermore, almost everyone can carry out an attack as hacking tools are available for anyone, too. Bringing both worlds together decreases the level of security to the rather insecure level of the Internet.

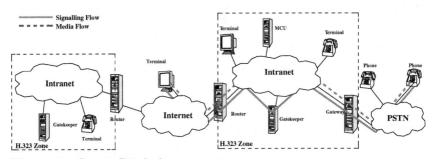

Figure 4.1. Generic IP telephony scenario.

To prove this we have looked for vulnerabilities in a H.323 based IP telephony scenario [3, 223, 2]. The following is an excerpt of this analysis and the insights. As illustrated in Figure 4.1 such an architecture comprises a signalling plane, a media transport plane and several telephony components. From a security point of view the following aspects should be considered:

– Both planes depend on the same infrastructure, the IP network. Compared to conventional telephony there is no physical separation between them.

- The network itself is not operated by a single, trustworthy provider. Parts of an IP telephony scenario typically depend on untrusted networks, components and operators.
- The IP network is also used by many other services. It is much more difficult to protect compared to a rather closed single-service network.
- The capabilities of components in an IP telephony scenario are not limited to telephony. Furthermore, they are full-fledged computers that can provide and use other distributed services and are therefore exposed to attacks.

The overall situation leads to an increased risk. Both signalling and transport lane are targets of attacks against integrity, confidentiality, and authenticity of the transmitted data. The audio payload as well as the signalling data is exposed to attacks such as eavesdropping, jamming, and modification. Compromising terminals or infrastructure components lead to additional risks regarding the user's privacy (i.e. who is calling to whom) and the misuse of IP terminals (e.g. using expensive lines to foreign countries). Furthermore specific functions of an IP telephony infrastructure component can be attacked, e.g. registration of terminals. The execution environment of IP telephony functions can also be attacked, e.g. the operating system of a terminal. Even systems that are not directly related to IP telephony can be attacked. For example, a firewall with support for IP telephony might be weakened as it temporarily opens certain connections. In particular we could conduct attacks with the following results during the analysis of certain IP telephony products and services:

Getting Control of a Terminal. With physical access to an IP telephone an attacker can restore the system's factory settings that include a well-known default password (written down in the telephone's manual). Furthermore, the passwords were inherently weak as they only consist of numbers and were often transmitted in plaintext. These attacks lead to full control of the device.

Denial-of-Service (1). Another attack is to send unexpected or incorrect signalling data. As a result the examined telephones were temporarily unavailable, locked up, or crashed. Later, we used such Denial-of-Service attacks in order to impersonate a legitimate terminal.

Denial-of-Service (2). Some phones used an integrated WWW-server in order to manage the device and to check its settings. Taking advantage of vulnerabilities in the implementation of the WWW-server we could crash the device with long URL requests (i.e. buffer overflow).

Eavesdropping. In IP telephony audio connections are negotiated dynamically on-the-fly. This seems to make it difficult to eavesdrop a call. However, studying the IP telephony protocol stacks and the corresponding documentation we were also able to design a simple tool that could record such calls on the fly.

Impersonation. Another attack was to deregister a regular terminal. This is only possible if the caller has the same IP address as the registered party. However, this information could be faked and a "malicious" device could be registered instead.

The discussed vulnerabilities are not due to limitations or shortcomings within technology, architectures and signalling protocols. The main reasons were severe flaws in design, implementation and default configurations of the examined products. The goal of this book is to develop an appropriate security approach based on patterns in order to prevent such problems which are basically well-known and where solutions should be available. In the meanwhile, security solutions for IP telephony are available [178, 180, 186].

4.2.2 Instant Messaging

As a rather new application IM enjoys a rapidly growing popularity: in August 2002 the number of users was estimated with 81 million users [55]. The main reason for the pervasiveness of this service is that IM has a severe advantage compared to e-mail that is still one of the Internet's popular applications: for a smooth online conversation you don't have to find, read, reply and send messages back and forth[1]. Being able to do this, all IM applications require at least the following services:

– Presence Service.
  The presence service provides a list of all people that are currently online. Being online your status can be requested by other people. You can restrict such requests setting up a list with people you want to interact with (called "buddy list"). The presence service allows to send requests in order to find out whether a particular person is online. It is also possible to be notified whenever a person connects to the IM network.
– Instant Messaging.
  This service is responsible for near to real time message exchange itself, i.e. you can directly exchange notes with another person being online. A message is the basic building block of IM. As the smallest unit of communication, all higher level services build on it.

The basic IM scenario is shown in Figure 4.2. The first step is always that a user connects to a messaging server farm providing username and password in order to be authorized. Location request for other users are redirected to servers that provide the presence service. Subsequent messages can be exchanged in two ways. They are either routed through the messaging server

---

[1] The `talk` program can be seen as an ancestor of IM. As written in the manual page, "it is a visual communication program which copies lines from your terminal to that of another user." The talk command appeared first in BSD 4.2 (1984).

farm servers or, once users located each other, messages can also be exchanged directly for higher-level services.

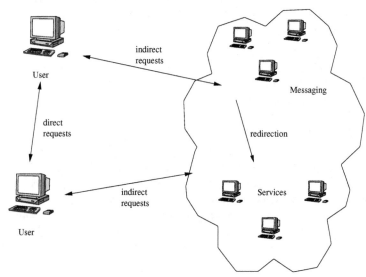

Figure 4.2. Instant messaging scenario.

A typical higher level service is a chat room, i.e. you can create a custom chat environment and send notes to a more or less closed group of people. Another popular service is file sharing, i.e. images, sound files, documents, etc. are shared among peers. The incorporation of streaming technologies even allows to talk to someone without using a phone or to exchange near-real-time news (e.g. stock quotes). Commercial applications also include collaborative games (e.g. sophisticated virtual worlds that last for months or even years). IM enables the coordination of activities in any distributed collaboration. The overall IM concept, however, introduces several security problems discussed in the following [55, 135, 173, 191]. Note, that we neither claim to provide a complete list of all security problems introduced by IM services or particular products, nor do we say that a given product features all of the above problems.

Subverting Firewalls. Usually, the network traffic of an organization is restricted by a firewall. Often inbound and outbound traffic is only allowed on well-known ports, e.g. HTTP connections on port 80. By default IM software is shipped with a well-known port, too. However, the configuration allows to set arbitrary ports, i.e. a firewall that makes decisions based on ports can no longer work.

Bypassing Virus Filtering. IM messages can also contain viruses, worms and Trojan horses. If the firewall is bypassed, we can also assume that anti-virus software at the network gateways does not work properly, too. Then everything depends on up-to-date and activated anti-virus software on *every* host.

Controlling the User's Computer. Software contains errors. Thus, many software packages are vulnerable due to buffer overflows that often give an attacker administrator privileges and allows to execute arbitrary code.

Loss of Confidentiality. Although it is possible all major IM products don't encrypt the messages. A sniffer tool allows the attacker to record all messages that might be interesting. If encryption is used at all, we can find weak algorithms (because they are fast) or proprietary ones (i.e. security by obscurity). Some products also store message protocols in plain-text, i.e. anyone with access to the local hard disk can basically read any message.

Impersonation. Sometimes even username and password are exchanged and stored as plain-text, i.e. the attacker can take over the user's identity. A recent bug in AOL's IM software (AIM) allowed to hijack user accounts due to a bug. The reason was a variable that is ignored by the sign-up process but prepended to the screen name when an account is created. For example, if this variable is set to "Ja" and the user name to "mes Kirk", an AIM account with the name "James Kirk" will be set up even if this name is already in use. Then the attacker can perfectly impersonate his victim.

Disclosure of Internal Information. Most IM messages contain the IP address of the user's computer. Especially direct connections will reveal this address and can give insights to internal network topologies. Furthermore, some clients export the / or respectively the C:/ directory by default. A request for a file named `passwd` might reveal interesting information for an attacker. Another problem is that some services use the same username for both e-mail and IM. This is an invitation for attacks such as harvesting and reselling of email addresses or password cracking.

Denial-of-Service. For example, an attacker can bring down an IM server farm if he controls many accounts on different clients and changes the state of each account from online to offline frequently and from many distributed clients. As these changes are published in the overall system they can simply lead to performance bottlenecks or to overloads. More serious are unexpected or incorrect messages that crash servers, clients, or both. Recently, a rather harmless worm spread successfully within a P2P network mainly used by the Kazaa software.

Client Software as Trojan Horse. The client software itself can have built-in Trojan horses. Until you don't use trustworthy open-source software that is frequently examined by the open-source community you cannot be sure whether the client software is in fact spy-ware or tries to use your resources (e.g. hard disk, memory, and processing power). IM platforms can even install more modules and updates during regular IM sessions without notification of the user.

Privacy Issues. As the IP address of the user's computer is sometimes transmitted along with each request, an attacker can try to build user profiles. Depending on the protocol some clients allow to display current searches together with the IP address. The attacker then knows what kind of information (e.g. software, videos, audio, etc.) someone is generally looking for.

IM is a new Internet application with a rapidly growing user community. Our analysis shows, however, that security is obviously not considered as a primary requirement. It seems that currently security is even treated as an after-thought by the majority of the available IM solutions. Many security weaknesses are caused by design or by accident (e.g. disabled or misconfigured security settings) and could have been avoided in advance. Nevertheless, there are efforts to make IM more secure in the next generation. For example, the IETF works on a secure IM solution.

4.2.3 Findings

In Table 4.1 we summarize the attacks described above together with the generic vulnerability and the overall consequences. The following interesting trends can be derived from this:

Firstly, the required knowledge for carrying out most of the attacks was obviously rather low. Furthermore, the principles of the attacks were not something new but well-known for years. Thus the incidents were no accident, i.e. it was only a matter of time when the first attacker starts exploiting vulnerabilities. Secondly, the vulnerabilities are not something new, too. They are well-known and countermeasures should have been available. Finally, the same is true for the consequences of the attacks. Although the consequences should have been well-known, it seems that security didn't play an important role.

Attack	Vulnerability	Consequences
sytem reset	weak password	full control
malformed input, buffer overflow	insufficient verification	denial-of-service, full control
eavesdropping	weak or no encryption	loss of confidentiality
spoofing, masquerading	weak or no authentication	loss of authenticity
tunneling	weak or no filtering	bypassing protection mechanisms

Table 4.1. Case studies: attacks, vulnerability, consequences.

Especially in new application domains it seems that the same errors are made over and over again. Observing security-related information sources we can see that security fails: almost every month we have severe security breaches in the news. Regardless of this alarming trend we can safely expect a high estimated number of unnotified cases, quite apart from near misses. As we know the technical reasons for security failures, we concentrate on the human factor in this book.

4.3 Why Security Fails

As stated in the previous section we assume that the main reason for the existing problems is that security failures are are no technical problem in the first place. Security is always implemented by humans on request of humans. Thus the human factor influences IT-security in significant ways. As put by Petroski who was quoted in the beginning of this chapter, humans will inevitably make errors when they build something new. As shown in the previous section, development and maintenance of secure systems can also be considered as situations in which humans will make errors. Such situations are complex, intransparent, dynamic, incompletely or wrongly understood [67]. These characteristics influence each other and complicate the development process. In this section we will underline this hypothesis by looking at findings of cognitive psychology [67, 116].

Repair-Service Behavior. Security can play a subordinate role in the engineering process. If security comes as an after-thought, this can lead to a situation where the people involved solve the wrong problems from a security point of view. Thus, good security solutions are often developed after an initial design and implementation with bad or no security. As the overall situation is difficult to handle, non-security experts start to solve obvious problems which, however, only play a minor role. They lose track and can overlook side-effects. Due to a lack of security-awareness and ignorance of time-dependencies it may be difficult to identify faults which are currently no problem but can become a problem in the future. Unclear objectives and no decomposition into sub-goals are further characteristics of such a "repair-service behavior". Nevertheless, examples such as Video on Demand systems [63, 99, 100, 101, 140], network infrastructures for mobile devices [113, 114], or NIS (Network Information System) infrastructures [4] show that it is possible to secure systems that have failed in first designs and implementations.

Ad-hoc Solutions. When people try to find a solution for a problem, they often follow an ad-hoc approach. In particular, "the average person cannot tell good security from bad security" [194]. The impact on elements aside the adopted solution are overseen in most cases [67].

A good example is the handling of system passwords: a system administrator wants to prevent that the users chose weak passwords. Thus he configures the system to enforce strong passwords, i.e. a user cannot enter passwords that don't meet certain criteria (password must not be contained in a dictionary). This solution is well-known and straight forward. Unfortunately, the administrator doesn't realize that nobody can remember strong passwords any longer. As a consequence, users might start to write their passwords on a slip of paper that could be found under their keyboard, or even worse, pinned on their monitor.

Another example is the application of firewalls in order to implement security at the network layer. They are applied in many occasions without thinking about the impact on other systems and applications. The other way round, most applications are developed without firewalls in mind [1, 185].

Side Effects. Security covers a very complex area with manifold dependencies [194]. Even if all dependencies are identified, it might be difficult to consider all of them appropriately. The IP phones are a good example for this. The developer could basically figure out whether the Web server software is secure or not. But probably he cannot decide whether the combination of Web server, operating system and hardware components is secure. The overall system is too complex to be considered as a whole. Often, the developer or administrator of a specific component doesn't even want to worry about security outside his area of responsibility, e.g. the Webmaster only cares about his Web server. Security engineering making sense should be possible without knowledge of the whole security scope and all its dependencies.

Time Dependencies. The level of security of a given system is also time-dependent [209]. A system that is considered to be secure today may be insecure tomorrow. Statements about the system's security are only valid with time references. For instance, the strength of cryptographic algorithms typically is founded on difficult mathematical problems. If a genius finds a solution for such a problem, security suddenly disappears.

Lack of Security Know-How and Awareness. With the exception of cryptography [34], the science of IT security is quite new and covers multiple disciplines such as operating systems, computer networks and software engineering. It is very difficult to make systems secure as there are many different components and mechanisms involved. In addition, trust relationships change frequently, which makes an analysis of all security requirements very hard. One cannot assume that the average system developer or architect is a skilled security expert, too. We should notice that in most cases security engineering is done by non-security experts. For example, the developer of a system has to implement the necessary security features to some extent as an add-on. In most cases the developer is an expert regarding the system's functionality but not regarding its security. Another problem is that "there aren't enough experts to go around" [194].

Rigidity of Experts. Finally, we also include security experts in our examination. A suitable quote comes from Maslow: "When the only tool you own is a hammer, every problem begins to resemble a nail." Having had success in previous situations can lead to a functional fixation where you adopt solutions that worked before although the context where the new problem occurred is different. This can basically lead to wrong conclusions, assessments, and decisions.

4.4 Related Work

In this section we present a few examples of other contributions which consider the human impact on security as integral part of their work.

The hypothesis of Krusl's PhD thesis is that programmers make assumptions which "frequently do not hold in the execution of the program" [139]. By nature, vulnerabilities caused by such a wrong assessment cannot be detected by tests. In order to improve the understanding of such vulnerabilities, Krsul developed a unified definition and classification based on previous approaches.

Petroski and Chiles present a couple of stories in more traditional engineering domains [170, 46]. The bottom line is always that humans have limitations that will lead to errors in complex situations. However, they stress that errors are a chance for improvements (or to put it more precisely - without errors there will be no improvement).

Anderson's work can be counted to the cornerstones of security literature focusing on the human factor [10]. He presents results of an examination of failures in retail banking systems. The main reasons were errors in the implementation and in the management. Anderson identifies the lack of a learning mechanism as the root of these typical situations.

4.5 Summary

In this chapter we have shown that the human factor has a significant impact on security. Looking at selected case studies which feature new application domains we saw that well-known errors are repeated. This can be generalized: although the principles of attacks are not new, the vulnerabilities are known, and countermeasures are basically available, the described problems have not been prevented in advance.

Looking for reasons we have considered aspects of cognitive psychology. Humans will inevitably make errors in complex situations such as developing and maintaining secure systems. Even experts can sometimes can be wrong. A statement from Anderson can serve as bottom line of our examination [10]:

> "When an aircraft crashes, it is frontpage news. Teams of investigators rush to the scene, and the subsequent enquiries are conducted by

experts from organisations with a wide range of interests - the carrier, the insurer, the manufacturer, the airline pilots' union, and the local aviation authority. Their findings are examined by journalists and politicians, discussed in pilots' messes, and passed on by flying instructors."

Examples as described before show that there doesn't seem to be such learning process for today's IT systems. As we have described in Section 3.2) there is no established security knowledge process. We take up Anderson's thoughts that a paradigm shift is underway, i.e. we have to look for new solutions for the described problem.

5. Classifying Security Improvement Artifacts

> Engineering is applied science.
> Engineering is the application of
> science for practical purposes.
> Engineers put theory into
> practice.
>
>

JOHN MCDONOUGH
>

> Structural engineering is the
> science and art of designing and
> making, with economy and
> elegance, buildings, bridges,
> frameworks, and other similar
> structures so that they can
> safely resist the forces to which
> they may be subjected.
>
>

THE STRUCTURAL ENGINEER
>

5.1 Introduction

We refer to a security improvement artifact as any approach, standard, role, method, technique, or tool that helps to improve security (analogous to the Zachman framework [219, 243]). In recent years a number of such artifacts have been developed to assist organizations in establishing and maintaining security. However, the increasing number of incidents indicates that there is obviously a gap between theory and the code of practice: in Chapter 4 we have shown that humans will inevitably make errors under certain conditions. Therefore our viewpoint is human-centered, i.e. we assume that the ordinary system engineer is no security expert. Thus, we use these and other important criteria in order to analyze a set of security improvement artifacts in this chapter. Note that the selection is influenced by the security expertise of the author and not necessarily complete. However, the examined security improvement artifacts are commonly used by security practitioners. The

M. Schumacher: Security Engineering with Patterns, LNCS 2754, pp. 57-86, 2003.
© Springer-Verlag Berlin Heidelberg 2003

goal is to identify gaps that have to be filled by our complementary security pattern-based approach.

We focus on developing systems that have to meet certain security requirements. The development of systems that provide security functionality themselves such as encryption software, firewalls, Intrusion Detection Systems (IDS), and virus scanner software, is out-of-scope of this book. We treat these as sub-systems or components that can be used as building blocks for security.

Outline. The outline of this Chapter is as follows: in the next Section we introduce our classification scheme for security improvement artifacts. First, we introduce steps of a typical security engineering process. Then we show the phases of system engineering. Based on an integrated view of security and system engineering, we present a set of important classification metrics. This view is used to organize the following Sections. In Section 5.3 we discuss typical security improvement artifacts that provide guidance for defining security requirements. Based on these requirements, an analysis of the system has to be conducted. From a security point of view this means to identify threats, attacks, and vulnerabilities which lead to a certain risk. Such concepts are presented in Section 5.4. Several security improvement approaches for specifying the architecture and the design of a system are examined in Section 5.5. The next step is to build the system. Accordingly, we discuss security improvement at the level of coding and configuration of system functions in Section 5.6. Then we discuss certain concepts for testing the system during integration and operation in Section 5.7. Finally, we summarize our findings and show that we need another approach to support security novices in solving security problems. As this chapter is rather extensive, we present intermediate results at the end of each section.

Results. In particular, the overall result of this chapter is that patterns are suitable as a security improvement approach. In order to classify security approaches, we introduce a framework that is based on an integrated view of security and system engineering. The comparison of a pattern-based approach with the other examined tools and techniques reveal that they are especially suitable for novices and help, for instance, to consider side-effects appropriately. However, we also identify some potential for improvements: there is no definition of what security patterns actually are and how they can be used. Besides, only a keyword-based search is possible, i.e. it is difficult to find and apply the right pattern efficiently. These findings draw up the agenda for the further chapters of this book.

We have presented a similar but less extensive comparison between patterns and security approaches first at PLoP 2001 [208]. A classification framework based on the Zachman approach has been discussed at our security patterns workshop at EuroPLoP 2002 [201]. Furthermore, we have examined vulnerability databases, security scanner, and prioritization schemes [198, 205].

5.2 Classification Framework

In security literature there is no commonly agreed classification scheme of security topics. Therefore we introduce a framework for classifying security engineering artifacts in this section. Our classification approach is based on a more integrated view of security engineering and other engineering domains - especially (software) system engineering. As security concerns are often treated as a separate task or - even worse - as an afterthought, it is important to understand the impact of security on system engineering tasks and vice versa. Therefore, we first introduce typical steps of security engineering. Then, we discuss human roles in a system engineering process. Based on the assumption that both approaches aren't integrated very well, we derive criteria for classifying security improvement artifacts.

5.2.1 Security Engineering

Security engineering is an evolving discipline. Thus an agreed and precise definition does not exist. Adapting the introductory quotes of this chapter, we can say that security engineering means to put security theory into security practice. This means that a security engineer designs and makes systems that are protected against threats, i.e. forces to which systems may be subjected. Amoroso defines (system) security engineering[1] as a "discipline that allows one to determine the optimal security approach for a particular system based on an identification of all relevant factors and impediments to security" [9].

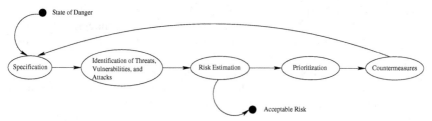

Figure 5.1. Security engineering approach.

The main objective of security engineering is to change from a state of danger to a state of acceptable risk, i.e. the assets associated with a computer system are protected in a sufficient way. As illustrated in Figure 5.1, several iterations including the following steps might be necessary:

Specification. All components and interfaces of the system have to be determined completely. If the specification of the architecture of a system doesn't cover all relevant components, some threats, vulnerabilities, and attacks might not be identified later.

---

[1] In this document the terms *Security Engineering* and *System Security Engineering* are used synonymously.

Identification of Threats, Vulnerabilities and Attacks. The basic threats and vulnerabilities for each component and interface of a system have to be identified. This helps to determine the corresponding attacks which can be expected.

Risk Estimation. The risk for a potential attack has to determined for all components and interfaces. Hereby, bias effects as a result of relationships between specific threats, vulnerabilities and attacks should be considered.

Prioritization. If a particular risk is too high, the corresponding vulnerabilities have to be prioritized. Vulnerabilities of a particularly jeopardized component or interface get a high priority. This step is very important in order to get an efficient order for carrying out the countermeasures.

Countermeasures. Appropriate countermeasures that eliminate the identified threats, vulnerabilities and attacks or at least minimize their effects have to be selected and carried out. Thereby the requirements of the owner of the system have to be considered (e.g. costs, usability, performance, etc.).

Especially technical countermeasures could lead to changes of the specification. Thus these steps build a loop and have to be repeated until the countermeasures lead to an acceptable risk, i.e. a state of security.

5.2.2 System Engineering

Several life cycle models for system engineering exist such as waterfall model, spiral model, and rapid prototyping model. These models define the steps and the workflow of the system engineering process. Although they follow different approaches, many life cycle models regard the phases as illustrated in the horizontal axis of Figure 5.2.

Humans play different engineering roles during the different stages of a system's life cycle. Many of such roles have been identified. For example, Sheard discussed 12 system engineering roles [216] and in the IT Baseline Protection Manual about 40 security-related roles can be found [33]. In order to narrow the scope of our following discussion we consider two major groups of participants that play basic roles in the overall life cycle. These roles describe *who* is involved in the engineering process and represent different perspectives on security. Considering the life-cycle we also discuss *when* they are involved and *what* they want to achieve.

Stakeholders. All people that need the system belong to the group of "stakeholders". In the early life-cycle phases, they provide the initial stimulus for new systems or new functions and perform viability checks. Technical management and executives should be expected at this level. Later, they will also run, maintain and use the system. Thus, administrators and end-users can be counted to this group, too.

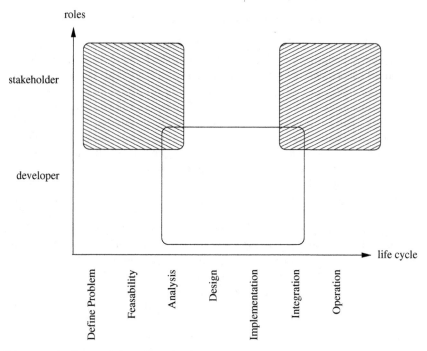

Figure 5.2. System life cycle and roles.

Developers. Between problem definition, feasibility studies and operation the "developers" come into play. Basically, systems can be developed in-house or by a team of external developers. In any case they have to consider the stakeholder's requirements. Their major tasks are analysis, design and implementation of the new system i.e. there are roles such as analysts, designers, and codifiers.

During the integration both parties work together more closely again. Figure 5.2 illustrates such an example for the assignment between roles and life-cycle phases. Hereby, the hatched areas represent the role assignment between stakeholders, developers and specific life-cycle phases. Although this scheme is rather coarse-grained, it shows that defining security objectives and actually implementing security is not necessarily carried out by the same set of people. Accordingly, overlaps indicate interfaces and interactions between different engineering processes and the corresponding roles as described before. Note, that the sequence of life-cycle phases might not be linear. Certain iterations are possible and some phases can be skipped, e.g. when COTS products are going to be used and integrated in order to provide new system functionality.

5.2.3 The Zachman Framework

State-of-the art security literature follows different approaches for structuring the security domain [9, 11, 71, 89, 90, 172, 194]. Usually, security topics are organized by problem domains such as encryption/decryption, access control, network security, etc.

The notion "artifacts" is taken from Zachman's Information System Architecture (ISA) Framework. The framework is two-dimensional. The rows represent different views on an architecture (i.e. roles) whereas the columns represent different perspectives of an architecture. The columns provide answers to *what, how, where, who, when,* and *why* questions. Architectural artifacts can be found in the cells of the framework. There are approaches to use or adapt the ISA framework for security, e.g. by Henning and Hybertson et al. [110, 119].

In contrast to Henning, however, we did not closely follow the Zachman Framework [110]. In fact, we adopted the basic concepts, i.e. using different views and identifying artifacts by asking certain questions. In contrast to Zachman we asked several questions to classify individual artifacts (answering usually "Zachman question" results in a single artifact). Such a composite of all cells in a single row leads to a complete model from the given perspective. That way we circumvented several drawbacks of the ISA approach. For example, it constrains engineering views to a fixed set and it does not have an explicit place for general solutions [119]. An example is provided in Table 5.1 on the next page.

5.2.4 Classification Metrics

Solving a security problem requires to incorporate security aspects into the overall system life-cycle. For the following discussions we look at an engineering scenario where we can observe different responsibilities and backgrounds of people which solve a (security) problem together. As indicated in Figure 5.3 it is basically possible to assign security engineering steps to system engineering steps. Hereby, we see the subsequent time phases of security engineering and, respectively, system engineering on the axes of the diagram. The bubbles show possible overlaps of the two processes. Based on our findings in Chapter 4 and the hypothesis that security engineering and system engineering aren't integrated yet. In fact, there is no defined integrated process today that is commonly accepted. Accordingly, we consider the following assumptions:

– System engineers have no adequate profile, i.e. they are security novices.
– System engineers have to focus on other aspects than security.
– Security comes as an after-thought and security engineering roles are not properly defined (if at all).

With this human-centered viewpoint we provide answers for several classifying questions, i.e. how can we achieve security improvements? The results

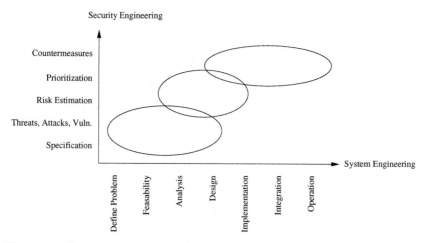

Figure 5.3. Integrating security and system engineering.

are security improvement artifacts at different life-cycle phases which are important for both security and system engineering. For example, one answer for the question *how* to identify threats and attacks (*what*) can be goal tree approaches used during analysis (*when*). An example for our approach is shown in Table 5.1.

	What	How	Who	When
Stakeholder	Security requirements	chose from pre-defined requirements	Management, technical executives	Problem definition

Table 5.1. Classifying security improvement artifacts.

Note that we sometimes categorize security improvement artifacts according to their focal point, i.e. it is basically possible to assign them to more than one category. For example, security management standards provide guidance for several life-cycle phases. Their focus is, however, on a higher level, i.e. they are usually used by the management and technical executives but not by developers or administrators. Another example is the IT Baseline Protection Manual that provides both rather high-level security concepts and technical information. The focal point is, however, on the technical security building blocks. Each artifact can be further classified by a set of properties introduced in the following. These metrics have been considered as important by the author during his security work. There might be more properties, however, the selected set is sufficient to classify the examined security improvement artifacts. Hereby, we also show some relationships between these properties.

Effort. Additional time and costs have to be taken into account for any security measure [210]. Therefore, the required effort for applying a security engineering technique can be used as a classification property.

Expertise. Experts solve problems better than novices [67, 116]. Thus, we can assume that there is a relationship between effort and expertise as experts usually solve problems more efficiently.

Structuring. We also consider structural differences of the overall representation of information as important [118, 198]. Such approaches can have a structured, semi-structured or unstructured representation. More structured representations together with defined semantics also help to formalize steps of security engineering.

Tool Support. Thus, a certain degree of structure improves the opportunities for tool support. A lack of supporting tools can be a major obstacle for the application of any engineering technique. Tool support helps to enhance "understandability, decrease the complexity [...], and eliminate terminological ambiguity [215]." Sophisticated tools can guide novices in the overall learning and problem solving process [214, 222]. Tool support is also an important classification criteria for security approaches [210].

Side-effects. The proper consideration of side effects is important for problem solving [67]. The focus of many approaches is often on isolated components. The results of missing side-effects are incomplete and wrong assumptions, i.e. the corresponding security measures will fail. A proper structuring of the required information is a precondition for the appropriate consideration of side-effects.

Time Dependency. Security is also a matter of time [209, 210]. The publication of new vulnerabilities and attacks can render the results of any security measure useless. Furthermore, the implementation of any security measure takes time, i.e. even if you know that you are vulnerable you are not immediately secure. As such, they are a special kind of side-effect.

These properties have direct effects on the applicability and usability of each security improvement artifact. The above set of properties might not be complete but sufficient to classify proven security approaches and to support our security pattern-based approach. Other properties such as scalability, consideration of relevant legislation, etc. are also important but out of scope of this book. Note that the sequence of criteria follows no specific order, i.e. there is no weighting for a given criteria. A weighting can only be given if the context for the application of a security improvement artifact is known (e.g. applied in a small company or in a global enterprise). Nevertheless, there are relationships between the criteria as described before.

5.3 Requirements Definition

Requirements describe the desired characteristics of the system such as usability or efficiency [124]. Balancing both security and other requirements usually means to find a compromise. Therefore, the definition of requirements is important for both security and system engineering. It might happen that not all requirements can be stated in advance, i.e. several engineering cycles can be necessary (e.g. a security policy defines requirements and requirements derived from running systems determine the policy). In this Section we discuss evaluation criteria, security management standards, and security policies. These are security improvement artifacts that can be used to derive security requirements.

5.3.1 Evaluation Criteria

When security is considered at a management or executive level, generic security standards play an important role. Especially the evaluation of the security of IT systems is very important for military, intelligence and more and more public organizations. Thus a variety of evaluation criteria and security guideline documents have been developed by various governments in cooperation with some large organizations. Prominent examples are the Information Technology Security Evaluation Criteria (ITSEC) [75] and the Common Criteria [121]. Although these standards are considered as means of evaluating a system, these standards provide also help for specifying a system.

Such criteria define different levels at which IT-systems can be evaluated and compared. The levels represent different sets of functional security requirements and hierarchical levels of assurance. The primary goal is to prove that the system fulfills certain requirements regarding its protection mechanisms and that the correctness of the implementation meets a certain assurance level.

Evaluation criteria help to create comparable security policy statements in a standardized way. Manufacturers are guided in the design and development of IT-systems and organizations can improve the specification of security requirements in contracts.

Findings. Independent of the expertise of the user, the specification of requirements of IT systems according to any criteria is a costly and time-consuming task. It is difficult for the layman to perform specifications (and evaluations) as the process itself is very complex and requires a lot of background knowledge. A first hurdle is to read and understand the documentation in order to be able to apply such a standard. For each step more or less structured documents have to be prepared. For example, the Common Criteria provide templates for Protection Profiles (PP). This increases the comparability and readability and enables at least a rudimentary tool support. Most standards focus on specific Targets of Evaluation (TOE) as an isolated entity. Therefore dependencies to other IT systems and components could be missed easily, especially by novices. As evaluation is expensive and time-consuming, it is difficult to keep the evaluation results of a TOE up-to-date (nevertheless, evaluated systems have a value for others as they can serve as a model for building or selecting systems). The overall goal of evaluation criteria and especially the Common Criteria is to improve security by enabling and establishing reusable protection profiles for certain classes of technology. The approach is to define sets of functional and assurance requirements for security. As our analysis shows they are no tools for the laymen and it can be expected that they will not be used in ordinary IT environments.

5.3.2 Security Management Standards

Security standards help to manage security appropriately. They are suitable for technical managers and executives. For example, the ISO standard 17799 is an internationally recognized generic information security standard. ISO 17799 provides a set of controls which comprise guidelines for information security management [123]. The standard also covers earlier activities such as development of a security policy and risk estimation. The main focus is, however, on the selection of security objectives and countermeasures: "Physical and Environmental Security", "Communications and Operations Management", "Access Control" and "Systems Development and Maintenance". It serves as a reference for given security problems. For each of these areas a set of controls is proposed. The standard is rather a top-down approach. As such it lists generic state-of-the-art countermeasures, i.e. it is said what could be done but not how. A similar approach is provided by the Standard of Good Practice of the Information Security Forum [92]. Although no specific recommendations are given, security standards are suitable for deriving requirements for a concrete implementation of countermeasures.

Findings. Security standards define organizational processes. Thus the effort depends on the level of organization, i.e. how good is the organizational structure and the organizational support for security. If a company shows a high degree of organization, security standards can be used in a straightforward way. Security management standards provide generic descriptions. Thus, it requires a certain amount of expertise to implement the identified security requirements. Typically such standards are structured by problem domains. There is no further meta-structure. However, workflow management tools can be used to support security management as their focus is on organization. Cross references are provided in corresponding security management documents. Therefore side effects can be considered. However, this requires a certain degree of completeness and up-to-dateness. Security standards can be used to improve security step by step. For example, baseline security is established first and piecemeal steps are made afterwards whenever necessary.

5.3.3 Security Policy

Many security standards consider the development of a security policy as an integral part of the overall security process. Nevertheless, security policies can be analyzed in isolation as a tool for specifying a system. Stakeholders should involve both technical management and staff members. As a result they deliver requirements that have to be met by the developers. In general policies describe what security objectives have to be met. If the security policy for an organization has to be created, the task of writing the document (developing the security policy) is typically assigned to a person (or group) within the organization. At first, it has to be determined which systems (objects) are used and which information (assets) they carry. Then it has to be defined what is allowed and what is forbidden. Thereby possible threats on the systems have to be identified and documented. Finally, the security-level envisaged is described [44]. To be more time invariant, concrete implementations and procedures should not be included. This has to be included in another document. Subsequently this security policy will be applied to the systems. All information is included in an informal text document. Examples for such a policy and corresponding procedures can be found at Vienna University of Technolgy (TUW)[2] [245] and Darmstadt University of Technology (TUD) [117]. The main focus of policies is to define the assets and to determine security requirements for subsequent implementations of security.

Findings. The effort for the determination of relevant systems and associated assets is high. The same is true for identifying relevant threats. Even if you have a "template" for the development of a security policy, the amount of time that has to be invested into the adaption on "local" circumstances should not be underestimated. Furthermore, a security policy should be evaluated continously. The effort is highly depending on the expertise of the developer or maintainer of the policy, as no aspect of security should be missed. Basically, a policy is an informal, unstructured text (i.e. without defined syntax and semantics). This makes it difficult to achieve tool support. However, there are formal approaches to describe policies at the finer-grained application or system levels, e.g. by Eckert [69, 70] or Sloman [56]. As an informal and more or less unstructured document a policy does not help to recognize dependencies between facts. It contains a rather monolithic and linear description of problems and solutions, interferences of different sections are not obvious. Many security policies don't reflect the actual security situation and are always out-dated, as many parameters (e.g. requirements or attacks) change frequently. Our evaluation shows that security policies are not a tool for the laymen. Beside the problems stated above it remains difficult that "everyone understands it, agrees with it and follows it diligently, all the time" [176].

---

[2] One of the people in charge for security at TUW said that the policy has been an approved guideline since 2 years and that it remained stable after crucial evaluations.

5.3.4 Summary

We have examined some security approaches for defining the requirements for a system. At this level of abstraction we can summarize that both effort and expertise is to high in order to consider evaluation criteria, management standards and policies as a security tool which is suitable for novices. In particular it is difficult to consider side-effects appropriately.

5.4 Analysis

From the system engineering oint of view, the goal of an analysis is to specify the new functionality of the system according to the requirements identifed before. From a security point of view an analysis means to identify threats, attacks, and vulnerabilities. Furthermore, the expected risk has to be identified and priorities have to be assigned to the identified problems.

As example we examine goal trees representing a methodological approach for the identification of threats, vulnerabilities and attacks. For the estimation of risk two general approaches are known in the security domain. With a risk analysis one tries to determine the likelihood for an attack to occur. This is typically used by the stakeholders. With the work factor approach the risk is determined corresponding the amount of the attacker's work. Developers can use this approach in order to find out how "strong" the system has to be inherently. Finally, we discuss corresponding prioritization schemes.

5.4.1 Goal Trees

Several approaches with symbolic tree representations have been developed. Each node represents a specific goal that has to be reached. Subsequently the overall goal is then decomposed into subgoals. Typically there are a variety of ways to achieve the high level goal. These goal trees are based on *AND/OR* trees that allow some basic calculations if values are assigned to the nodes such as the cost of a particular attack. The values can be propagated up the tree to the root. Another result could be which attack would be the most likely one, if the values `possible` and `impossible` are assigned to the tree nodes. Furthermore, goal trees facilitate "what if" experiments, e.g. what would happen if you have more budget than expected. In the following we briefly describe two tree approaches with different goals: threats and attacks. As threats and attacks describe a (potential/concrete) danger for a system, the stakeholders are involved.

Threat Trees. The goal of threat trees is to identify threats to a system [9]. They are a methodological approach to identify threats. The threats to a system are identified and divided into sub-threats. The result is a threat tree structure that contains a list of threats for every leaf.

Attack Trees. Attack trees are used to identify possible attacks to a system [193]. The usage of attack trees has been made popular by Bruce Schneier. The root node of an attack tree is the goal of an attack, e.g. get a user's password. The leaf nodes represent different ways of achieving that goal, i.e. newly created leafs are sub-goals. If these steps are repeated, you get a tree structure that represents attacks against a system. It is possible to combine several attack trees to a bigger one. It can happen that identical leaf-nodes occur in different locations. In that case the same sub-tree will be used.

Findings. It isn't clear when the process of identifying the tree node goals terminates, as you could easily add more and more details of specific goals. As a sufficient coverage of all considered aspects (e.g. attacks or threats) is desired, something like a (e.g. public) tree repository is needed. The effort for developing goal trees is dependent on the expertise of the user. The process of creating any of the above trees still requires a lot of security know-how. If you are a novice in the field of security, it is very likely that you will forget some aspects but "creating (attack) trees requires a certain mindset and takes practice" and "you'll get better with time" [194]. Goal trees are both human and machine readable. Therefore, they are easy to understand and an automated analysis is possible. Goal trees are well suited for describing side effects of a given goal. In fact, trees can be combined in order to see how certain nodes have influence on other paths through the tree. To be really useful - especially for novices - a repository of trees developed before could be necessary. The more concrete the trees are, the more time-dependent they become. Especially for attack trees, a continuous review process has to be defined in order to keep the trees up-to-date. This would be supported by a tree repository, too.

5.4.2 Risk Analysis

A quantitative approach for the risk analysis originates from the world of insurances. The basic idea is to calculate the probability of the occurrence of certain events in order to calculate appropriate insurance coverage. This approach is widely applied within the IT world [175]. The quantitative approach to risk analysis is based on the assumption that critical factors can be precisely calculated. The qualitative approach concentrates on magnitudes instead of precise values.

Applying the quantitative approach two parameters have to be determined in order to calculate if a certain security risk is acceptable: the expected loss and the probability for the occurrence of a malicious event. The multiplication of both values results in the expected value for the security risk.

A serious determination of these values is, however, difficult. First, the expected loss can only be a rough estimation as multiple aspects have to be considered: manpower for repairs, money for broken hardware/software, loss of reputation, loss of secret information, etc. Second, as attacks are not random events, there is nothing like a "mean time between failure" as for example known in the area of fault tolerance. One important reason for this is that not every incident is reported. This is due to fear of a negative public image but also due to undetected incidents or more trivial reasons like lack of time and lack of awareness why it might be important to report an incident. No matter why, there is no reliable data pool. Thus nobody can really know how often certain attacks occur.

Findings. Conducting a risk analysis is a straightforward task. The input is a list of possible threats, vulnerabilities, and attacks which were determined by previous steps. For each list item two values have to be determined. This is correlated with the amount of input and the expertise of the user. The determination of reliable values for loss and probability for an incident is difficult for experts and even more difficult for the laymen. The representation of "risk" is simple as it is just the multiplication of two values that result in the risk. If the values are known, this can be easily automated. Besides, tools for supporting risk analysis are available such as Risk Watch 17799 [184] (that helps to assess compliance against the ISO 17799 standard) or The Buddy System [53]. During a risk analysis threats, vulnerabilities, and attacks are usually treated in isolation, i.e. side effects are not considered. Nevertheless, this depends on the input of the previous steps. The results of a more generic risk analysis (i.e. the focus is on threats) are less time independent, whereas the results of a more concrete risk analysis (i.e. the focus is on vulnerabilities and attacks) are more time dependent. To be up-to-date, a risk analysis can be repeated as often as needed. In particular, it should be repeated regularly, at least when new threats, vulnerabilities, and attacks are made public.

5.4.3 Work Factor Concept

The work factor concept is mainly applied in the field of cryptography in order to find out how strong a specific cryptographic protocol is. It is defined as "the amount of work an attacker must perform to overcome security measures " [218]. It is assumed that the underlying algorithms are secure, i.e. the amount of work for an attacker is directly related to the length of the cryptographic key: the longer the key, the longer a brute-force attack takes (on average).

Much earlier this approach was applied to make statements about the qualities of safes. There are different categories for safes, depending on the safe's protection against breaking-in or fire. A "TL-15" safe of the company Underwriter Laboratories does for example guarantee that a sophisticated safe-breaker with standard tools needs at least 15 minutes to open the safe [195].

Yee analyzes the work factor concept in the context of software vulnerabilities [241]. He splits the total effort into the work required "to discover a security vulnerability", "to engineer an attack based on the vulnerability" and "to run the engineered exploit". However, he identifies two major drawbacks of this approach. First, the time to identify a vulnerability highly depends on the amount of know-how and skills of the analyst. Second, the publication of vulnerability information alters the metric. Even if there are no automated exploit scripts, subsequent attacks are easier the more details of a vulnerability are made available.

Findings. Dependent on the expertise of the user the work factor concept is not a straightforward task. One has to be able to simulate the criminal energy of an attacker in order to get serious values. Furthermore, there might be several ways to attack the target. Especially the discovery of (new) vulnerabilities is difficult and requires a high level of expertise. For experts it is easier to develop an exploit and even more easy to run the (automated) attack. Analoguous to a "risk" value, a "work factor" has a very simple representation. Accordingly, tool support would be possible. The work factor concept helps to get a clear image of attacks. Trying to play the role of the attacker it is easier to select appropriate countermeasures. The user has to be creative when he tries to simulate an attack. This includes - dependent on the user's expertise - combined attacks. Complex scenarios can only be considered with corresponding expert knowledge. The results of a work factor analysis are very time dependent. As soon as an exploit is published, almost everyone can conduct an attack without high efforts. It can certainly be assumed that - even for laymen - the actual work factor will be dramatically reduced with more and more automated penetration tools available. As noted by McHugh the "value that could be assigned to any work factor metric [...] is vanishingly small" [152]. By nature, the work factor concept can be combined with attack trees. Besides all its limitations, the work factor concept is important for the internal assessment of any security team (e.g. CERTs) dealing with a still unpublished vulnerability.

5.4.4 Prioritization Schemes

Almost all approaches for the identification of security problems we discussed before also provide a prioritization scheme. A detailed analysis of such schemes is available [205]. The stakeholders apply prioritization schemes in order to determine what problems have to be solved first. Accordingly, developers can find out, what security features have to be available immediately.

Severity-based Approach. A value between 0 and 180 is assigned to each entry in the CERT database. The intention is to roughly declare the severity of the vulnerability. The "calculation" considers different aspects such as:

− Is information about the vulnerability publically available?
− What are the consequences of an exploitation of the vulnerability?
− How difficult is it to exploit the vulnerability?

According to CERT different weights are assigned to each of these factors, i.e. the final value cannot really be used to directly compare different vulnerabilities. Moreover, the metric is not linear, i.e. a "40" vulnerability is not half as severe as a "80" vulnerability. The CERT metric is mainly for internal use. Its main purpose is to decide if a CERT-Advisory should be published. Only if the value is higher than 40 there will be a *decision* whether information about the vulnerability is going to be published[3].

Findings. The effort for getting a value for the priority depends on the user's expertise. If he is familiar with the subject, it should be straightforward. As CERT does not provide more precise information about how the metric can be calculated exactly, it is only of limited general expressiveness. Therefore it cannot be applied from an end user perspective. Although several aspects are considered they don't remain visible in the overall result. Therefore the advantage of a finer-grained representation is lost. Basically, tool support is possible and would help to determine approriate values (e.g. based on decision trees). Dependent on the underlying vulnerability database, side effects are not considered. As CERT does not follow a full-disclosure policy, priorities might not be up-to-date.

Risk-based Approach. In many vulnerability databases and security scanner tools three-level prioritization schemes are used. However, there are different definitions for the range of each category.

X-Force. This database contains a "risk factor" attribute [227] . The value high is assigned if an attacker can gain administrator privileges or is able to bypass a security mechanism such as a firewall. A medium rating is given if an attacker can gather information dramatically increasing the probability for an attack. A low value means that an attacker can gather information possibly leading to a compromised system. However, this rough classification is problematic as the definition of the values is not always clear-cut. For example it is always a matter of discretion, if a vulnerability is classified as low or medium. Furthermore, the prioritization scheme does not cover vulnerabilities that can lead to DoS attacks.

ICAT. Every ICAT database entry contains a "severity" attribute [164]. Although the possible values are high, medium and low, the definition is different compared to the X-Force database. Vulnerabilities with a high severity enable remote attacks with increased privileges, enable a local attack with full access to the target system, or have a corresponding CERT advisory. Vulnerabilities with a low severity don't allow direct access to the target but they can reveal information that make an attack easier. Vulnerabilities in the medium class don't fulfill the criteria of high or low vulnerabilities.

---

[3] The highest value ever was 180 and was calculated for a buffer-overflow in the widely used BIND software. There are, however, many entries with a severity of 0, i.e. there is an average of only 18,5.

NIST mentions that is difficult to apply this prioritization scheme in different environments. However, there are more problems. First, the rating scheme basically consists of only two classes as the medium class contains no additional properties. Second, the recourse to the CERT scheme is somewhat questionable as we have already shown the liabilities of this scheme. Finally, Denial-of-Service attacks cannot be rated, too.

Security Scanner. The prioritization schemes of tools such as the Internet Security and System Scanner are only of limited use as they rely on the vulnerability databases discussed before [226]. The SecureScan tool uses a three-level classification, too. However, a more subtle definition of classes is given:

A high risk is assigned to a vulnerability if it is possible to compromise the target without further efforts. Vulnerabilities at the medium level can lead to a compromise, but more work will be required. In combination with another medium level vulnerability, however, a high level classification can be reached. Similarly, several low level vulnerabilities together with a medium level one can lead to a compromised target. Furthermore, all DoS vulnerabilities are classified as medium. Finally, all vulnerabilities that increase the risk but aren't sufficient to lead to a damage are at the low level. Additionally, a threat category is assigned to each vulnerability: theft of information, manipulation, loss of data and DoS. In comparison with X-Force and ICAT a more fine-grained prioritization is possible therefore.

Findings. As most prioritization schemes are rather simple, laymen should basically be able to classify a vulnerability properly. Nevertheless, this requires some security background. Especially vague definitions of classes require a certain amount of expertise. Basically such schemes are good candidates for tool support. For example, the assignment of a vulnerability to priority class can be done by decision trees. Dependent on the underlying vulnerability database, side effects are not considered. Dependent on the underlying vulnerability databases the values can be updated frequently. This increases the effort for prioritization.

System and Software Manufacturers. We also had a look at prioritization schemes of leading IT and software manufacturers. We investigated the Linux distributors Caldera, Debian, Mandrake Linux, RedHat, S.u.S.E. Linux and Turbolinux. Furthermore, we had a look at UNIX companies such as SCO, SGI, and SUN as well as the BSD derivates FreeBSD, NetBSD and OpenBSD. Finally, we searched for rating schemes used by companies such as Cisco, Compaq, Hewlett Packard, IBM and Microsoft. Although most of them offer a vulnerability-related mailing list with additional information on their web-site, we couldn't find a prioritization scheme with the exception of the Linux distributor S.u.S.E. They explained that there is no strict scheme but that the following criteria of a vulnerability are considered: local or remote exploitation, Denial-of-Service possible, extension of privileges possible, and relation to a default package. An additional weighting is given on a "gut level"[4].

5.4.5 Summary

The examined security improvement artifacts which support the analysis phase of a system show all a structured representation of the relevant security information. As such, they are all well suited for tool support. However, all of them are no tool for novices and require a certain amount of expertise. Furthermore, the possibility for considering side-effects appropriately is not used - although it would be possible.

5.5 Architecture and Design

When the requirements are determined, the risk for a new system is determined, and the security problems are prioritized, architecture and design investigations are conducted. Often, semi-formal modeling techniques are used for this task. When verification is also an issue, formal methods can be used instead or as a complementary approach.

5.5.1 Modeling Techniques

Data-, function- and object-oriented modeling methods are counted among the semi-formal approaches and are typically used by developers. They are characterized through different graphical elements but also linguistic elements. An example of data modeling techniques is Entity Relationship Modeling (ERM), for object-oriented modeling the Unified Modeling Language (UML). UML can be made more formal by writing constraints in Object Constraint Language (OCL) as part of the model. Rensing demonstrated this approach based on the specification of security services of the RADIUS protocol [179]. Jürjens is working on UMLsec that is an UML extension for representing security in UML models [128]. The usage of UML class diagrams offers the possibility to describe a role, its characteristics and relations between roles. Statecharts can be used to describe the behavior of elements or roles. Activity graphs, sequence diagrams, and collaboration diagrams are used to describe the cooperation of the different elements of the whole system.

Findings. The effort for specifying the system architecture with semi-formal approaches is also highly dependent on the expertise. As many software developers are familiar with such techniques, it should be a natural way to model the security aspects, too. The semi-formal approaches are human-readable.

---

[4] E-mail correspondence with Thomas Biege, who is responsible for the S.u.S.E. security advisories.

Therefore they are more useful for non-modeling experts, too. The average software developer can be expected to easily understand a UML-based security model. Nevertheless, one still has to know how to model a system appropriately from a security point of view. Semi-formal approaches, especially UML, offer a structured way to describe systems. Wheras the syntax of UML is defined, security related semantics are not yet commonly agreed. As it is possible to specify especially security aspects more explicitly, tool support is possible (e.g. for automated verification). Such tools are available that support the usage of modeling techniques during development. It is possible to show dependencies between elements of a system with semi-formal approaches. Thus it should be basically possible to model side effects of security related aspects, too. As semi-formal specifications are easy to understand it should be rather easy to adapt them to changing requirements. However, this depends mainly on the complexity of the system.

5.5.2 Formal Methods

Security is a current hot topic in the formal methods community. During development formal methods are powerful tools to show that a system meets the requirements. Typically formal methods are applied to protocols such as authentication, fair exchange, electronic commerce, and electronic auctions. A well-known result of the formal method approach is the Bell-LaPadula model for access control that was used in the Orange Book [16]. Formal methods provide benefits in several ways [240]. As you can specify the interface between the system and its environment, they help to narrow the system's boundary. Furthermore, you can characterize the behavior and the properties of a system in a precise way.

Another important aspect, especially in the field of security, is that you can prove that a system meets its specification. During the process of specification, formal methods help to focus the developer's attention. During the process of verification, they provide additional assurance in order to increase the trustworthiness of a system. Formal approaches cover descriptive techniques such as specification languages, models, and logics as well as analysis techniques like model checking, theorem proving, and their combination.

Formal methods can be grouped in logic-based methods and status- or process-based methods. Using logical methods, such as Z, the predictable properties of a system are described. Additionally they provide means to validation by test. With status- and process-based methods structures and flows are described. These provide validation by simulation only and can be classified as asynchronous (e.g. Petri Nets) or synchronous methods.

Policies in a formal way and especially authorization policies are used in the area of management of distributed systems. There exist different languages [56] to describe policies in a formal way and also mechanisms to check consistency and conflicts [224].

Findings. Typically formal methods are applied only to specific problem areas such as smart-cards or cryptographic protocols. Larger systems cannot be handled with formal methods due to increased complexity and dependencies. This could be a difficult task as systems become more and more complex. Although formal approaches deliver important contributions to the field of security, the layman cannot be expected to have the required mathematical background. Formal methods allow highly structured representations. This is also reflected in a variety of available tools. However, the verification of a system can be only as good as the assumptions that have been postulated. Thus, the biggest challenges of the formal method community will always be to improve the specification capabilities and to find adequate model assumptions. Today formal methods can be used for systems with a certain level of complexity. It is rather difficult to model large, distributed systems and to consider side effects appropriately. Remaining exercises will be to push the integration of formal methods into the overall process of engineering and to cope with partial specifications. The results of a formal specification cannot be adapted easily to changing requirements as they require a high level of expertise.

5.5.3 Summary

The modeling techniques as well as formal methods usually show a high degree of structured information. Thus, the tool support is good. It is even possible to consider side-effects and time dependencies. On the other hand the required expertise for developing the architecture and the design of a system with these approaches is high. Note that patterns can be integrated in this life-cycle phase, especially when we consider the semi-formal modeling techniques. For instance, UML diagrams can be found in patterns very often.

5.6 Building

Building a new system means to codify the design for given runtime platforms. Thus, we look at approaches at the code-level such as secure programming guidelines and checklists. In a broader sense we also count the proper selection and configuration of systems and sub-systems for implementing security functionality to the building phase. With this understanding we examine security building blocks and best practice documents.

5.6.1 Secure Programming Guidelines

At the code level, certain security programming guidelines are available such as NCSA Secure Programming Guidelines [159], Secure Programming for Linux and Unix HOWTO [238] and Security Code Guidelines from SUN

Microsystems [155]. The intention is to avoid typical pitfalls during codifying and resulting security weaknesses such as buffer overflows or extended privileges. These guidelines focus on specific features of given programming languages, e.g. how to write **suid** programs in C, how to write secure CGI programs, or how to write secure Java code. They offer advice on what to do (e.g. "keep privileged code as short as possible") and what mustn't be done (e.g. "never use the unix **system()** call").

Findings. Using programming guidelines is straightforward and leads only to minimal overhead. Before, during and after coding the programmer looks up how to implement sensitive parts. Security know-how is not required but security awareness. After a while we can expect that he gets familiar with the problems and adopts the secure programming paradigm. As programming guidelines are rather low-level, there is no high degree of structuring. Nevertheless, there are certain tools that help the programmer to identify problems and propose solutions at the code level. Usually, side effects are not mentioned. Often, security measures at the code level lead to decreased performance. As programming languages are available for a long time, programming guidelines are rather stable. For example, we know for more than 30 years how to prevent buffer overflows (nevertheless, they are still a major reason for security breaches).

5.6.2 Security Building Blocks

The implementation of security can be seen from a module-based point-of-view. This means that countermeasures are identified separately for each building block of the system. For example, the German IT Baseline Protection Manual describes standard countermeasures that should be considered for a set of typical IT systems [33]. These countermeasures can be applied if overall, typical threats can be assumed. Going beyond this baseline, additional countermeasures have to be identified and implemented in high-risk scenarios.

For each component a set of the typcial threats is provided. These threats are taken from a threat catalog. Furthermore, detailed descriptions of corresponding countermeasures are given which are also taken from a catalog. The IT Baseline Protection Manual is organized in several hierarchical layers including infrastructure, IT systems, networks and applications. The standard covers both general and product-specific countermeasures of commonly used IT components. The IT Baseline Protection Manual also features an underlying matrix that assigns threats to countermeasures. Together, this should lead to a consistent description of security building blocks. Nevertheless, we identified inconsistencies, e.g. the threat "disruption of power supply" is assigned to a networked UNIX server but not to a networked server based on the Windows NT operating system. As a consequence, the countermeasure "local uninterruptible power supply" could be missed. Obviously, the benefits of structuring are not used consequently[5].

Findings. The selection of appropriate building blocks depends mainly on the results of the analysis phase. The implementation itself is straightforward and mainly an organizational effort. As detailed information is provided, security expertise is basically not required. Nevertheless one has to know the corresponding configuration parameters and how they can be adapted. Furthermore, one should be aware of side-effects that might lead to new problems. The documents are typically loosely structured. We can find an introduction section, a description of threats and countermeasures, and references to documents that provide further information. Due to a good degree of structuring the IT Baseline Protection Manual is suitable for tool support and a variety of tools is available on the market. Side-effects can basically be considered. However, the documents usually don't describe the drawbacks of certain countermeasures. Approaches based on building blocks are based on typical generic threats and are therefore not very time-dependent. For example, the IT Baseline Protection Manual is reviewed and updated twice a year. As a consequence, the countermeasures have to be reviewed regularly, too.

5.6.3 Best Security Practices

Best security practices are usually compiled by organizations or people which offer security services based on a long-lasting experience such as the CERT/CC that provides a couple of documents about improving the security of networked computer systems [8]. The information is organized in three hierarchical levels: security improvement modules, practices, and implementations. The modules cover top-level topics such as "Security for Information Technology Service Contracts", "Responding to Intrusions", "Securing Public Web-Servers", etc. Each module is structured in a rather uniform way. First, the terminology is clarified and the target audience is addressed. Each module also defines the scope, i.e. what is covered (and what not). Then the security issues (i.e. what kind of problems can occur) and a top level summary of how security can be approved are provided. Each module refers to corresponding security improvement practices and related modules/documents. The practices describe security improvement in a procedural way. They are organized in several areas such as hardening and securing systems, preparing detection, responding to intrusions, etc. The practices are structured, too. First, a motivation is given ("Why this is important"). Then guidelines are provided how to improve security. Finally, policy considerations and links to implementations are given. The implementations are concrete instructions for specific systems and applications. They contain "backward references" to the corresponding practices. If available, they contain scripts that help to

---

[5] This was approved by an e-mail conversation with a member of the BSI team which is responsible for the IT Baseline Protection Manual.

carry out certain tasks. The implementations themselves are not uniquely structured.

Findings. The main effort in applying security best practices lies in finding the right document. Once identified, the steps are straightforward. It can be expected that you get more and more familiar with the approach using the documents several times. Problems occur, however, when you leave the typically narrow focus of such security improvement approaches. The target group is always mentioned. Expert security know-how is not necessarily required. The documentation seems to be suitable for security novices. Especially the structure of the CERT/CC documents is convenient. It helps to get familiar with them and to compare them efficiently. However, the structure gets blurred the more concrete the documents become. Furthermore, the structural elements seem not to be mandatory, i.e. there are some variations. Currently, only a HTML-based web-interface is provided. However, the underlying structure would make tool support possible. The three-level hierarchy along with bi-directional references shows the dependencies between the documents. This helps to identify side affects and increases the comfort of browsing this collection of knowledge. By nature, the more concrete documents are more time dependent and should be updated on a regular basis.

5.6.4 Summary

The security improvement artifacts at the implementation level of a system are very suitable for novices. Most of them are mature and address well-known problems at the code and configuration level. However, there is still room for improvements. Especially, the tool support as well as the consideration of side-effects can still be improved. Furthermore, we could realize a trend that security-related patterns emerge at this area [201].

5.7 Testing

During integration and especially during the operation of a system it is necessary to look for vulnerabilities that have been discovered recently. This can be achieved by querying vulnerability databases that list known vulnerabilities of a given system. In contrast to these more conceptual approaches, such tests can also be conducted based on automated tools that usually detect problems locally or remotely during runtime.

5.7.1 Conceptual Testing

In a broader sense we define a vulnerability database as structured collection of information about vulnerabilities. At present there is already a multitude of various vulnerability databases. These databases are driven publicly or privately by various organizations. All vulnerability databases offer a web-frontend for keyword-based searches. Therefore, they serve as a tool for the analytical identification of vulnerabilities and attacks. This approach can be used by stakeholders in order to derive requirements and by developers in order to secure re-used components (e.g. application servers). The content of vulnerability databases is typically limited to flaws in implementation or configuration.

CERT/CC. An approved source of vulnerability information is the CERT/CC (see also Section 7.5.2) [42]. An entry in this database contains an overview of the vulnerability, a more detailed description, the impact of the vulnerability and a solution, e.g. apply a patch. Furthermore the affected systems are listed. Pointers to information can be found in the references section. At the end, all people having contributed to a database entry are acknowledged.

Bugtraq. In contrast to CERT/CC the Bugtraq vulnerability database is operated under a full-disclosure policy, i.e. information is published as soon as possible and there is basically no censorship [213]. The database entries are similar to the CERT/CC database. However, it contains detailed information regarding the exploitation of a vulnerability.

X-Force. The X-Force database is operated by the company Internet Security Systems [227]. It is the data pool for the company's security tools. Again, the database schema is similar to the previous ones.

ICAT Metabase. The National Institute of Standards and Technology (NIST) operates a meta database called ICAT [164]. It contains entries of other vulnerabilities and references to them. According to NIST these are all CERT-Advisories, the X-Force database, information from the mailing lists Bugtraq and NT Bugtraq as well as the corresponding database. Additionally, several security related notifications from vendors are included. In contrary to the other databases, the ICAT database offers extensive search capabilities. More than 40 vulnerability attributes can be used to narrow the results of a query.

Findings. The usage of vulnerability databases is very convenient for the identification of vulnerabilities. Web-based query interfaces simplify the overall process. Almost everyone can use vulnerability databases. Without expert knowledge everyone can look up whether there are known vulnerabilities for a given system. However, the installation of fixes or updates - if available - is more difficult. Vulnerability databases belong to the structured or highly structured sources of security related information [118]. This enables efficient search and retrieval of relevant information and tool-support (ranging from GUI frontends to automated security analysis tools). A severe shortcoming is the isolated treatment of vulnerabilities. Thus relationships and bias effects cannot be considered. With a vulnerability database only single vulnerabilities can be rated as specific context information is not available [205]. The time dependency depends on the disclosure policy of the operator of a vulnerability database. Databases with a full-disclosure policy are updated frequently and usually are always up-to-date. The advantages for the user yield a rather high effort for the maintenance of the database on the operator's side. Furthermore, little effort is made to strive for standardized data and provider models which in turn leads to a high data redundancy and an aggravated information search on the user side since information on vulnerabilities may be a competitive advantage [198]. On average information about a particular vulnerability can be found only in two of ten major vulnerability databases [6].

5.7.2 Runtime Testing

Security scanners are tools for the automated detection of vulnerabilities. For example, they can be used by developers in order to identify problems in prototypes (the stakeholders also use them later to find problems in running systems). Typically, they rely on an internal vulnerability database - often a snapshot of one of the databases discussed before. The functionality is as follows: the software is started on a remote system, then the entire network is analyzed. If the running services are determined, the next step is the identification of vulnerabilities. In order to identify vulnerabilities that are locally exploitable additional scanners which are locally installed have to be used. The following tools give an overview for this kind of software.

Internet Scanner. The Internet Scanner by Internet Security Systems (ISS) has been an established product [226]. The first version of the software was released in 1992 and lead to an unpleasant amount of work for CERTs at that time[7]. A recent version is shipped with about 40 categories (e.g. "Backdoors", "CGI-Bin" or "TCP/IP") and 728 security tests. The Internet Scanner relies on the X-Force database.

System Scanner. A supplementary tool is ISS's System Scanner which is executed locally on the target of evaluation [226]. Thus the local exploitation of vulnerabilities can be considered.

SecureScan. The company VIGILANTe offers the product SecureScan which is also a remote analysis tool [233]. Its distinguishing feature is that it can be combined with other products, e.g. with the ISS Security Scanner or Network Associates' CyberCop NT. Therefore a higher recall factor can be achieved.

Findings. The main effort lies in the configuration of the scanning process, i.e. what kind of systems are analyzed, what kind of vulnerabilties have to be tested, etc. Then the tool runs autonomously and after a while the user gets a report. As there are also free tools available (such as Nessus [59]), the

---

[6] The MITRE Corporation, Editorial Board Teleconference Summary, June 2001.

[7] Personal conversation with Klaus-Peter Kossakowski who worked several years for different CERTs and wrote his PhD thesis about such incident response capabilities [138].

purchasing costs can be minimized. Security scanner tools are very convenient for users. They provide "point & click" interfaces and help to automate the process of identifying vulnerabilities. Some tests may be dangerous (e.g. a test for DoS vulnerability could bring a system down), i.e. one should be careful configuring such tools. As most tools rely on vulnerability databases, the representation is equally suitable. Furthermore, such tools provide structured reports, i.e. what vulnerabilities have been identified. As a consequence, testing is very suitable for automation and tool support. However, the results are limited to the underlying databases, i.e. flaws in architecture and design can typically not be found automatically. As discussed, most vulnerability databases don't treat relationships between vulnerabilities. Thus, using testing tools cannot go beyond the capabilities of the underlying databases, too. As it is simple to carry out a security scan, the list of identified vulnerabilities can be easily kept up-to-date. This depends on the vulnerability databases, too[8].

5.7.3 Summary

The strength of the examined testing tools lies in the high degree of structured information which make them suitable for automation of the testing process. As they offer convenient user interfaces, they are also suitable for novices - however, the results should be treated with certain care in order to avoid a false sense of security. Although it would be possible, they do not, however, consider the side-effects of a vulnerability.

5.8 Summary and Conclusions

Every security improvement artifact discussed before is a valuable resource for making systems more secure. However, our analysis reveals that the human factor is often not considered appropriately. Furthermore, there are always interrupts as security and system engineering are separated tasks. In the following we provide a summary of our examination. Furthermore we discuss how patterns fit into our framework and what is missing in order to understand them and make them suitable for security engineering.

5.8.1 Summary

In Table 5.2 we summarize our findings and evaluate each security improvement artifact according to the following simple scaling scheme. From the viewpoint of a given classification criteria, a security improvement artifact

...

---

[8] The business model of commercial tools is to make money with updates of the vulnerability databases.

- strongly supports security novices (++).

- somewhat supports security novices (+).

- provides only limited support for security novices, more convenient for experts (-).

- provides no support for security novices at all, even inconvenient for experts (- -).

For example, *security programming guidelines* require no special security knowledge from the programmer. However, a certain degree of security awareness is necessary. Therefore, the *expertise* criteria is rated with a (+). For the sake of clearness we underlay (-) and (- -) with a light-gray box. Our evaluation reveals the following trends:

- Security improvement artifacts at early life-cycle stages (requirements definition, analysis, architecture and design) are not suitable for novices. They require significant levels of both resources (effort) and security knowledge (expertise). At lower levels, i.e. building and testing novices find a variety of convenient concepts which guide them during building and operating systems securely.
- Most approaches show a significant degree of structuring that enables tool support. In particular, goal trees, modeling techniques, and testing approaches are suitable for novices.
- Most of the examined artifacts don't support the consideration of side effects - a situation where failures creep in. An exception are the CERT/CC security improvement modules that show bi-directional linkage between documents.
- Especially during building and testing time dependencies can be considered appropriately. Approaches at earlier phases are either too generic or too heavy-weight (effort, expertise) in order to produce up-to-date results.

As indicated by the last row of Table 5.2, patterns as introduced in Chapter 2 feature most of the advantages mentioned above: the effort for using them is low, security expertise is not required by definition, patterns have a structured representation (context, problem, forces, etc.), they are linked to other patterns, and ideally they are time invariant. Furthermore, patterns can be found at different levels of abstraction and for different life-cycle phases. As such they seem to be an ideal complement for the discussed security improvement artifacts and a solution for the human factor problem. For example, security policies doesn't seem to be an adequate approach at all - although security cannot be done without them. We come back to this later and show how patterns can compensate such limitations. However, some features are missing that make patterns suitable for *security engineering*. This is discussed in the following.

	Effort	Expertise	Structuring	Tool support	Side effects	Time dependency
Requirements.						
Evaluation Criteria:	(- -)	(- -)	(+)	(+)	(-)	(- -)
Management Standards:	(+)	(-)	(-)	(+)	(+)	(+)
Policy:	(-)	(-)	(- -)	(- -)	(- -)	(- -)
Analysis.						
Goal Trees:	(-)	(-)	(++)	(++)	(-)	(-)
Risk Analysis:	(- -)	(- -)	(+)	(+)	(-)	(-)
Work Factor Concept:	(- -)	(- -)	(+)	(+)	(-)	(- -)
Severity Prioritization:	(-)	(- -)	(- -)	(+)	(- -)	(- -)
Risk Prioritization:	(+)	(-)	(+)	(++)	(- -)	(-)
Architecture & Design.						
Modeling Techniques:	(+)	(-)	(++)	(++)	(+)	(+)
Formal Methods:	(-)	(- -)	(+)	(+)	(-)	(-)
Building.						
Programming Guidelines:	(++)	(+)	(-)	(+)	(- -)	(++)
Building Blocks:	(+)	(+)	(+)	(++)	(-)	(+)
Best Practices:	(+)	(++)	(+)	(+)	(++)	(+)
Testing.						
Vulnerability Databases:	(+)	(-)	(++)	(++)	(- -)	(+)
Runtime Testing:	(++)	(+)	(++)	(++)	(- -)	(++)
Pattern Approach.	(+)	(++)	(+)	(- -)	(++)	(+)

Table 5.2. Strengths of common security approaches.

5.8.2 Conclusions

Elementary drawbacks of patterns can be found in the patterns-discussion FAQ maintained by Doug Lea [145]. The first important question for our discussion is about finding relevant patterns:

9) Where can I find published or online patterns about XXX?

There is not a central clearing house for patterns, but it is not too hard to find them. Here are some starting points:

* Hillside Patterns Home Page
* Linda Rising's book, The Pattern Almanac (also its predecessor, The Patterns Handbook), that contains references to most patterns that have been published.
* Wiki
* Pattern Depot
* Open directory
* Your favorite search engine

We don't agree that is is not too hard to find a particular pattern for a specific problem. Given the growing number of pattern-related events, the number of new patterns is steadily growing. For example, about 40 contributions were submitted to EuroPLoP 2002 as well as to PLoP 2002. If we assume this as the average number of new patterns for each conference, we will have a total number of nearly 300 pattern contributions where each contribution often contains more than one pattern (e.g. a pattern language). Even worse, not all related patterns are merged into a larger system of patterns[9]. It is far from being convenient to browse several web sites/books in order to find the pattern that really solves your problem. And as search engines are usually keyword based, you cannot type in your problem expecting to retrieve the right pattern immediately.

More sophisticated queries would be possible, however, if we took advantage of the *structure* of patterns. As user we have a problem in a given context. It would improve search and retrieval capabilities if we were able to utilize this semantic information for looking up the right pattern (assuming that they can be accessed through a single interface). Nevertheless, we still have the problem of different templates, i.e. some patterns have more structure than others. Basically, this is a good thing as it doesn't constrain the authors freedom. On the other hand, a value-added *tool-support* is more difficult to achieve if not impossible. The reason for this can be found in another patterns-discussion-FAQ item:

19) What is the theoretical basis of Patterns?

No formal basis in the usual sense. [...]

However, a theoretical model that describes the syntax of security patterns would be an important pre-requisite for (tool-)supporting novices in

---

[9] Recognizing this the community started several events for merging and integrating related patterns and pattern languages.

finding and using the right pattern. Concluding our discussion the we derive the following requirements for a pattern-based approach for security improvement:

- We need to understand what security patterns actually are and how they can be used.
- We need a theoretical model in order to improve search and retrieval of patterns.
- We need an interface to access *all* relevant patterns.

An important boundary condition is that existing patterns considered as a piece of written knowledge cannot be changed as it would require a lot of effort to unify all patterns. Even more important is that the community would not accept to be forced to use a mandatory template (in fact such a proposal would very likely be ignored). Based on that we present our pattern-based approach for integrated security and system engineering in the following chapters.

6. Toward a Security Core Ontology

> Such concept and terminology
> inconsistency is a symptom of
> the relative immaturity of the
> field of computer security.
>
> EDWARD AMOROSO

6.1 Introduction

In this chapter we provide definitions of security concepts and relations between them as used in this book. On the one hand these are required as many different definitions are used in security literature. A clarification of the relations between the concepts helps to get a better understanding of the overall concept "security". On the other hand the development of such a "security ontology" enables the automated processing of security-related information. As such, we consider a security ontology as an important prerequisite for specifying security patterns and improve their applications in the security domain.

Outline. This chapter is organized as follows: first, we outline and assess related work which deals with ontologies concerning security in Section 6.2. In Section 6.3 we briefly present the methodology we have used for the development of our security core ontology. In Section 6.4 we introduce definitions of top-level security concepts. We discuss the relations between these concepts in Section 6.5. Finally, we summarize our findings in Section 6.6.

Results. The result of this chapter is a small core ontology which contains key definitions of security concepts and relations between them. As it is based on an intuitive understanding of security – i.e. a state of security is achieved when there is protection against known threats – virtually any community security terminology (e.g. ontologies derived from security standards) can be integrated seamlessly.

M. Schumacher: Security Engineering with Patterns, LNCS 2754, pp. 87-96, 2003.
© Springer-Verlag Berlin Heidelberg 2003

6.2 Related Work

Comparatively early, Filman and Linden published a paper about an ontology for security (OntoSec) [88]. The scenario are software agents - so called SafeBots - which should implement software security controls. The overall goal was to make defenses more cost effective and to make attacks much harder as the vision is that the agents are distributed and pervasive enough. Important preconditions were that the agents communicate and that they can be generated dynamically from a predefined specification. OntoSec is the language to fulfill these requirements. "Security requirements, specifications, goals, actions, events, and knowledge of agents" can be represented.

Grill introduced a framework for comparing and querying Certification Practice Statements (CPS) [98]. In the context of Public Key Infrastructures (PKI) CPS are documents which describe practices and procedures applied when a certificate is issued. The approach was to represent these statements with Description Logics in order to make them processable by computers. That way, end users can be supported by judging whether certificates are trustworthy or not. This work is a step toward an ontology in this particular security domain.

Denker developed a security ontology for DAML+OIL in order to control access and data integrity of Web resources [58]. That way, the security requirements of a Web resource can be annotated and taken into account by Web applications. Thereby, well known security methods and techniques are considered such as password-based login or X509 certificates for authentication. A hook to the XML Signature Syntax and Processing Rules [14] is also provided in order to specify more details of the access restrictions. This approach was also implemented for data integrity. As a proof-of-concept an integration within DAML-S service specifications as well as a wrapper for the Security Assertions Markup Language (SAML) is provided.

Raskin et al. presented an ontology-driven approach to information security [177]. They remark that a security ontology could increase the systematics, allows for modularity and could make new phenomena predictable within the security domain. In particular, an ontology approach is a prerequisite for the inclusion of natural language documents (e.g. incident reports or vulnerability notes). Furthermore, a precise specification of the security know-how could help to improve prevention and reaction capabilities. The largest ontology of this project was also described in a book of Nirenburg and Raskin [163] and can be accessed by a Web interface. According to the authors a glossary of security-related terms has been compiled and added to the ontology[1].

In summary, most of these approaches are rather close to the technical aspects of security and particularly of specific application domains. As such, we

---

[1] About 400 concepts without claiming "to be fully representative, let alone exhaustive".

cannot use them as they don't describe a generic model of security that can be used for specifying patterns. However, Nirenburgs and Raskins work go into this direction as it contains entries taken from glossaries and an English lexicon. However, it doesn't define the general relation between countermeasures (i.e. means of protection), threats and attacks (i.e. which represent danger). Thus, their ontology is not yet suitable for our specification of security patterns as we cannot express our core model of security. Nevertheless, we can basically import concept from this ontology if they fit in on of the concept classes described in this chapter.

6.3 Methodology

We develop an ontology that contains the core concepts and relations of the security domain. Thus, we haven't followed a fully-fledged process of ontology development. We rather focus on a simple representation of a security paradigm that can be applied both in theory and in practice.

In particular, we followed the pragmatic, collaborative approach to ontology design as discussed by Holsapple and Joshi [115]. The basic idea is to let a group of people work together in order to develop and improve a given ontology iteratively. Such an approach helps to identify and eliminate inconsistencies and ambiguities. In principle, this approach can be combined with any of the ontology development methodologies such as discussed in Section 3.4.2. For example, the Enterprise Model Approach or TOVE could be used. We proceeded as discussed in the following paragraphs.

Consideration of Design Requirements. The first step is to specify how we meet the design criteria for the ontology design (see Section 3.4.1). The overall goal is to define the core security concepts as the basis for a theoretical model for security patterns. Thus, the boundary conditions are that we basically want to describe practicable solutions to well-known problems. Thus, we limit our approach to the identification of a small set of core security concepts. Finer-grained taxonomies going beyond the first level of abstraction are out of scope.

Our prime directive is to adopt standard names and definitions of security concepts. For example, we have looked in the glossary of the Common Criteria [121], the Internet Security Glossary [182] as well as definitions given in state-of-the-art security textbooks or articles. This proceeding ensures the *clarity* of the resulting ontology (see Section 3.4.1). For each concept we provide natural language documentation.

The *coherence* requirement states that inferences should be consistent with the given definitions. We show that this requirement is met by the derivation of our theoretical model and its applications in Chapter 8 and Chapter 9. As we can prove that the defining axioms are logically consistent, the ontology fulfills this criteria.

We restricted our effort to the identification of disjoint core security concepts which are related to patterns. We can use the security core ontology as a generic structure for plugging in security terminologies of different sources. Thus, the requirement *extendibility* can be met, too.

As we avoided to use proprietary elements of the selected representation language (namely F-Logic), we also have a *minimal encoding bias* as the ontology can virtually be codified in any representation languages as for example discussed in Section 3.4.3.

Our basic assumption for the core security concepts is our understanding of "security" as a condition of security (i.e. protection against threats and attacks) achieved by a set of safeguards and countermeasures. As there are no more assumptions, we also considered the requirement of making only *minimal ontological commitments.*

Task Definition. This book defines security patterns and shows how to make use of their added values. In order to specify the purpose of our ontology in more detail, we identified a set of competence questions by conducting interviews with a couple of selected security professionals. Thereby, we briefly introduced security patterns based on our PLoP submission in 2001 [208]. Then we asked the participants what features they would expect from a useful security patterns query engine. It turned out quickly that the individual answers could be generalized to a set of competence questions which are listed in Appendix C. The key concepts of our security core ontology can be derived from the competence questions contain.

Anchoring and Improvement. For each identified concept we provide a natural language definition. These definitions are derived from standards, textbooks and articles and have been proven to be useful in both educational and project work of the author (see Appendix E). During our development process of the ontology, a small set of 15 people contributed to the security core ontology. In particular, they all have different backgrounds covering education at universities, security consulting, development of secure systems and some members of the pattern community. This is neither a representative nor significant set of people, but nevertheless the feedback process has helped to identify some inconsistencies and ambiguties. We have been in the position to improve some definitions considerably.

6.4 Definitions of Concepts

In the following we present definitions of the core security concepts used throughout this document. As scenario for the following definitions we think of a small company that develops and sells software products. We don't claim that the ontology is complete but as we considered the design criteria discussed in the previous section, it is possible to integrate further concepts and instances. We always indicate such possible extensions.

Asset. Security is defined in the context of (objective or subjective) perceived threats. A threat is always directed against an asset, i.e. statements about security have to be seen in the context of such an asset. We define the concept Asset as follows:

Definition 3 (Asset). Assets are information or resources which have value to an organization or person.

A set of typical assets in an IT environment is, for instance, provided in the IT Baseline Protection Manual [33]. For example, applications, systems, or networks can be counted among these assets. Beside this rather "material" things assets can be seen more abstract. For example, human-related assets are intellectual properties, documents, know-how, etc. Accordingly, it is possible to add sub-concepts of assets. Considering our example, the source-code of the software products represents an asset for the company.

Stakeholder. The important aspect of the previous definition is that assets belong to or are needed by someone. As this doesn't necessarily need to be the owner of an asset, we prefer to use the concept Stakeholder:

Definition 4 (Stakeholder). A stakeholder is an organization or person who places a particular value on assets.

The stakeholders use the assets in order to conduct his "business" properly. As such they place a certain value on them. Ideally they should take care that they could rely on them. As there can be different types of stakeholders (with different size, different number of employees, etc.) the ontology can be extended that way. In our imaginary company the chief executive officer and the developers probably put a value on the source-code.

Security Objective. Now we make our understanding of security more precise in the context of assets as defined before. Especially this means to specify what objectives have to be expressed in order to achieve a certain level of protection.

Definition 5 (Security Objective). A security objective is a statement of intent to counter threats and satisfy identified security needs.

Typical security objectives are that the protection of confidentiality and integrity of an asset has to be guaranteed. Basically, there can be many other, more finer-grained security objectives. The core ontology can be extended with a corresponding taxonomy of such concepts [200]. It is likely that the stakeholder of our company want to ensure confidentiality, integrity and availability of the source-code.

Threats. In principle, threats can only be perceived as a problem if security objectives are expressed. If one is not aware of threats one believes to be secure although one isn't.

Definition 6 (Threat). A threat is a potential for a security breach of an asset.

According to this definition threats are abstract but there is the danger that something or someone abuses the assets. Threats can be materialized in different ways, for example by a force majeure (lightning, fire, water, etc.), technical failures, human error, or deliberate acts. Again, the ontology can be extended. We could, for instance, refer to corresponding threat trees (see Section 5.4.1) or threat catalogs (see Section 5.6.2). In our example, typical threats are that an attacker either modifies (i.e. change or delete) the source-code or steals it.

Attack. Attacks are one way to realize a threat. We use the following definition of Attack:

Definition 7 (Attack). An attack is an action that violates the security of an asset.

We don't distinguish deliberate actions from human errors (which are other ways to realize a threat but can have the same effects as an attack). Furthermore, attacks can have several relations to other concepts, e.g. the corresponding action (create, destroy, modify, listening, etc.). Usually, a successful attack leads to a certain damage of the target of an attack. Attacks bring some advantage to the attacker (e.g. administrative rights) or security objectives can be violated. Extending the ontology with subconcepts we could refer to attack trees (see Section 5.4.1). An attack in our scenario could be that an attacker eavesdrops the source-code during transmission.

Attacker. The attacker himself is a main reason why we have to care for security. We use a very simple definition for the concept Attacker:

Definition 8 (Attacker). An attacker is the entity which carries out attacks.

Formally, security standard terminology often refers to attackers more generally as threat agents. This would also include other threat sources as discussed before. If required, this super-concept could be included into the ontology without changing the sub-concepts and instances of Attacker.

Attackers can be divided in several sub-classes. Thereby, we can refer to relations to the concepts behavior (e.g. well-defined, by chance, planned, etc.), motivation (e.g. sabotage, espionage, revenge, etc.), know-how and skills (e.g. script-kiddies, professional, amateur, etc.) and physical access (e.g. local, remote, etc.). Furthermore, the attacker has always more possibilities inside the security perimeter. We distinguish such insiders from externals. Insiders often have access to internal assets and can misuse them more easily (on the other hand, it could also be easier to detect them). Besides, we can distinguish between passive and active mode of an attacker. Conducting an attack actively means to manipulate assets somehow whereas passive attackers try to gain information on the basis of observing assets (e.g. data exchanged on a network or stored at a system).

In our example, an attacker could be a competitor in business or a former employee.

Vulnerabilities. A precondition for attacks are vulnerabilities in the assets. We define Vulnerability as follows:

Definition 9 (Vulnerability). A vulnerability is a flaw or weakness that could be exploited to breach the security of an asset.

Many different attributes (or relations to other concepts) are known. For instance, Krsul provides a very sophisticated taxonomy of vulnerabilities [139]. He refers to the impact and the location of a vulnerability, the objects affected, etc. A more pragmatic classification has been provided by Knight [136]. He distinguishes the following types of vulnerabilities: logical fault, weakness, social engineering and policy oversights. These can be classified by two factors. First, the specific target of an attack. Here he distinguishes between systems and persons. Second, how quickly can the attacker exploit a vulnerability (either immediately or after a while). This approach is neither complete nor generally applicable but it is definitely useful for a first, coarse-grained classification.

Looking at vulnerabilities of assets in the IT context, the logical faults and weaknesses should be considered in particular [118]. Here it is possible to classify the vulnerabilities further by the time of their introduction, i.e. the life-cycle of an asset should also be considered. As such there can be, for instance, flaws in designs, implementation, integration, etc.

Vulnerabilities in our scenario could be that the company uses a ftp server for uploading source-code. Such software is known to have implementation (e.g. leading to buffer overflows) and configuration errors (e.g. publically accessible directories). Furthermore, files are usually not encrypted (this could be considered as a design flaw).

Countermeasure. In order to reach a state of security there need to be some kind of protection. In this case we speak of countermeasures as defined in the following:

Definition 10 (Countermeasure). A countermeasure is an action taken in order to protect an asset against threats and attacks.

Countermeasures can be implemented according to the strategies described by the Prevention, Detection, Correction model [21]. Implementing preventive countermeasures means that one tries to foresee the most likely threats. This could mean to use hardened software, operating systems, etc. An extreme interpretation of this strategy would be to give up the usage of certain assets at all. Other countermeasures could also act as a deterrent, e.g. immediate layoff of employees (acting as inside attackers). Detecting an attack is very important in order to know that something is going wrong. Here one should take care of minimizing false positives and especially wrong negatives! As such these countermeasures are a prerequisite for a proper correction cycle. First, one has to react (in an optimal case according to prepared plans), then one has to fix the vulnerability in order to prevent further attacks.

In our example, the company could use a VPN or switch to a secure replacement of ftp such as ssh/scp.

Risk. The concept Risk is always used when the dangers related to a certain activity should be estimated. We define Risk as follows:

Definition 11 (Risk). The risk is the probability that a successful attack occurs.

The estimation of risk in the IT context is used in order to determine if certain countermeasures are required and how much effort (costs, time, etc.) should be spent. In order to determine if a certain security risk is acceptable, two parameters have to be determined: the expected loss and the probability for the occurrence of a malicious event. The multiplication of both values results in the security risk (see Section 5.4.2).

In our scenario, the risk that a successful attack occurs is not acceptable. The source-code is the basis for all business and represents a very high value. As it is rather easy to exploit vulnerabilities in the described scenario, countermeasures must be taken.

6.5 Relations between Concepts

Although we have only a rather limited set of concepts and relations between them, an overall graph which concludes all of them is already too confusing. On the other hand, a visualization of the concepts and relations allows to look at them from different points of view and to discuss the relations more explicitly (in contrast to implicit declarations within the definitions and the accompanying text). Therefore, we gradually explore the relations between the security concepts introduced above with a sequence of coherent illustrations. Each figure contains only the examined concepts and its direct neighbors within the overall graph. Each concept is drawn as a named circle and each relation is indicated as an arrow between the corresponding concepts. In the accompanying text we *emphasize* the relations between the concepts.

We start with Figure 6.1 that shows the direct relations of asset. The most important relation is, that stakeholders *place value on* certain assets. As assets usually *have* vulnerabilities, the property or functionality of the assets cannot be guaranteed. Thus, certain threats can *cause harm to* assets.

Now we look at the direct relations of the concept stakeholder as illustrated in Figure 6.2. Considering the above, the stakeholder should *express* security objectives which (by our definition) determine what threats should be countered. Based on these security objectives, the stakeholder *implements* countermeasures in order to protect the value of his assets.

Figure 6.3 shows the relations of the concept threat clarifying the complementary relation between countermeasures and threats. On the one hand

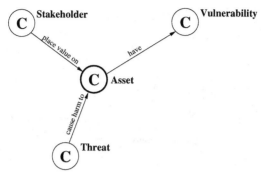

Figure 6.1. Characteristics of Asset.

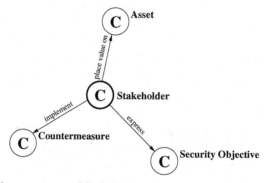

Figure 6.2. Characteristics of Stakeholder.

countermeasures *reduce* risk. On the other hand threats *increase* risk. Besides, we can see that threats *cause harm to* assets. Furthermore, particular attacks *realize* specific threats. That way, attacks are indirectly related to countermeasures, i.e. a countermeasure should also protect against attacks. In principle, countermeasures *protect against* threats. As such they are means to achieve and maintain a certain level of security. This relation also reflects that attackers and stakeholders are virtually opponents in the IT world. It is important to note, that the perception of threats depend on the security objectives. Only if security objectives *address* certain threats, countermeasures can be justified.

Other important relations of attacks are shown in Figure 6.4. Basically, attacks *exploit* vulnerabilities in order to breach the security of an asset and take illegal advantages. The attacks themselves are *carried out* by attackers. This sounds trivial but the skills, motives, and capabilities of an attacker have a great impact on the likelihood of a successful attack. We see that attacks are considerably determined by the attacker and an exploitable vulnerability. As we have already mentioned attacks *realize* threats.

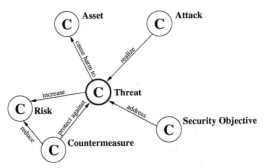

Figure 6.3. Characteristics of Threat.

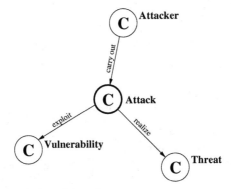

Figure 6.4. Characteristics of Attack.

6.6 Summary

In this chapter we have defined a security core ontology which contains well-known key security concepts. We have roughly followed an approach of collaborative ontology design in order to identify blind spots, inconsistencies and ambiguities in the ontology. Whether our core ontology will be used by a broad community of users cannot be predicted today. However, such ontologies "have value in and of themselves" [134]: they help to clarify "inconsistencies" in terminology as mentioned in Amoroso's quote in the beginning. Nevertheless, the combination with other ontologies (as indicated in the accompanying text of the definitions) will realize the full power of such an ontology. An immediate value of our security core ontology is that we can integrate any community terminology which follows the given structure. Furthermore, it is possible to define mappings between different ontologies [239]. Such an integrated ontology can then be applied to security patterns and make their added values accessible.

7. Foundations of Security Patterns

> Most interesting of all, however, is the lesson that the bulk of computer security research and the development activity is expended on activities which are of marginal relevance to real needs. A paradigm shift is underway, and a number of recent threads point towards a fusion of security with software engineering, or at the very least to an influx of software engineering ideas.
>
> ROSS ANDERSON

7.1 Introduction

In this book we apply the pattern paradigm for improving security. Security patterns are a solution to the human factor problems stated in Section 4 and Section 5. Namely, they help to solve security problems avoiding repair-service behavior and ad-hoc solutions. Taking patterns into account, side effects and time dependencies can be identified more systematically. As security patterns contain expert's "wisdom" they increase security know-how and awareness. Even for experts they are a powerful vehicle to work more efficiently at a higher level of abstraction. As such security patterns fill a gap between theory and the code of practice. The identification of their limitations for being suitable as a security improvement artifact draws up the research agenda for this book.

Outline. In this chapter we introduce the concept of security patterns: we show an example pattern in Section 7.2 for getting a first impression on security patterns. In Section 7.3 we outline the history of security patterns. Then we introduce what a security pattern actually is in Section 7.4, i.e. we describe the semantics of the elements of a security pattern. We discuss the distinguishing properties of a security pattern, describe how security patterns are

M. Schumacher: Security Engineering with Patterns, LNCS 2754, pp. 97-119, 2003.

supposed to be used, show security-related forces, and present an approach for organizing security patterns. In Section 7.5 we describe where and how security patterns can be found. Thereby we classify typical security-related information sources. Mostly, they contain knowledge about how things actually went wrong. We also show how material for security patterns can be derived from security standards as discussed in Chapter 5. We summarize and conclude this chapter in Section 7.6.

Results. In this chapter we will present several important contributions for both the pattern and the security community. Namely, we introduce our security pattern template which shows how regular patterns become a security pattern. Furthermore, we identify and discuss two basic approaches for mining security patterns as well as selected, representative sources. A result is that one source for mining security patterns is not sufficient as they usually don't contain all required elements of patterns.

We have already discussed parts of these results in certain conference articles, a journal publication and a book [199, 200, 208, 207]. Furthermore, we initiated the establishment of the security pattern community. In particular, we organized the first workshop dedicated to security patterns at EuroPLoP 2002 [201]. A follow-up workshop is held in 2003.

7.2 Security Pattern Example

Before we start to specify what security patterns actually are, we introduce a short example in order to provide a first glance at the security pattern approach. The example is taken from a pattern language of passwords and choosing passwords which consists of 16 patterns [183]. Note that this example represents one particular style of representing a pattern. Other style are more detailed and contain further pattern elements.

Without knowing security patterns in detail, we can already learn several things from this example. The pattern has a name PASSWORD EXTERNALIZATION that identifies the concept the pattern stands for. The pattern starts with a summary which explains the problem and the solution in one sentences. This helps to find out whether the user should read pattern. All patterns share the same context, namely chosing and handling passwords. Thus, the context isn't explicitly given in each pattern. However, the context is also determined by previous patterns as the implementation of a solution usually changes the context.

The next paragraph describes a problem that occurs when you have to chose and handle a password. The solution starts with a *Therefore* and contains a rule, design, etc. that helps the user to solve the problem. Examples can be used to underline that the solution is in fact a proven way to solve the problem.

Password Externalization

Synopsis: Use visual or other helps that play to your individual capabilities to remind you of passwords..

Singleton passwords are frequently difficult to remember, because of their arbitrary nature. Stopping short of writing them down somewhere, you need a way to externalize them so that you can look them up.

Therefore, use your primary trait to encode a password in something that plays to your trait. If you are a visual person, use something visual, like a tree, or a crossword puzzle in which you encode your password. If you are an auditory person, use the patterns you recognize in the Ode to Joy or something similar. If you are an olfactory person, I can't help you, but you probably know best how to associate textual patterns with the smell of your beloved one.

For example, some banks gave customers credit-card-sized prints that featured a matrix of digits into which customers visualized their pin codes. Also, some people hide pin codes in their phone books as phone numbers.

Previous pattern: CODE BOOK.
Next pattern: MASTER ACCOUNT FILE.

Figure 7.1. Security pattern example.

There are previous and next patterns. This indicates that the pattern is somehow integrated into an overall set of patterns. Depending on the type of these relations, temporal sequences of applying the patterns are described.

7.3 History of Security Patterns

The work on security patterns has steadily evolved over the past few years. Today a mixture of single patterns, frameworks and pattern languages is available. For a better comprehension of security patterns we outline an example for a pattern language. This "Architectural Patterns for Enabling Application Security" was the first contribution to the pattern literature explicitly dealing with security. Then we introduce other cornerstones of security patterns. The overall trend led to a perception of "security patterns" as own problem-specific pattern domain which resulted in the establishment of a community in 2002.

7.3.1 Pioneering Security Patterns

Yoder and Barcalow were the first that published a paper with security-related patterns in 1997 [242]. Their focus was on patterns which enable security at the level of general software applications. They present seven patterns and put them in perspective describing the relations between them. As real-world analogy they referred to a military base in order to clarify context, problem, and solution of the patterns. Furthermore, they refer to real-world software examples where the patterns were successfully used.

The overall pattern language (i.e. the patterns and some relations between them) is illustrated in Figure 7.2. In the following we briefly show "thumbnails" of the patterns: each item starts with the name of the pattern followed by a short description of the problem and the corresponding solution.

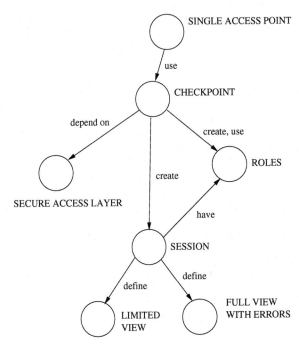

Figure 7.2. Security pattern system example.

SINGLE ACCESS POINT. It is difficult to secure applications basically having arbitrary access points. Accordingly, the solution is to restrict access to a single point of access.

CHECK POINT. Different users have different security requirements. A typical problem is how these requirements can be implemented independent from the design of the application. The solution is to encapsulate a corresponding procedure that can implement such (changing) requirements.

ROLES. The administration of users having different rights is only manageable to a certain, rather small extent. Therefore, users with the same rights are grouped by assigning roles to them.

SESSION. The different modules of an application need access to security-related information such as the user's identity. Such information should be encapsulated globally relying on the concept of sessions. That way the information can be made accessible locally independent from the user's rights.

FULL VIEW WITH ERRORS. Users can call operations only if they have the corresponding rights. Based on these rights, error messages can be displayed whenever "illegal" operations are called.

LIMITED VIEW. As alternative solution to the previous pattern, a user is offered only those operations that he is allowed to call. Both solutions solve the same problem but resolve the forces differently.

SECURE ACCESS LAYER. Applications can only be as secure as their environment. Based on external security mechanisms (e.g. at the level of operating system, network or databases) a secure access layer should be established in order to protect messages from and to the application.

Yoder and Barcalow stressed the relations between the patterns of the language. They included a concise explanation how each pattern is related to other patterns (including non-security patterns). Using interaction and collaboration diagrams they showed how the patterns work together. Note that the problem with retrofitting security has also been recognized: ideally, security should be considered from the beginning of any software development.

7.3.2 Other Contributions

After this cornerstone publication, other patterns were published with the focus on security. Most of them consider previous results and refer to them.

Tropyc. Cryptography is a classical area of security. Braga et al. presented a set of nine patterns for building cryptographic software components [27]. The focus is on the traditional aspects of security, i.e. confidentiality, integrity, authentication and non-repudiation. Four core patterns are used to compose other proven cryptographic services (e.g. SECRECY WITH AUTHENTICATION which is derived from INFORMATION SECRECY and MESSAGE AUTHENTICATION. Together they form a "Generic Object-Oriented Cryptographic Architecture" (GOOCA). Additional information about structure and dynamics of the patterns is provided, too. Furthermore, relations with other patterns are discussed separately (including the SECURITY ACCESS LAYER.)

Authenticator Pattern. Brown et al. presented a single pattern that "performs authentication of a requesting process before deciding access to distributed objects" [31]. The authors identified relations to patterns for authorization as introduced by Fernandez and Hawkins [83] as well as Neves and Garrido [161].

Access Control Patterns. A couple of contributions deal with authorization. Hays et al. combined the security functions of authentication, access control and data filtering within a distributed environment in a framework [108]. This framework integrates the following patterns: DATA FILTER [91], BODYGUARD [161], RPC CLIENT [111] and AUTHENTICATOR [31]. Together these patterns and an accompanying security model build the "Object Filter and Access Control Framework". As such it was a first step towards integrating individual security patterns into a larger framework.

Fernandez also presented some authorization patterns: AUTHORIZATION RULES and ROLE-BASED ACCESS CONTROL [84]. The clue is that meta-data constraints are used to define authorization. Furthermore, architectural levels (based on the LAYER pattern [35]) are defined where each level has its own security mechanism and security enforcement. The combination of a layered architecture that includes a meta-level and patterns are a promising approach for a larger security pattern system.

Picking up this work, a pattern language for security models was published [85]. There are patterns for established security models: the AUTHORIZATION pattern (access matrix), ROLE-BASED ACCESS CONTROL pattern and MULTILEVEL SECURITY pattern (implementing the Bell-LaPadula model). It is suggested how these abstract patterns can be applied to all levels of the layered architecture, e.g. the FILE AUTHORIZATION pattern is a specialization of the AUTHORIZATION pattern at the system layer.

7.3.3 Security Pattern Community

Step by step the recognition of security as a new "branch" for the pattern community got on its way. After our general discussion of security patterns [208] the key persons started to work together more closely based on a mailing list. Eventually, we have planed and organized the focus group "Thinking about Security Patterns" at EuroPLoP 2002 that represents the kick-off meeting of the security pattern community [201]. There, the basics of security patterns were discussed. The major results have been the identification of existing security patterns and candidates which we are going to publish in 2004 [204]. Since then, results of the security pattern community are published at our corresponding Web-site http://www.securitypatterns.org where an up-to-date list of security patterns and related work can be found.

7.4 What Is a Security Pattern?

From Chapter 2 we know what a "regular" pattern is. Proceeding from Alexander's informal definition of a pattern and its structure as presented in Section 2.3 we can derive an analogous definition of a security pattern:

Definition 12 (Security Pattern). A security pattern describes a particular recurring security problem that arises in a specific security context and presents a well-proven generic scheme for a security solution.

Applying this definition to the example in Section 7.2 on page 98 we can find all elements of this definition. The recurring security problem is that you cannot remember strong passwords easily, the security context is chosing and handling passwords and the security solution is to use visual or other helps that play to your individual capabilities to remind you of such passwords. In this section we introduce the key elements of patterns from a security point of view. This includes the presentation of a typical security pattern template, forces which usually occur in security environments, and different approaches of how security patterns can be organized.

7.4.1 Security Pattern Template

In general, the structure of security patterns is identical to traditional patterns. They have an expressive name, a context, a problem and a solution. There are relations to other security patterns as well. Nevertheless, specific *security concepts* can be assigned to these structural pattern elements. We introduce our security pattern template in the following:

Security Context. Based on a scenario the context of the security pattern is illustrated. As we discussed earlier, the *life-cycle* phases and the *layer* of abstraction are important attributes of a security pattern context. This context describes the general conditions under which the security problem occurs. It can be useful to list context setting (e.g. the previous pattern in our example in Section 7.2 on page 98) security patterns, too.

Security Problem. The problem statement defines the security problem that occurs in the specified security context and will be solved by the security pattern. In the field of security a problem occurs whenever a system is protected in an insufficient way against abuse. Generally spoken we have to deal with *threats* which represent a possible danger that something or someone violates security. Generic threats are, for example, disclosure, deception, disruption and usurpation. An *attack* is an action that materializes a threat. Usually, there can be one or more attacks which lead to a specific threat. Within the problem the forces have to be considered. As security related forces we can consider the *security objectives* and other, non-security requirements. A security solution has to balance these requirements with other aspects such as usability and performance.

Security Solution. Ideally, the security solution solves the overall security problem. It is a set of one or more countermeasures which have to be applied in order to reduce the *risk*. For each *threat/attack* there should be at least one countermeasure. It is also useful to warn from typical pitfalls, e.g. how could this pattern become an anti-security pattern. As the solution resolves the forces it is also important to discuss the consequences of the application of a security pattern.

Security Pattern Relations. Some solutions may introduce new problems or only a part of the problem might be solved. Thus, additional security patterns should be considered. Similarly, problems could only be solved partly or certain side-effects couldn't be addressed within the given security pattern. That way a pattern hierarchy will be formed.

As with regular patterns there can also be some optional elements that can be used if they improve the comprehension of a security pattern (e.g. aliases, diagrams for dynamical and structural aspects, examples, counterexamples, etc.).

7.4.2 Application of Security Patterns

The elements of a security pattern also imply how they are supposed to be used. The user reads the pattern. If he finds himself in the described context, he has to decide whether the problem is important for him. If yes, he can apply the solution knowing that he acts "on expert advice". Furthermore, he knows what has to be done next, as the pattern is linked to subsequent patterns.

We illustrate this by the following example: recall the case studies we have examined in Chapter 4. In Table 4.1 on page 51 we have summarized the weaknesses, namely weak passwords, insufficient verification, weak or no encryption, weak and no authentication, and weak or no filtering. These problems could have been avoided, if the developers and users would have had the chance to look at security patterns.

Vulnerability	Security Pattern
weak password	PASSWORD PATTERNS [183]
insufficient verification	AUTHORATIVE SOURCE OF DATA [187]
weak or no encryption	CRYPTOGRAPHIC PATTERNS [27, 147]
weak or no authentication	AUTHENTICATOR, I&A PATTERNS [31, 120]
weak or no filtering	ACCESS CONTROL PATTERNS, FIREWALL PATTERNS, AUTHORATIVE SOURCE OF DATA [108, 207]

Table 7.1. Case studies resolved.

In Table 7.1 we show that security patterns for the described problems would have been available, i.e. solutions for such well-known problems have already been captured in patterns. Furthermore, there are patterns which increase the awareness for security problems and help to determine the right security objectives [74, 73].

However, the following requirements have to be met: the patterns have to be integrated into an overall set of security patterns. In particular, the relations between the patterns have to be drawn as this is a precondition for considering side-effects appropriately and for covering all relevant patterns. In fact, such an integrative process is in progress since 2002 [201]. Furthermore, it is necessary that the set of security patterns contains all relevant problems (as in the above example). Our approach of specifying security patterns and their relations is a contribution to meet this requirement. However, even an incomplete pattern system has its value today, as the problem boundaries are specified and can be identified by the user.

7.4.3 Forces Related to Security

The perception of threats is largely determined by both context and forces. Only if we consider certain security requirements (= forces) in a given context as important, a threatening situation can occur. For example, eavesdropping is not a problem if confidentiality is not a security requirement. We briefly introduce two sets of forces. First, we present a set of characteristics of a software product defined in the ISO/IEC standard 9126 "Software engineering - Product quality - Part 1: Quality model" [124]. Second, we discuss the functional security requirements provided by the Common Criteria [121]. Finally, we discuss some relations between these two sets of forces.

Software Quality Metrics. The ISO/IEC standard 9126 provides a set of software quality characteristics and a corresponding quality model. These can be used to specify and evaluate the quality of a software system using "validated and widely accepted metrics" [124]. As illustrated in Figure 7.3, the product quality is defined by six characteristics which are further split into several sub-characteristics. For each main characteristic the compliance with "standards, conventions, or regulations in laws and similar prescriptions relating to" the specific characteristic is also taken into account.

The focus of the quality characteristics introduced in ISO 9126 is to consider all relevant aspects of a software product. As such, these characteristics can be considered as forces which occur in any problem domain. Thus, security only plays a subordinate role within the set of all characteristics. It is interesting that security is considered as sub-characteristic of functionality (indicated by the shaded box in Figure 7.3)! This reflects the understanding that a system cannot work properly if there is a security breach.

Functional Security Requirements. The Common Criteria define a set of functional security requirements. Although the authors of the standard don't claim that they are complete, these requirements are considered as "well understood" and represent "the current state of the art in requirements specification and evaluation" [122].

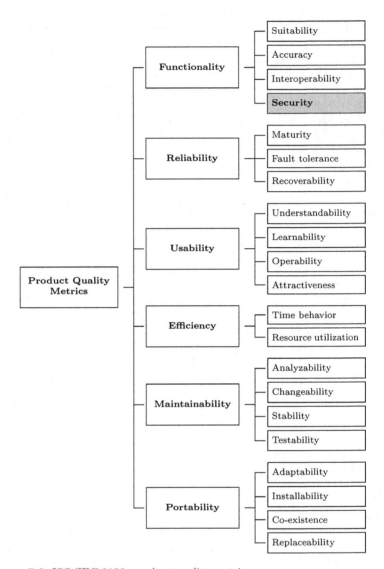

Figure 7.3. ISO/IEC 9126: product quality metrics.

As depicted in Figure 7.4 the requirements are organized by functional "classes" such as *Security audit* or *Cryptographic support*. For each class there can be subordinate class "families" which describe objectives and requirements of lower level functionalities (e.g. *Security audit* has the families *Automatic response, Data generation,* etc.). These families are further subdivided in "components". Although this sounds a little bit complex, a hierarchical representation of functional security requirements is achieved that way. From these requirements, forces for security patterns can be derived directly [200]. For example, the following statements are taken from the Common Criteria:

- Class: user data protection, family: data authentication → *A system should "be capable of generating a guarantee of authenticity of the information content of objects (e.g. documents)."*
- Class: identification and authentication, family: authentication failures → *A system should "be able to terminate the session establishment process after a specified number of unsuccessful user authentication attempts."*

As the Common Criteria also specifies some dependencies between the functional security requirements, it is possible to find a convenient and complete set of relevant sets of forces very efficiently.

Qualitative Balancing of Forces. In this section we looked at two different possibilities of organizing the forces of security patterns by various points of view. Thereby we can see that the forces are weighted in a different way. For example, the product metrics described in ISO 9126 consider *security* as a somehow subordinate functional requirement that is at the same level than the other requirements. On the other hand, the Common Criteria don't even mention other requirements than security related ones. Instead they provide a rich and fine-grained set of security requirements.

Apart from this observation we want to point out that the forces described before have a certain impact on each other. Intuitively, we can examine a qualitative balancing of forces. For example, a certain solution can be better to learn, slower, more difficult to use, etc. This helps us to understand the consequences of the application of a security mechanism in a better way. Based on the user's preferences (e.g. performance is an important issue) the most suitable solution can be identified. Note, that it is hard to get precise values for requirements such as usability and suitability (this can only be achieved if "rigorous metrics are used" consistently throughout all life-cycle phases of the system [124]).

7.4.4 Organizing Security Patterns

As we discussed in Section 2.5 patterns can be organized in different ways. These approaches can also be applied to security patterns. One way is to consider the context of a security pattern as classification criteria. For example, you can classify them by the life-cycle phase, i.e. when should a security pattern be applied? This is directly related to the question when a problem effectively occurs. Another way is to use a layer approach, i.e. at what level should security be considered?

It can be useful to combine such approaches. A multi-dimensional approach which combines both life-cycle and layer could be useful. Our approach is driven by the observation that many security activities take place

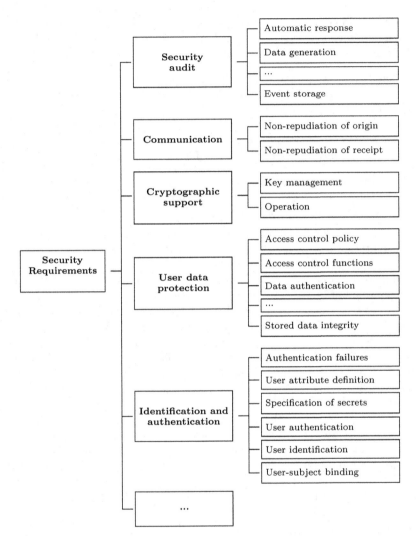

Figure 7.4. Common Criteria: functional security requirements.

at the following levels of abstraction: *enterprise, system* and *application*. As the most important life-cycle phases we consider *architecture, design* and *operation*. That way, almost all security patterns can be classified today. For example, SINGLE ACCESS POINT [242] is an architectural pattern applied during development of applications and WHITE HAT HACK THYSELF [187] is a pattern at the any level of abstraction applied during operation. Such a framework can be easily extended, e.g. by adding more life-cycle phases or levels of abstraction, and is similar to our approach of classifying security improvement artifacts in Chapter 5. The framework is illustrated in Figure 7.5.

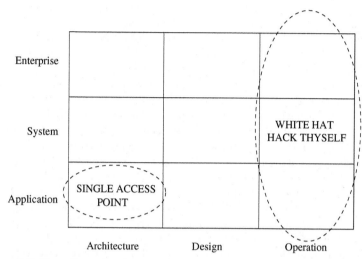

Figure 7.5. Two-dimensional organization of security patterns.

As a third dimension the problem domains of a security pattern are often considered. For example, this can be structured analogous to the classes of security requirements in the Common Criteria. Furthermore, different classes of threats and attacks can be taken into account. As a supplement it could also be useful to classify security patterns by the type of the provided solution (e.g. prevention, detection, or reaction).

Such rather simple schemes are preferred in the pattern community as they can be easily understood and applied [35]. We have used similar schemes in order to compile a first overview of all security patterns [201].

7.5 Mining Security Patterns

In the following, we first discuss what the completeness of a system of security patterns means and how this is going to be achieved. Then we identify artifactual approaches for mining security patterns (see also Section 2.6.1). Basically, we consider two different ways: on the one hand we can learn from typical errors and try to find out how they could have been prevented in advance. Most of today's security information providers follow this approach. Security holes are discussed and solutions are provided after a new vulnerability has been discovered. The opposite approach is to try and get security right the first time. Following this paradigm, many security standards are available as a source for mining security patterns.

7.5.1 Completeness of Security Pattern Collections

In Section 2.4 we have discussed the evolution from pattern catalogs to pattern systems to pattern languages. Thereby, the latter are a complete set of patterns which belong to a given problem domain. In the next chapter we take for granted to have such a complete set of all *known* security patterns. Only then we can achieve protection against all known threats/attacks, i.e. establish a state of security by applying patterns.

This statement can be examined from different points of view. Discovering all known security patterns means that in principle there can be security patterns which haven't been identified yet. Therefore, it should be possible to integrate them into a system of patterns as soon as they are discovered.

Another important issue is the principle of seeing patterns as a hypothesis. This says that patterns are evolving, i.e. they are going to be refined and improved constantly until they reach a stable, alive state [6, 5]. Therefore, all collections of patterns should reach the state of a language eventually. Besides it is better to have a rather "thin" security pattern than no security at all. The pattern community processes should guarantee that all relevant patterns of a given domain will be identified and captured over time. Later, we will define the pragmatic criteria of "coverage" of a security pattern system (see Section 8.6) which enables us to give evidence whether a system of security patterns is complete or not under the assumptions given above.

7.5.2 Security Information Providers

Security-related information is offered by different sources. Typically, anti-security cases are discussed as it is much easier to describe a failure and to provide workarounds or long-term solutions after an incident occurred. There are several types of security information providers which we have characterized by the following set of features: respectability, reliability, and speed of reaction [207]. After we introduce representative security information providers, we classify them according to the given attributes.

Computer Emergency Response Teams. Being engaged in security improvement since the Morris Internet Worm incident in the late eighties, Computer Emergency Response Teams (CERT) are counted among the most respected security information providers. Very often, CERTs are non-profit organizations evolving from larger security projects or organizations. The ancestor of all CERTs is the CERT Coordination Center (CERT/CC) at the Carnegie Mellon University [37]. In Germany there are, for instance, the DFN-CERT [62] evolving from the German Research Network (Deutsches Forschungsnetz, DFN) and the RUS-CERT [188] established at the University of Stuttgart. Another well-known example is the Australian CERT-AU [36].

A primary goal of any CERT organization is to assemble, process and provide information about vulnerabilities. By means of *advisories* they warn regularly about severe vulnerabilities which could have a large impact. Besides, they observe areas such as Viruses and Trojan Horses, too. As CERTs attach great importance to the completeness of the information included in the advisories, these are not always up-to-date. It always requires some time to collect and verify all information about a specific vulnerability and how it can be fixed. Furthermore, CERTs follow a non-disclosure publication policy, i.e. they only publish an advisory when a fix or workaround is guaranteed. Often this holds up the publication of an advisory, too.

Beyond advisories, CERT/CC offers two other types of notifications. On the one hand there are *vulnerability notes* which contain information about recently discovered vulnerabilities [41]. Basically, these notes can evolve to advisories at a later point in time. On the other hand there are *incident notes* [39] which contain information about the occurrence of exploitations of potential vulnerabilities.

Beside these public, national CERTs there are a couple of other organizations which provide security-related information and consultation. Often, these are state-run organizations such as the Computer Incident Advisory Capability (CIAC) that is a service of the U.S. Department of Energy (DOE) [47]. CIAC supports DOE facilities and contractors in case of any security-related incidents. The Federal Computer Incident Response Capability (FedCIRC) plays a similar role for the U.S. government and its facilities [80].

Hacker Groups. Other important security information providers are hacker groups. Motivated in different ways and typically with high expertise these groups of people are engaged in uncovering vulnerabilities. Some of them also publish their insights. In contrast to CERT-like organizations they often don't care whether a too early disclosure of a vulnerability and its exploitation could lead to severe damage. Exchanging information hacker groups often operate WWW sites and sometimes public newsgroups in the USENET or instant messaging channels. Hacker groups which offer their own Web content are, for instance, the Chaos Computer Club (CCC), Phrack, and L0phT, which have also been under contract for a security consultancy.

Security Companies. Many consulting companies for security as well as manufacturers of security software publish security-related information on a regular basis. By nature this is not an unselfish act rather than a proof of competence. In the case of a software manufacturer it can also be seen as advertising for the own product portfolio.

For example, the Australian company INFILSEC Systems Security called its vulnerability database a "vulnerability engine" that should serve as a tool for manufacturers, system administrators, security consultants and analysts. The idea was to develop and operate a central repository for vulnerabilities of operating systems, applications, and protocols. Besides, information about solutions should have been stored. As input a mailing list such as Bugtraq should be used. A search engine was planned as interface for the resulting database. Furthermore, an online update interface was considered in order to submit information to the system.

Another example is the company Internet Security Systems (ISS) which sells security software and offers consulting services. They also operate the vulnerability database X-Force (see also Section 5.7.1).

Software and IT Companies. Software and IT companies represent another source of security information on their own. They publish information about security problems and corresponding solutions concerning their products. However, we can safely assume that almost no company publishes such information on a voluntary basis. Typically, information is only released, if a vulnerability is publically discovered by a third party (CERTs, hacker groups, etc). Thus, such information is usually available before an official announcement of the affected company. As an example for such vendor-driven publications about product-related security information is Microsoft's security mailing list [154].

Newsgroups and Mailing Lists. Presuming that "real" hackers have always up-to-date information about security holes, newsgroups in the USENET and dedicated security mailing lists represent the most up-to-date information sources which are publically accessible. Contributions come form hackers, employees of IT companies and other IT professionals. As representatives for such newsgroups we refer to the following examples:

- `comp.security.unix`
- `comp.security.ssh`
- `comp.security.misc`
- `de.comp.security`
- `comp.lang.java.security`
- `comp.os.ms-windows.nt.admin.security`
- `comp.os.netware.security`
- `comp.security.firewalls`

There are also several security mailing lists – Bugtraq [212] and Alert [229] belong among the most considerable of them. A more complete list of both security-related newsgroups and mailing lists is provided by Hurler [118].

Articles and Textbooks. Finally, we also discuss articles and textbooks as a source of security information. By nature, articles and especially textbooks cannot cover highly topical subjects. However, the required middle- and long-term background knowledge is captured in such documents.

Findings. In Table 7.2 we summarize the findings of our examination of security information providers by classifying them qualitatively according to the characteristics mentioned above. Regarding the respectability, CERT-like organizations can be classified high whereas hacker groups have a rather dubious reputation. With respect to the reliability, the quality of information is at a high level from both CERTs and hacker groups whereas the other sources offer a broad fluctuation. The speed of reaction is remarkable in so far as CERTs are rather slow and especially mailing lists operated under a full-disclosure policy offer information very quickly - even if it isn't complete or verified.

	Respectability	Reliability	Speed of reaction
CERT (Advisories)	high	high	low
CERT (other)	high	high	medium
Hacker groups	low	usually high	high
Security companies	medium - high	medium - high	low - medium
News/mailing lists	low - high	low - high	high
Articles and books	medium - high	medium - high	very low

Table 7.2. Classification of security information providers.

In order to cope with the problem of security holes in a sufficient way, it is necessary to call in more than one security information provider, i.e. a balanced mix of sources is required. Our experience with training of both students and professionals, however, revealed that this is a very time consuming task [207]. Furthermore, we can see that not enough effort is made to fix solutions in running systems [181]. As a consequence it is even more important to get security right the first time.

7.5.3 Security Standards as Sources for Pattern Mining

We consider security standards such as the German IT Baseline Protection Manual [33] or the ISO/IEC Standard 17799 [123] as a source for the mining of security patterns [199, 200]. Typically, relevant threats, examples for attacks, security requirements and corresponding countermeasures can be found. As we have discussed in Section 7.4.1, we can relate instances of these concepts to the structural elements of security patterns. We show how this can be achieved in this section.

A major advantage of using standards as a source of inspiration is that experts usually clearly know solutions to given problems but if you ask them to write down their know-how, they will run into trouble because they rely on knowledge that is a result of long lasting experience, i.e. this knowledge is not explicitly available in their mind. Thus, security standards help to express the rather "difficult" aspects of security patterns and the authors can fully concentrate on the solution.

Other advantages of mining patterns in security standards is that you can expect that security experts have written them. Public feedback helped to improve them over time, i.e. they should be sound in both form and content. One can also expect that following security standards contributes to the completeness of a security pattern system.

Furthermore, security standards help to achieve a more standardized terminology and a more formalized structure for security patterns. Additionally, this approach might help to improve the integration of patterns from different authors into a larger pattern system. Although many pattern practitioners think that formalisms and standardization should not be applied to patterns [35] such approaches are justified in the security domain as they help to ensure that standard security requirements are indeed met.

Mining security patterns in those standards requires an assignment between concepts in the standards and the elements of security patterns. In the following we show this by selected examples[1]. For each standard we provide a table that summarizes what parts of the standard can serve as input for security patterns.

Common Criteria. The Common Criteria define an international security standard. National security organizations from the governments of the Netherlands, Canada, France, Germany, Great Britain, and the USA developed the Common Criteria in order to merge their own security standards. In the following we show how context, problem and solution elements of a security pattern could be more standardized and formalized according to the Common Criteria (see also Section 5.3.1). Note that the Common Criteria do not provide possible solutions and hints for relations between patterns. The overall relationship between security patterns and the Common Criteria is illustrated in Table 7.3.

Security Pattern	Common Criteria
Context	Environmental assumptions, policy statements
Problem	Security objectives, threats, attacks
Forces	Functional security requirements
Solution	-
Relations	-

Table 7.3. Mining security patterns: Common Criteria.

---

[1] A comprehensive study of relevant security standards was compiled by Project Team 5 of Initiative D21 [210].

The *environmental assumptions* describe security aspects of the environment in which the IT system is intended to be used. There are several assumption categories that cover assumptions about administrators, users, data protection, communications, physical protection and procedural protection. The *user assumptions* do, for instance, help to determine what kinds of users there are, i.e. what are their motives, attitudes and access privileges. Basically such assumptions have to be assured by other security patterns on which the given security pattern relies. Often the IT system must comply with security *policy statements*. Thus an optional description of them helps to specify the context more precisely. A general policy statement could be for example that all information must be marked and labeled.

The *security objectives* address all of the identified security aspects. They "reflect the stated intent and shall be suitable to counter all identified threats and cover all identified organizational security policies and assumptions." Threats are directly related to the security objectives. One only perceives a threat if a security objective applies to the environment or the IT system (and vice versa). The security objectives are something one wants to achieve (i.e. goal) whereas the threats are something one wants protection against (i.e. non-goals). The Common Criteria provide certain categories of *threats* and lists of detailed *attacks*. As such the security objectives, threats and attacks can be assigned to the problem section of a security pattern.

Specifying the forces helps to clearly define what *functional security requirements* have to be met by the IT system and its environment in order to counter the identified threats in a reasonable way (see also Section 7.4.3).

IT Baseline Protection Manual. The German IT Baseline Protection Manual offers default security countermeasures which should be considered for any IT system. Thereby, overall threat scenarios are assumed. Furthermore, a process for the establishment and preservation of an appropriate security level is described. Besides, a straight-forward procedure for the determination of the current security level conducting a plan/actual comparison is provided. As such it is not necessarily limited to national usage and another valuable source for mining security patterns. As illustrated in Table 7.4 the elements of security patterns can be related to the elements of the IT Baseline Protection Manual.

Basically, the IT Baseline Protection Manual provides countermeasures against threats that can occur at different layers [33]. This seems to naturally fit to the pattern terminology. However, there are several important differences. Regarding the context, a 5-tier IT baseline protection model is provided. This covers universally applicable aspects, the infrastructure, IT systems, networks, and IT applications. Within these layers several modules can be identified. For example, the module "UNIX system" belongs to the layer of IT systems. Each module is assigned to a layer and a description of the module specifies the context in more detail. Within this description assumptions concerning the module and its environment are made.

Security Pattern	IT Baseline Protection Manual
Context	Layer model, description
Problem	Threat scenario, Threats catalog
Forces	-
Solution	Safeguard catalog
Relations	Limited support

Table 7.4. Mining security patterns: IT Baseline Protection Manual.

Threats are organized in five catalogs where each of them represents a class of threats which characterize them by their origin. Namely there are threat catalogs for force majeure, organizational shortcomings, human failures, technical failures, and deliberate acts. There are several hundred individual threats where about a third of them belong to the class of deliberate acts. Beside a description of each threat references to related threats are provided. Furthermore, examples of recent occurrences of corresponding attacks are given sometimes. Each module contains a threat scenario which is a list of typical threats which are assumed regarding IT baseline protection of the given module.

The safeguard catalogs which contain sets of countermeasures are also organized in classes. The characteristic of each class is where a countermeasure is going to be applied. Namely there are safeguard catalogs for infrastructure, organization, personnel, hard- and software, communications and contingency planning. For each safeguard a responsibility for initiation and implementation is assigned. A description how to implement the safeguard is provided. If available, relations to complementary countermeasures are listed. Furthermore, additional controls are mentioned (like check-list questions).

As discussed in the previous paragraphs, the IT Baseline Protection Manual features several types of relations. First of all, there are explicit relations between the modules. This can be seen as a sort of precondition. That way a sense of a hierarchy is implemented, i.e. countermeasures of a more general module hold also for a lower-level module. Furthermore, there are relations between threats as well as between countermeasures. However, each module covers more than one problem and more than one solution in a given layer-based context. This is not consistent with the pattern paradigm (one context, one problem, one solution) and blurs the relationships between threats and countermeasures. As a consequence each module contains more than one pattern and the relations and dependencies between them are not obvious to pattern authors. Although a matrix which shows the assignment of threats and countermeasures is available, this additional knowledge cannot be used in a straightforward way as one would always have to check explicitly which countermeasures protect against what threats.

ISO 17799. The focus of the ISO 17799 standard is the management of security [123]. The standard was developed by the British Standards Institute
(BSI) as the British Standard 7799. As it was widely used beyond the national level, however, it finally became an international standard adopted by
ISO. Today it is used all over the world and several tests and audits which are
compliant to ISO 17799 are available. In the following we discuss the overall relationship between security patterns and ISO/IEC 17799 statements as
illustrated in Table 7.5.

Security Pattern	ISO 17799
Context	Chapters and sections
Problem	Rudimentary support
Forces	Objectives
Solution	Controls
Relations	References

Table 7.5. Mining security patterns: ISO 17799.

The standard is organized in a Chapter/Section hierarchy which represents topics and sub-topics of security management. For example, the topic
"Physical and Environmental Security" is subdivided into "Secure Areas",
"Equipment Security" and "General Control". Pattern authors can refer to
this as an analogous context hierarchy.

Each sub-topic is introduced with a brief discussion of the objectives, i.e.
what should be achieved by the application of the subsequent controls. This
can be seen more as a description of forces than the actual problem as the
objectives describe requirements in a given context. The actual problem is
outlined in the description of each control. However, this is only a rudimentary support for pattern authors as the level of detail doesn't go beyond very
short (and sometimes vague) statements of what the problem actually is (e.g.
"Equipment should be sited or protected to reduce the risks from environmental threats and hazards, and opportunities for unauthorized access").

The controls describe best practices in the different areas of security management. By nature, these controls are at a rather high level and should be
supplemented with additional and more detailed documentation.

If available, relations to other controls are mentioned as references to the
corresponding section.

Findings. Our examination shows that is is necessary to have a look at more
than one standard as the required elements of a security pattern cannot
always be found in the desired level of granularity. Furthermore, the standards
have a different scope and can be seen as a supplement for each other. Note
that no standard mentions the consequences of the application of a control

or countermeasure. Furthermore, the importance of relations doesn't seem to play a major role.

7.6 Summary and Conclusions

Security patterns are a solution to the problems stated in Chapter 4 and Chapter 5: they capture the expertise of security professionals and assist novices to get security right the first time in a systematic and generative way. In this chapter we have specified the semantics of the core concepts of security patterns and how security patterns can be identified.

7.6.1 Summary

From a syntactical point of view, security patterns are the same as regular patterns for the development of software. Representing a specific view on software there are, however, certain distinguishing features. The semantics of the elements of security patterns is described in our security pattern template. Typically, security has to be considered in different life-cycle phases and at different layers of abstraction. Furthermore, problems in the security domain are represented by threats and the corresponding attacks. Solutions to the described kind of problems are countermeasures which provide protection and help to establish a certain state of security. We have discussed these relationships by introducing our security pattern template.

Then we have discussed forces which arise in the security domain. We found out that security related forces have always an impact on other forces such as usability and performance. Therefore, applying a security pattern has always some consequences based on a qualitative balancing of forces. This can be used to make statements about the quality of the state of security that can be achieved with patterns.

After that we have introduced an organization scheme for security patterns. This basically relies on categories for different classes of security pattern contexts. Besides, we consider the problem domains of security as an important criteria for classifying security patterns.

In the next section we have discussed different approaches for mining security patterns which we have identified. First, we briefly discussed why we can speak of a complete set of security patterns. This can be assumed if we consider pattern collections as evolving knowledge. Over time, a collection of patterns of a particular domain will be mature and complete.

In principle, we have identified two approaches: one can identify proven solutions by learning from errors or one can mine patterns from collections of established security solutions. The first type of information is offered by certain types of security information providers which we have classified by their respectability, their reliability, and their speed of reaction. As none of the information sources satisfies all of these requirements it is necessary to monitor several of them. The other type of sources for mining security patterns are security standards. These provide certain statements which can be directly transferred to elements of security patterns. We show this by discussing several examples of such standards. Our examination has also revealed that it is necessary to look at more than one standard as these usually don't contain all elements required for describing a pattern.

7.6.2 Conclusions

In this chapter we have provided core definitions of security patterns and how they can be identified. Our pattern template has been introduced first at PLoP 2001 and is used since then. Our approach of mining patterns from security standards has been adopted by the security pattern community and is going to be applied in subsequent work on security patterns [200, 204]. For example, Lehtonen and Pärssinen have found the right forces of their pattern in the Common Criteria [147].

In particular, both authors and users of security patterns can benefit from security standards. Although the patterns become more standard-oriented and more formalized, they are still human-readable. As context, problem and solutions can be identified more precisely, this increases trust in the overall pattern which is important in the security domain. Our approach helps to identify (i.e. find new patterns) and match (i.e. search and retrieve) security patterns more precisely. Furthermore, our approach accelerates the overall writing process as authors can rely on standard descriptions of context, problem and forces while spending their full attention to the elaboration of the solution. In particular, we have published selected patterns in order to prove our point that security standards are a valuable resource for pattern mining [200].

Our examination in this chapter has revealed that security information providers and security standards are valuable sources for mining security patterns. However, a repository of dedicated security patterns can be much more helpful and specific than such sources of information: patterns are more clearly structured and provide explicit linkage to other security patterns.

8. A Theoretical Model for Security Patterns

> A problem well-stated is a
> probem half solved.
>
> ——————————————
> CHARLES KETTERING

8.1 Introduction

Security patterns are best security practices. We identified them as a suitable tool for novices supporting them in solving security problems more efficiently. Nevertheless, there are still some features missing in order to take real benefit from them (see Section 5.8.2). The basic problem is to find the "right" security pattern. Due to a lack of defined syntax it is not possible to ask meaningful questions and to get semantically meaningful results. Therefore, we develop a theoretical model for security patterns in this chapter. The fundamental idea is to share security patterns (and related information) utilizing the ontology paradigm. Based on a security core ontology (see Chapter 6) we can define the syntax of security patterns at a different level. The result is a model for security patterns that helps to understand what security patterns precisely are and that enables sophisticated search and retrieval of security patterns.

Outline. We proceed according to the following steps: we introduce related work in the area of modeling patterns in Section 8.2. Hereby, we show that the known approaches are not sufficient for security engineering. In Section 8.3 we give an introduction into our approach of modeling security patterns. In Section 8.4 we provide syntactic definitions of core security pattern concepts, i.e. context, problem, solution. Building up on this we define the syntax for security patterns and security pattern systems in Section 8.5. Thereby, we focus on refinements of the definitions for the *specializes* and *requires* security pattern relationships. In Section 8.6 we explain the notion of *coverage* which basically means that there must be a countermeasure for each threat in order to achieve security. Equipped with this set of definitions we can derive the key result of our formal model: based on our understanding of the term security we prove that coverage implies security in Section 8.7. Finally, we provide a summary and conclusions in Section 8.8.

M. Schumacher: Security Engineering with Patterns, LNCS 2754, pp. 121-140, 2003.
© Springer-Verlag Berlin Heidelberg 2003

Results. In Chapter 5 we have found out that patterns don't have defined syntax and semantics. These limitations are the main reason for the restricted usage of security patterns today. For example, the search and retrieval capabilities don't go beyond keyword-based searches. Thus, we have developed a theoretical model for security patterns in order to overcome this shortcomings. Our approach is unique and combines the ontology paradigm with the pattern approach in order to make patterns suitable as a security engineering tool. Hereby, we meet the requirement that patterns should remain prose as we assign meta-information to the documents and operate on this syntactical model.

8.2 Related Work

Borchers has introduced a formal syntactic notation for a generic pattern system [25]. His intention was to clarify pattern concepts in general and to lay down a foundation for computer support. He also implemented the Pattern Editing Tool (PET). This software parses patterns prepared in XML and displays them in a suitable way (i.e. each pattern element can be easily recognized). It is possible to customize the representation of patterns, e.g. show only context, problem, solution and hide details such as illustrations and examples.

PET also supports a navigation through the pattern graph based on hyper-links. Furthermore, PET automatically builds a graphical representation of the pattern graph that can be used for navigation, too. The PET prototype serves as proof-of-concept and as feasibility study that a tool support is basically possible.

The above approach is a first step toward a generic, theoretical model of patterns. However, it makes no use of the semantics which are provided by patterns (in general as well as domain specific), Therefore, it isn't possible to get more meaningful answers from PET than from an ordinary search engine.

8.3 Modeling Security Patterns

In this section we motivate and introduce our approach of specifiying the syntax and the semantics of security patterns. We discuss the notion of pattern linguistics and show the mapping between ontology concepts and security patterns. Furthermore, we outline the steps of our specification approach.

Motivation. As we have shown in Section 5.8 a theoretical model for security patterns is required if we want to understand security patterns and make their added values accessible. In particular, we use an ontology-based approach to define a model for security patterns. By that way we can, for instance, achieve tool support going beyond keyword-based search and retrieval of security patterns (see Chapter 3). The specification approach of security patterns and the resulting model represent integral contributions of this book.

We advocate the usage of patterns for improving security, especially when security novices are in charge. When we specify more precisely security patterns, we are able to show the conclusiveness of our approach. Furthermore, a such theoretical framework is required for any kind of tool support. Especially when we want to use security patterns in a more efficient way a model is an indispensable precondition. Defining the intuitive and common sense knowledge, we can also clarify the internals of security patterns, i.e. a theoretical model also contributes to an inter-subjective understanding within the community.

Developing a formal framework makes the added-value of security patterns accessible: we have a provable semantics and can find relationships which might not be obvious. Beside our theoretical model the patterns themselves remain prose! However, they can be used more efficiently with corresponding meta-information.

Pattern Linguistics. In this paragraph we introduce the notion pattern linguistics. Being part of the domain of language science, linguistics provides theories for the structure of human languages [137]. The overall goal is to identify principles for classifying any language-related data. A branch of linguistics focuses on the language system, i.e. form, function and structure of a language. For our discussion it is important that this includes the examination of syntax and semantics of languages. As implied by the term "pattern language" our goal is to find such principles for patterns, too.

As part of the grammar, the syntax describes the formal structure of a language. The target of examinations is a set of rules which describe how the words of a language can be combined. Following Alexander's definition as quoted in Section 2.3 a pattern is such a (three-part) rule that fixes the core elements of a pattern (see Figure 8.1(a)). As such, a pattern is the basic building block for bigger units reflected in the pattern language.

Beside syntax, the semantics of patterns are important. Again we can continue our linguistical consideration. Following de Saussure, a linguistic sign (= a pattern) consists inseparably of a signifying and a signified element [57]. Accordingly a pattern consists inseparably of a name and the pattern concept (as illustrated in Figure 8.1(b)). For example, assume that you develop a secure application including the SINGLE ACCESS POINT pattern [242]. In order to conduct the right steps there has to be a link between your representation of the pattern concept ("What does SINGLE ACCESS POINT stand for?") and a representation of the verbal form of the pattern's name. Therefore, one goal of patterns is to establish them as "words" from the expert's vocabulary.

Semantics basically arise from human interpretation. However, the unit of identifier and concept has no meaning from a syntactical point of view where only the structure is important. This is especially true for machine-based processing of language structures, i.e. computers don't understand the

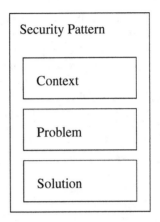

(a) Three-part rule.

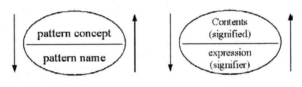

(b) Expert's vocabulary.

Figure 8.1. Patterns as linguistic signs.

concepts. The other way around the result of an automated processing has to be formally correct in the first place. However, syntactically correct units only make sense if they are also meaningful semantically. We pick up this issue again in the next paragraph.

Security Patterns and Ontologies. If we speak of pattern linguistics and want to process patterns with tools we have to think about machine-readable representation and meaningful results: ontologies are one way to represent both syntax and semantics. As illustrated in Figure 8.2 we apply the ontology paradigm at two levels of abstraction:

1. At a higher level of abstraction we consider a "security pattern ontology" (i.e. security pattern system). This ontology consists of patterns as concepts and the corresponding relations between patterns.
2. The patterns themselves provide a structure for the structural elements of a pattern: context, problem, solution. These elements consist of concepts of the security ontology which are at a lower level of abstraction.

As stressed with the dotted lines in the middle of Figure 8.2 the elements of the security pattern ontology define a structure over a composite of the elements of the security ontology. This "mapping" defines which pattern elements are assigned to concepts of the security ontology. Later we use the security ontology concepts and particular ontology relations between them, namely the *specialize* and the *protects against* relation, to define the security pattern ontology relations. The semantics of the former relation represents a partial order of concepts which belong to the same class. That way, hierarchical taxonomies can be described. The latter relation has been explicitly specified between countermeasures and threats/attacks in the security core ontology in Section 6.4.

Definition 13 (*specializes$_{ont}$*). If a concept x from the security ontology specializes a concept y, we write x *specializes$_{ont}$* y.

We use this security ontology relation to define the relation *specializes$_{pat}$* at the higher level of patterns (indicated as a directed dashed line).

Definition 14 (*protects_against$_{ont}$*). If a concept x (which specializes the concept *countermeasure*) from the security ontology protects against a concept y (which specializes the concepts *threat* or *attack*), we write x *protects_against$_{ont}$* y.

We are going to use this security ontology relation to define *requires$_{pat}$* relationship at the higher level of patterns (indicated as a directed solid line).

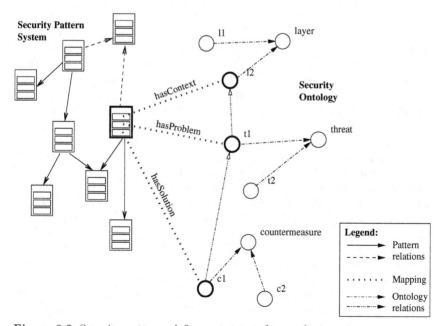

Figure 8.2. Security patterns define a structure for ontology concepts.

As a consequence of these definitions, the correctness of patterns depends on correctness of the security ontology. The ontology is "correct" if the concepts, relations and inferences match with the human intuition and interpretation. For example, countermeasures are concepts that are the source of a $protects\_against_{ont}$ relation that has to be met by the security ontology. This is the case if the security ontology reflects the common sense of the users. Thus, we kept the core of the security ontology rather simple in order to avoid misunderstanding and ambiguity (see Chapter 3). However, any community terminology which follows our definition (e.g. threat and attack taxonomies can be derived from security standards as we have shown in Section 7.5) can be integrated into the core ontology. We show some concrete examples in the next chapter.

Approach. Our approach can be summarized as follows: we build on a security ontology that defines core security concepts and semantic relations. Whether these concepts and relations are valid in reality cannot be determined from a syntactical point of view. As discussed in Section 7.5 we can assume, however, that the ontology is correct as domain experts codify the knowledge (e.g. the ontology is derived from an established security standard). As such we consider the security ontology as basis for the truth values of statements about security patterns.

The security patterns are a means of consolidating ontology concepts in a certain kind of structure. With security patterns we can represent security knowledge at a different level of abstraction than ontologies. The security patterns create additional structures between subsets of ontology concepts: concepts which describe context, problem and solution are put into a perspective. Furthermore, interactions such concepts can be considered as patterns are related to other patterns. For example, the consequences of implementing a countermeasure could introduce new problems which are covered by another related pattern. In fact, such information comprises the added value of security patterns.

The overall goal is to show that the application of a set of security patterns helps to establish security. Thereby, we first define what it means for a set of security patterns to be "secure". This definition is based on our understanding of security as a state of being free from danger which is achieved by countermeasures (as such the definition is based on a $protects\_against_{ont}$ relation between concepts of the security ontology). Hereby it is important to have only sets of security patterns that follow our definition of security. However, security is a more "global" criteria, i.e. we cannot prove this within the security patterns themselves. Thus, we define "coverage" as a second, effective "local" criteria. The semantics of this criteria also rely on the ontology: coverage means that there is at least one countermeasure for each security problem. The next important step of our formal approach is to relate the definitions of "coverage" and "security" and show the non-trivial implication that a covered security pattern system leads to a state of security. If we then have such a covered security pattern system (i.e. the semantic relations which define coverage hold true), the semantic relations which describe security are true, too.

Proof Methodology. In this chapter we present proofs concerning the correctness of certain clauses. The representation of the proofs follows a structured notation that is comparable to an interactive theorem prover. This form has been introduced by Lamport who claims that following this style it is much more difficult to prove a clause which is wrong [143]. Such a proof is a sequence of numbered steps. Each step either contains a short justification why the step is valid or the step itself will be refined to another sequence of steps. The numbering follows the structure, e.g. step 1.2. is the second step at level 1. The structure allows to read a proof selectively, i.e. steps at lower levels could be skipped when not required. Usually a proof starts with a proof sketch.

8.4 Core Definitions

Before we can define a security pattern, we need to define its components. Briefly spoken, a security pattern consists of a security context, a security problem and a security solution. First, we specify these elements of a security pattern. Based on that we are able to provide a theoretical model for security patterns and security pattern system. We now define these terms.

Security Context. The term security context is used in many different ways. Following the definition of pattern context we have to look at characteristics which describe *situations* in which security problems occur, e.g. time and location[1]. As described in Section 5.2 the *time* of the occurrence of a problem is one important characteristic, i.e. when does a problem occur? Another important characteristic is to narrow at which level of abstraction a security problem occurs. Hereby, we refer to a *layer* approach as described in Section 2.5.

Definition 15 (Security Context). A *security context* Γ is a set of life-cycle phases and hierarchical layers.

This notation can be extended freely as long as new characteristics are disjoint. Values for both time and location are taken from the security core ontology. Typical examples for life-cycle phases are *analysis, design, implementation, integration,* and *operation* (see Section 5.2.2). This fits perfectly to the terminology of patterns, e.g. there are design patterns or idioms which are related to particular implementation aspects (see Section 2.5). A layer

---

[1] Researchers in the domain of Ubiquitous Computing also work on definitions of context and context-awareness. They consider time and location as important characteristics of context, too [61, 60].

model can, for instance, be found in the IT Baseline Protection Manual. According to this model the context can be physical *infrastructure*, *IT systems*, *networks*, and *IT applications*. Again, the elements of Γ, like those given above, are concepts taken from the underlying ontology. For example, the following would be a valid security context according to Definition 15:

$$\Gamma = \{\text{analysis}, \text{infrastructure}\}$$

Security Problem. In such a security context a security problem can occur. As presented in Section 6 threats and attacks are counted among typical security problems.

Definition 16 (Security Problem). A *security problem* Π is a set of threats and/or attacks.

Basically, the elements of Π are again sets of concepts from the ontology. For example,

$$\Pi = \{\text{denial of service}, \text{ping of death}\}$$

and

$$\Pi = \{\text{eavesdropping}, \text{sniffing}\}$$

are possible instances of a security problem. Both, threats and attacks can, for example, be taken from community specific threat and attack taxonomies which can be integrated to the security core ontology directly. Thereby, threats represent a potential for a security breach and attacks are in fact security breaches. Note, that one or more attacks can lead to a specific threat.

Security Solution. The security solution solves the security problem that occurs in the security context. Intuitively, a security solution should contain only countermeasures which are concepts from the ontology that stand for solutions to particular threats or attacks.

Definition 17 (Security Solution). The *security solution* Σ is a set of countermeasures.

The countermeasures are also concepts of the ontology. For example,

$$\Sigma = \{\text{asymmetric encryption}\}$$

and

$$\Sigma = \{\text{mandatory password protection, restrictive access rights}\}$$

are possible instances of countermeasures. Countermeasures can address one or more problems. However, the proper assignment of countermeasures and threats also depends on the context. Thus, such an assignment can only be made at the level of the security pattern itself.

Security Pattern. Based on the previous definitions of the elements of a security pattern we can now provide a definition of a security pattern, too.

Definition 18 (Security Pattern). A *security pattern* is a triple $P := (\Gamma, \Pi, \Sigma)$, where Γ is a security context, Π is a security problem, Σ is a security solution.

The security pattern intuitively relates countermeasures (stated in the solution) to threats and attacks (stated in the problem) in a given context. A possible instantiation of P would be for example:

$$P = (\{\text{local area network}\}, \{\text{eavesdropping}, \text{sniffing}\}, \{\text{encryption}\})$$

In fact, this can be seen as a rudimentary thumbnail of a security pattern consisting of the relevant meta-information in the correct syntactical notation. Whether this description is true depends, however, on the underlying security ontology which actually captures the semantics.

As described in Section 2.3, the *name* of a security pattern is an important property in order to identify and use them efficiently - the name is the sign that signifies the pattern concept. Being formal the name is, however, only a symbol without further semantics. Thus we don't consider the name in our theoretical notation. In fact, the semantics are contained in the concepts and relations of the corresponding security pattern ontology (see also Chapter 3 and Section 9.3.1) and how they are mapped to security patterns (see the security pattern template in Section 7.4.1).

Security Pattern System. As regular patterns, security patterns don't exist in isolation, too. There are many interactions with other security patterns, e.g. one pattern *requires* that another pattern has to be applied before. Similarly one pattern can be more *special* (or more general) than another pattern.

Although the relationships are usually listed in the text of the security pattern, they can be assigned to the security pattern system where the emphasis is on the relationships. As we draw the analogy between ontologies which consist of concepts and security patterns, we provide a corresponding definition:

Definition 19 (Security Pattern System). A *security pattern system* is a directed acyclic graph $PS = (\wp, \Re)$ with nodes $\wp = \{P_1, \ldots, P_n\}$ and edges $\Re = \{R_1, \ldots, R_n\}$. Each node $P \in \wp$ represents a *security pattern*. There is a *relation* between two nodes $P, Q \in \wp$ if and only if there is a directed edge leading from P to Q.

Some natural relations between security patters are induced by some semantic relations between them. The two main relations are "requires" and "specializes". Both are defined in the following section. Apart from that, other relations can be defined by a user of a security pattern system. A cycle of relations having the same type should not occur[2].

8.5 Primary Security Pattern Relations

As for example depicted in Figure 7.2 on page 100 there can be different kinds of relations between patterns. Noble showed, however, that all pattern relations can be traced back to a set of primary pattern relations, i.e. all "secondary" relationships can be expressed in terms of the primary relationships namely *refines*, *uses*, and *conflicts* (see Section 2.5) [165]. Currently we focus on the first two relations and discuss conflicts again in Section 9.4.1. We refer to the relation *refines* as *specializes*. Similarly, we refer to *uses* as *requires*. We now define these relations building on the security ontology.

Specializing Security Patterns. Making a security pattern more special basically means to make both the context and the problem of the pattern more specific. As an example we consider a pattern with a network context where a typical problem is the protection of the confidentiality of transmitted data against eavesdropping attacks. If we now step into a context of an Ethernet-based Local Area Network (LAN) that is obviously more special than the network context we can also see more specific attacks: in an Ethernet-based LAN it is possible to capture and interpret packets intended for other stations. Such *sniffing* attacks are for example typical in Ethernet-based LANs.

To define what it means for a security pattern to specialize another security pattern, we first define a *specializes* relationship on contexts and problems. As discussed before, the $specializes_{ont}$ relationship can only be applied to concepts that share a common class of the security ontology, e.g. the relationship {local area network} $specializes_{ont}$ {analysis} does not hold true.

Definition 20 (Γ_1 *specializes*$_{con}$ Γ_2). Let Γ_1 be the context of a security pattern P_1 and Γ_2 be the context of a security pattern P_2. We say that Γ_1 specializes Γ_2 (written as Γ_1 *specializes*$_{con}$ Γ_2) if and only if

$$\forall x \in \Gamma_2 : \left[x \in \Gamma_1 \lor (\exists y \in \Gamma_1 : y \ specializes_{ont} \ x)\right]$$

Intuitively, a context Γ_1 specializes a context Γ_2 if all elements of Γ_2 occur in Γ_1 or a specialization (in terms of the ontology) of the elements in Γ_2 occur in Γ_1. For example, we consider four contexts $\Gamma_1 = \{\text{Ethernet}, \text{Bank}, \text{Linux}\}$, $\Gamma_2 = \{\text{Network}, \text{Bank}\}$, $\Gamma_3 = \{\text{Ethernet}, \text{Bank}\}$, and $\Gamma_4 = \{\text{Network}\}$. For these sets holds that Γ_1 *specializes*$_{con}$ Γ_2 but not Γ_3 *specializes*$_{con}$ Γ_4. The terms Ethernet, Bank, Linux, and Network are taken from a part of an ontology that contains definitions of possible context concepts. In a similar way we can define what it means for a problem to specialize another problem.

---

[2] A cycle would indicate a "hen & egg" problem, e.g. P_1 *requires* $P_2 \ldots P_n$ *requires* P_1.

Definition 21 (Π_1 specializes$_{prob}$ Π_2). Let Π_1 be the problem of a security pattern P_1 and Π_2 be the problem of a security pattern P_2. We say that Π_1 specializes Π_2 (written Π_1 specializes$_{prob}$ Π_2) if and only if

$$\forall x \in \Pi_2 : \left[x \in \Pi_1 \vee (\exists y \in \Pi_1 : y \; specializes_{ont} \; x) \right]$$

As an example, the following relation holds:

{Sniffing, Denial of Service} specializes$_{prob}$ {Eavesdropping, Denial of Service}

but the following relation does not hold:

{Sniffing} specializes$_{prob}$ {Denial of Service}

Hereby, the terms Sniffing, Denial of Service, and Eavesdropping would belong to an attack taxonomy described by the ontology. With Definitions 20 and 21 we can now define what it means for a security pattern to specialize another security pattern.

Definition 22 (P_1 specializes$_{pat}$ P_2). Let $P_1 = (\Gamma_1, \Pi_1, \Sigma_1)$ and $P_2 = (\Gamma_2, \Pi_2, \Sigma_2)$ be security patterns. We say that P_1 specializes P_2 (written P_1 specializes$_{pat}$ P_2) if and only if Γ_1 specializes$_{con}$ Γ_2 and Π_1 specializes$_{prob}$ Π_2.

Changing the context of a security pattern basically means to change the level of abstraction. The above definitions show that there are several possibilities to specialize a security pattern depending on whether the context and/or the problems are made more specific. This is illustrated by the following examples.

1. The context is specialized and the problems remain the same:

$$P_1 = (\{\text{Ethernet LAN}\}, \{\text{Eavesdropping}\}, \Sigma_1)$$

$$specializes_{pat}$$

$$P_2 = (\{\text{Network}\}, \{\text{Eavesdropping}\}, \Sigma_2)$$

This helps to distinguish solutions for a problem that occurs in different contexts. Depending on the context different solutions could be given, e.g. encryption at the network layer and encryption at the link layer. This case is an indication that the problem section might not be detailed enough.

2. The context remains the same and only the problems are specialized:

$$P_1 = (\{\text{Network}\}, \{\text{Sniffing}\}, \Sigma_1)$$

$$specializes_{pat}$$

$$P_2 = (\{\text{Network}\}, \{\text{Eavesdropping}\}, \Sigma_2)$$

This helps to distinguish solutions for more specific problems. Whereas encryption generally protects against eavesdropping, a switched network usually helps against sniffing attacks. This case indicates that the assumptions in the context of the pattern might not be detailed enough.

3. Both, context and problems are specialized:

$$P_1 = (\{\text{Ethernet LAN}\}, \{\text{Sniffing}\}, \Sigma_1)$$

$$specializes_{pat}$$

$$P_2 = (\{\text{Network}\}, \{\text{Eavesdropping}\}, \Sigma_2)$$

This is the most natural application of the $specializes_{pat}$ relationship as the level of abstraction changes in a homogenous way: the more specific the context the more detailed threatening events (i.e. attacks) can be described.

4. Both, context and problems remain the same. As the solution is unambiguously determined by context and problem statement, this case doesn't seem to make sense as both patterns should be identical then. However, this fact can be indicated by a tool and the user of the pattern repository can get a hint that a new pattern covers the same topic as an existing one. If the solution differs, an additional pattern that is more general than both patterns, could be necessary. It could also be possible that a *conflict* can be detected that way, i.e. you detect competing patterns. If the solution is the same, pattern aliases can be detected and double entries in a pattern repository can generally be avoided.

Although example 3 seems to be the most reasonable implementation of $specializes_{pat}$ we decided to go beyond such a rigid subset relationship. That way the pattern author's freedom can be respected and the piecemeal growth of a security pattern repository can be better supported.

Requiring Security Patterns. Requiring another security pattern has the following intuitive interpretations. First, a particular threat or attack is not addressed by the pattern and has to be solved in another pattern. Second, the application of a pattern can lead to a new problem. We will illustrate this in some examples.

Assume a security pattern that solves the problem eavesdropping with the countermeasure encryption. Although this problem is obviously solved, the threat of a traffic flow analysis still remains [208]. This problem has to be solved in another pattern in order to achieve a high level of security.

Another example is the protection against eavesdropping in a local area network on a lower layer. The basic problem here is the usage of a shared medium, i.e. network stations are able to capture any packet including those which are not intended for them. This is usually solved by using a Switch device. However, this introduces new problems such as protection of the administrative interfaces and manipulation of the Switch's address register (e.g. ARP cache flooding and poisoning) [207].

In order to define what it means for a security pattern to require another security pattern we rely on relation $protects\_against_{ont}$ which comes from the security ontology again.

Definition 23 (P_1 **requires**$_{pat}$ P_2). Let $P_1 = (\Gamma_1, \Pi_1, \Sigma_1)$ and $P_2 = (\Gamma_2, \Pi_2, \Sigma_2)$ be security patterns. We say that P_1 requires P_2 (written P_1 $requires_{pat}$ P_2) if and only if

$$\exists p \in \Pi_1 : \qquad [\forall s \in \Sigma_1 : \neg(s \ protects\_against_{ont} \ p)]$$
$$\wedge \quad [\exists s' \in \Sigma_2 : s' \ protects\_against_{ont} \ p]$$

From this definition follows that a pattern P that includes countermeasures for each problem within the pattern doesn't require another pattern. We discuss this in more detail in the next section. Note that this relation can also be defined transitively. For example, if for patterns P, P' and P'' holds that P $requires_{pat}$ P'' and P'' $requires_{pat}$ P' then we would say that P requires not only P'' but also P'. This is the case when there is a chain of requirements which have to be considered subsequently in order to achieve protection against a set of related problems as discussed above.

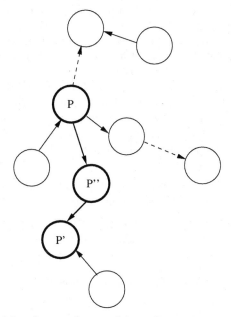

Figure 8.3. Transitive closure of a set of depending patterns.

Definition 24 ($P\ \widetilde{requires}_{pat}\ P'$). Let P, P' and P'' be patterns. We say that P requires P' transitively (written as $P\ \widetilde{requires}_{pat}\ P'$) if and only if

$$P\ requires_{pat}\ P' \vee \left[\exists P'' : P\ \widetilde{requires}_{pat}\ P'' \wedge P''\ requires_{pat}\ P'\right]$$

Note that Definition 24 is recursive. Intuitively, a pattern P requires another pattern P' transitively if there is a "path" from P to P' using just the relation $requires_{pat}$ (see Figure 8.3). Using definition 24, it is possible to define the transitive closure of a set of security patterns with respect to the $\widetilde{requires}_{pat}$ relation. For any security pattern P we define $PM(P)$ as the set of patterns including P which is closed under $\widetilde{requires}_{pat}$, i.e.:

$$PM(P) = \{P'|P\ \widetilde{requires}_{pat}\ P'\} \cup \{P\}$$

A central assumption we must make is that for a given problem domain a security pattern system contains "all known and useful" patterns. Basically this means that for a given security pattern system $PS = (\wp, \Re)$, if a pattern $P \in \wp$ requires a pattern P', then $P' \in \wp$ as well. We formulate this as an axiom.

Axiom 1 (Containment Axiom). Let $PS = (\wp, \Re)$ be a security pattern system. Then for all $P \in \wp$ holds that if $P\ \widetilde{requires}_{pat}\ P'$ then $P' \in \wp$.

The Containment Axiom is not difficult to justify. In practice, all security patterns which have proved useful to provide countermeasures to particular attacks should be integrated into the security knowledge base (i.e., the security pattern system) of the problem domain. In fact, we discussed in Section 7.5.1 that our assumption holds. Without the axiom it would be impossible to achieve security with applying patterns.

The following lemma, which will be used in our final theorem, is a simple reformulation of the Containment Axiom. Intuitively, the lemma states that there cannot be a pattern "outside" a security pattern system that provides a solution for a problem stated in a pattern inside the security pattern system. We consider this lemma that is inline with the previous definitions as a shortcut for this statement.

Lemma 8.5.1 (Containment Lemma). Let $PS = (\wp, \Re)$ be a security pattern system. Then the following holds:

$$\forall P \in \wp : \forall P' \in PM(P) : P' \in \wp$$

Proof. ASSUME: $P \in \wp$ and $P' \in PM(P)$
PROVE: $P' \in \wp$

PROOF SKETCH: The proof follows almost directly from applying the Containment Axiom.
1. $P' \in \{P'|P\ \widetilde{requires}_{pat}\ P'\}$
   PROOF: Follows from the assumption that $P' \in PM(P)$ and the definition of $PM(P)$. $\square$

2. $P \ \widetilde{requires_{pat}} \ P'$
   PROOF: Follows from step 1. □
3. $P' \in \wp$
   PROOF: Follows from the assumption that $P \in \wp$, step 2 and the Containment Axiom. □
4. Q.E.D.
   PROOF: Step 3 states the consequent of the lemma. □

8.6 Internal and External Coverage

According to our understanding, a state of security "is achieved by a set of safeguards and countermeasures applied to maintain the condition of being safe from threats." However, this is intuitively only true if there is a countermeasure that addresses each threat. We define this as the coverage of a security pattern.

In the following we distinguish between internal and external coverage. Intuitively, a pattern is internally covered if it does not require another pattern to provide countermeasures to all of its problems (i.e. threats and optionally a set of corresponding attacks). Again we rely on the $protects\_against_{ont}$ relation of the security ontology.

Definition 25 (Internal coverage). Let $P = (\Gamma, \Pi, \Sigma)$ be a security pattern. We say that P *is internally covered* if and only if

$$\forall p \in \Pi : \exists s \in \Sigma : s \ protects\_against_{ont} \ p$$

Not all security patterns are internally covered. All patterns that require another pattern are not internally covered. For these patterns we define what it means for a security pattern P to be externally covered by the set $PM(P)$ of required security patterns. This is the case if either P is internally covered or, in case there is a problem p without a solution in P, there is another security pattern P' in $PM(P)$ that provides a countermeasure to p.

Definition 26 (External coverage). Let $P = (\Gamma, \Pi, \Sigma)$ be a security pattern. Then we say that P *ist externally covered relative to* $PM(P)$ if and only if

$$\forall p \in \Pi : \quad [\exists s \in \Sigma : s \ protects\_against_{ont} \ p]$$
$$\vee \quad [\exists P' \in PM(P) : \exists s' \in \Sigma' : s' \ protects\_against_{ont} \ p]$$

The internal coverage is a special case of external coverage when $PM(P)$ is an empty set. The defintion of coverage can now be applied to an overall security pattern system, too.

Definition 27 (Coverage of a Security Pattern System). Let $PS = (\wp, \Re)$ be a security pattern system. We say that PS *is covered* if and only if

$$\forall P \in \wp : P \text{ is externally covered relative to } PM(P)$$

In the next section we use the definitions for coverage in order to prove why coverage implies security. This is an important step because coverage is a "local" property and security (as defined in the next section) is a "global" property.

8.7 Why Coverage Implies a State of Security

Intuitively, the fact that a security pattern system is covered should mean that there is a solution for every problem within the security pattern system. In fact, this property follows from the above definitions and is proven in the following theorem. For a security pattern system $PS = (\wp, \Re)$ we define

$$\text{problems}(PS) = \bigcup_{P=(\Gamma,\Pi,\Sigma)\in\wp} \{p : p \in \Pi\}$$

and

$$\text{solutions}(PS) = \bigcup_{P=(\Gamma,\Pi,\Sigma)\in\wp} \{s : s \in \Sigma\}.$$

Thereby, problems(PS) is the set of all problems which occur in the pattern system, and solutions(PS) is the set of all solutions (or countermeasures) occurring in the pattern system. Based on the security ontology, we can now define what security of a security system means.

Definition 28 (Applying security patterns implies a state of security). The application of pattern from a security pattern system PS *implies a state of security* if and only if

$$\forall p \in \text{problems}(PS) : \exists s \in \text{solutions}(PS) : s \; protects\_against_{ont} \; p$$

In the following we prove that a covered security pattern system implies a state of security according to our definitions. The theorem shows that it is sufficient to speak about coverage in order to draw conclusions about a state of security. This takes for granted that the security pattern system contains all known problems of a problem domain (see Section 7.5.1) and that the underlying security ontology meets the ontology requirements (see Section 3.4.1). We conjecture that the implication can be strengthened to an equivalence.

Theorem 8.7.1 (Coverage Theorem). *Let PS be an arbitrary security pattern system. If PS is covered, PS implies a state of security.*

Proof. Assume: $PS = (\wp, \Re)$ is covered.
Prove: PS implies a state of security.

PROOF SKETCH: We need to show that PS implies a state of security, i.e. that for every problem $p \in$ problems(PS) there is a solution $s \in$ solutions(PS) that protects against p. The proof takes an arbitrary problem p from a security pattern P and then applies the definition of coverage which yields two cases: either p is catered for in the same security pattern it came from (i.e. P), or there is a security pattern P' which is required by P (i.e. $P' \in PM(P)$) and protects against p. In the latter case, we apply the Containment Lemma to show that P' must be part of the original PS. Therefore, every problem has a solution in PS, and hence, PS implies a state of security.

1. All $P \in \wp$ are externally covered relative to $PM(P)$.
   PROOF: Follows from the assumption and Definition 27 (Coverage of a security pattern system). $\square$
2. Take an arbitrary security pattern $P = (\Gamma, \Pi, \Sigma)$ and any problem $p \in \Pi$. Then $p \in$ problems(PS).
   PROOF: Follows from the definition of problems(PS). $\square$
3. For p holds that either (a) $\exists s \in \Sigma : s \ protects\_against_{ont} \ p$, or (b) $\exists P' = (\Gamma', \Pi', \Sigma') \in PM(P) : \exists s' \in \Sigma' : s' \ protects\_against_{ont} \ p$.
   PROOF: Follows from step 1 and Definition 26 (external coverage). $\square$
4. ASSUME: $\exists s \in \Sigma : s \ protects\_against_{ont} \ p$
   PROVE: Q.E.D.
   PROOF SKETCH: This is case (a) which was identified in step 3. We need to show that p has some solution in PS, which is rather easy in this case, since the solution is contained in the same security pattern as the problem.
   4.1. $s \in$ solutions(PS)
      PROOF: The solution s guaranteed in the case assumption is in Σ which is the set of solutions provided by P. From the definition of solutions(PS) follows that $s \in$ solutions(PS). $\square$
   4.2. $s \ protects\_against_{ont} \ p$
      PROOF: Follows directly from the case assumption. $\square$
   4.3. Q.E.D.
      PROOF: We needed to show that $s \in$ solutions(PS) and that s protects against p. The former was shown in step 4.1 and the latter in step 4.2. This completes the proof for this case. $\square$
5. ASSUME: $\exists P' = (\Gamma', \Pi', \Sigma') \in PM(P) : \exists s' \in \Sigma' : s' \ protects\_against_{ont} \ p$.
   PROVE: Q.E.D.
   PROOF SKETCH: This is case (b) from above. We need to show that the solution s' guaranteed by the case assumption belongs to solutions(PS). This can be shown by applying the Containment Lemma.
   5.1. $s' \ protects\_against_{ont} \ p$
      PROOF: Follows directly from case assumption. $\square$
   5.2. $P' \in PM(P)$
      PROOF: Follows directly from case assumption. $\square$

5.3. $P' \in \wp$
PROOF: Follows from step 5.2 and the Containment Lemma. $\square$
5.4. $s' \in$ solutions(PS)
PROOF: Follows from step 5.3 and the definition of solutions(PS). $\square$
5.5. Q.E.D.
PROOF: From step 5.1 we know that s' protects against p and from step 5.4 we know that $s' \in$ solutions(PS) which concludes the proof for case (b). $\square$

6. Q.E.D.
PROOF: Step 3 guarantees that steps 4 and 5 cover all cases, i.e. in any case there is a solution s in the set of solutions provided by PS such that s protects_against$_{ont}$ p. By Definition 28 this means that the security pattern system PS implies a state of security, completing the proof. $\square$

As said above, coverage is a "local" criteria, i.e. a tool could systematically check all "requires" relations for solutions to a given problem. It is not necessary to search in the overall pattern system. Whenever a pattern system is not covered, either a "requires" relation is missing or the pattern system is not yet complete. Note, that we consider patterns as means of establishing and maintaining a state of security. So far, we haven't made any assumptions about the quality of such a state, e.g. is a particular solution more secure than an alternative solution. However, it is possible to extend the model in that way: one the one hand, the problem statement of patterns is narrowed by forces which express security requirements and other attributes. On the other hand, the solution resolves these forces in a certain way, e.g. confidentiality is increased but performance and usability are decreased. We show an example for this approach in the next chapter.

8.8 Summary and Conclusions

Establishing patterns as a source of security improvement, especially suitable for non-experts, requires to think about a way to make the added values of patterns available. As tool support is one important requirement, we have identified the need for a theoretical model that lays down the basics of syntax of security patterns. Considering tool support another important boundary condition is that the patterns considered as written piece of knowledge shouldn't be touched in order to respect the author's freedom writing expert knowledge in the most suitable way.

8.8.1 Summary

Proceeding from the notion of pattern linguistics we draw an analogy between ontologies (consisting of concepts and relations) and pattern systems (consisting of patterns and relations). In order to establish patterns as "linguistic signs" it is necessary to define both syntax and semantics of patterns.

This analogy represents the starting point for our formalization approach. We have defined core definitions of security patterns referring to concepts of the security ontology, namely security context, security problem and security solution. These elements are part of each security pattern. Furthermore, we defined a security pattern system as a directed acyclic graph which consists of patterns (= nodes) and relations (=edges).

Accordingly, we have defined the primary security pattern relations "specialize" and "requires" referring to concepts and relations of the security ontology. Based on that we have been in the position to define the Containment Axiom which demands that all security patterns which provide countermeasures to particular threats/attacks should be integrated into the security knowledge base. Furthermore, we have proved the corresponding Containment Lemma which proves that there cannot be a pattern outside the pattern system providing a solution for a problem occurring within the pattern system.

Equipped with the core definitions and primary relations of security patterns we have introduced the concept of "coverage". We have distinguished between internal coverage (i.e. no other pattern to provide countermeasures to all problems within a given pattern is required) and external coverage (another pattern is required to "cover" all problems). Again, we have relied on concepts and relations of the security ontology.

The coverage of a security pattern system is a "local" criteria that can be checked by referring to concepts and relations which are assigned to security patterns. Following a common sense definition of security which basically states that security can be achieved by countermeasures against all threats, the coverage criteria can be used to conclude that a pattern system implies a state of security (which is a "global" criteria). Based on our definitions given before, we have been in the position to prove this statement.

8.8.2 Conclusions

As we have discussed in Section 5.8.2 patterns can be applied as a security improvement artifact. Especially for security, the pattern approach has to be extended in order to understand security patterns and to take advantage of the added value that they basically offer. The important drawbacks are that there are no sophisticated search and retrieval capabilities for the majority of patterns. One reason is that patterns are understood as prose today and, as a consequence, that there has been no applicable model for security patterns available. Thus, our theoretical model for security patterns and some basic relations between them is an important contribution for both the security and the pattern community.

The benefit for security engineers and security novices is that security patterns help to integrate security into software development tasks in a natural way - assuming that patterns are used during development anyway. Furthermore, security patterns complement any other security improvement artifact as they can virtually be applied in any life cycle and at different layers of abstraction.

The benefit for the pattern community is that we don't touch the patterns themselves respecting the author's freedom and creativity in selecting an appropriate pattern template and writing proven solutions in a convenient way. Enhancing security patterns with corresponding meta-information helps to transfer the core concepts of security into the pattern world. With defined syntax (and semantics) sophisticated tools are now possible that show, for instance improved search and retrieval capabilities. Thus, users can take advantage of pattern features more efficiently. Furthermore, defined terminology and structures can also support authors of patterns by writing the parts of a pattern which are rather difficult to write according to the author's experience.

Recall that any theoretical model is vulnerable if the suitability of the modeling approach will be questioned. Thus, our definitions rely on common sense statements that are typically used in the security domain. Furthermore, we have applied the pattern approach in a straight-forward way without changing the core concepts. As a proof of concept we discuss several new applications of security patterns in the next chapter. We even show that it was possible to develop a security engineering tool that can fulfill the expectations of the intended group of users (i.e. security experts, security novices, and authors/maintainers of security patterns).

9. New Applications of Security Patterns

> The value of an idea lies in the using of it.
>
> ———————————
>
> THOMAS A. EDISON

> Failure is simply the opportunity to begin again, this time more intelligently.
>
> ———————————
>
> HENRY FORD

9.1 Introduction

The intention of this chapter is to show the conclusiveness of our approach by presenting new applications of security patterns which were all implemented with a prototype for a security pattern search engine. Before we step into this proof of concept, we briefly summarize the problems and how we have solved them.

The core premise of this book is that the human factor has to be considered by any security improvement approach. In fact, patterns support this requirement as they help to reduce complexity. Problems are divided in manageable parts and can be solved in a structured way. Thereby, side-effects and time-dependencies can be considered as patterns are related to other patterns. In order to make these added values usable, it was necessary to represent the pattern elements appropriately and to model the structure and the rules of security pattern systems. After doing this, we are now enabled to build a tool which can support both professionals and novices by improving the security level of their systems in a structured and comprehensive way. As patterns come from software engineering, we also achieve a certain level of integration between security and traditional software development.

Outline. The outline of this Chapter is as follows: first of all we introduce our approach for implementing a "security pattern search engine" in Section 9.2. Section 9.3 deals with the representation of the security core ontology,

M. Schumacher: Security Engineering with Patterns, LNCS 2754, pp. 141-159, 2003.
© Springer-Verlag Berlin Heidelberg 2003

the integration into the structure of security patterns as well as the rules for deriving new information and queries which are used to access the knowledge base. We also show first basic applications of our model: annotating patterns, supporting pattern authors and integrating non-pattern sources. In Section 9.4 we step into more sophisticated applications of security patterns. We introduce improved search and retrieval capabilities for security patterns. Furthermore, we show advanced techniques such as the consideration of side-effects or the maintenance of security pattern repositories. Finally, we summarize our results in Chapter 9.5.

Results. This chapter proves that the theoretical model developed in the previous chapter can also be implemented. Even more important is that we can show several new applications of patterns which make them useful as a security improvement tool. With a rather loosely structured meta-information we are able to make the added values of security patterns available and develop a prototype of a security pattern search engine. That way we can show that, for instance, security patterns help to solve problems in a structured way, help to consider side-effects and time dependencies.

9.2 A Security Pattern Search Engine

In order to demonstrate the applicability of our pattern-based security improvement approach we developed a so-called "security pattern search engine". In this section we discuss in how far this system can be called an expert system, present the main use cases, introduce the architecture of the prototype and discuss related work.

9.2.1 A Pattern-Based Expert System?

Basically, security patterns help to solve recurring security problems in a proven way. As such a corresponding tool should support the users in doing so. Thus, the question arises whether our security pattern search engine can be called an expert system.

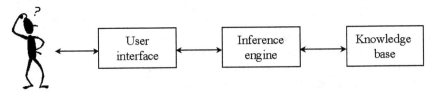

Figure 9.1. General architecture of an expert system.

As illustrated in Figure 9.1 the key components of an expert system are the knowledge-base, the inference engine and the user interface [68, 126].

Discussing these components we can introduce our tool and its relation to expert systems.

Knowledge Base. Generally spoken the knowledge base contains a symbolic representation of the specific knowledge of the given problem domain. This includes concepts, instances (or facts), relations as well as rules which can be used to derive additional knowledge from facts. In our case this is the security core ontology with additional taxonomies taken from a specific terminology, the mapping between the structure of security patterns and the security core ontology, and rules which express our theoretical model.

Inference Engine. The inference engine processes the user's queries, applies them to the knowledge base and presents corresponding answers according to the implemented reasoning mechanism. Based on both the facts and the rules it is possible to derive knowledge that might not be obvious. In fact we used such an inference engine in order to implement the prototype.

User Interface. The user interface is responsible for input from the user (i.e. queries) and for displaying both intermediate and final results. In our case the user interface is implemented with a Web browser and a remote Web server which interacts with the inference engine which in turn interacts with the knowledge base.

Findings. After all, we can say that our search engine can be called an expert-system as it shows all required components. However, the notion of a knowledge-based system seems to be more feasible: First, this term is more general as "any system which performs a task by applying rules of thumb to a symbolic representation of knowledge" is in fact a knowledge based system [126]. Second, we expect that the practical focus of our approach is not on the rules written by experts. Particularly, the rules are fixed by our theoretical model. Thus, the expert's main task is to add new facts (i.e. new security patterns) to the knowledge base.

9.2.2 Use Cases

In this book we apply the pattern approach to security engineering, e.g. to solve typical security problems at different layers of abstraction. In this context we discuss use cases which are, for instance, derived from the competence questions we gathered while defining the task of the security core ontology (see Section 6.3 and Appendix C). A more general view of use cases for our system is illustrated in Figure 9.2. This is derived from our work within the Pattern Editing Toolkit (PET) project [24] and represents a subset of possible use cases.

As major roles we identified the expert, pattern authors and regular users (which can be subdivided into further categories such as manager, developer, end-user, etc.). In the following we outline the use cases assigned to these roles.

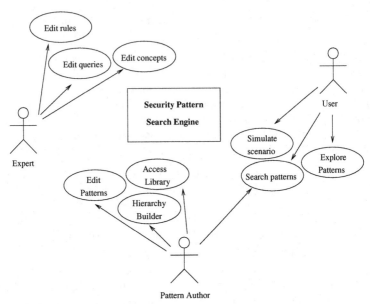

Figure 9.2. Security engineering with patterns: use cases.

On the one hand, the task of experts is to implement and maintain the knowledge base which represents the theoretical model. Thus, they should be able to *edit concepts, edit rules* and *edit queries*. Namely, they should be able to modify, add and delete these items. As we expect the knowledge base to be stable, the interventions of experts shouldn't occur very often.

On the other hand, both pattern authors and users will use the system frequently. Another obvious task of authors is to *edit patterns*. In our case this includes the annotation of patterns with meta-information. Thereby, they can *access a library* which contains predefined pattern elements, e.g. threats, forces or countermeasures. The intention of a *hierarchy builder* is to identify relations between patterns. Thus, a pattern hierarchy can be computed. Furthermore, pattern authors would like to *search patterns* that are somehow related to the pattern they are going to write.

This is also a key use case for regular users. In the end they want to find the pattern(s) that solve their problems. Thereby, it is useful to *explore patterns*, i.e. browse a pattern hierarchy in order to get an overview of the dependencies between patterns. Furthermore, it could be useful to *simulate scenarios*, i.e. conducting some sort of "what-if" experiments.

9.2.3 Prototype

Before we implementing the prototype we have had to make certain decisions with respect to the architecture and the actual implementation environment. We will outline this in the following.

Conceptual Decisions. Basically, several conceptual approaches can be imagined. Our prototype can be classified as a problem-specific tool as it integrates security knowledge (the ontology) and provides a strategy for problem-solving (the pattern approach) [174]. Thereby, further criteria should be taken into account. First, we prefer to use open components and interfaces whenever possible as this helps to extend and integrate the tool in an existing environment. Furthermore, it is easier to exchange certain components. Second, it should be possible to design an attractive user interface as the prototype should help the user to solve problems in a convenient way. Thus, the time for adjustment for using the tool should be minimal, too.

Architecture. We can implement the prototype following a centralized or decentralized approach. A strictly centralized implementation would mean that the content is collected, maintained and published by a single authority. This could work if the users have trust in such an organization. An example could be Hillside.net as non-profit corporation which promotes the pattern movement. Especially, a pattern repository dedicated to a particular topic such as security can be realized in that way. Taking into account the results of a general survey on vulnerability databases we expect that this approach could be acceptable for a majority of potential users [107]. Therefore, we decided to use this variant for our prototype.

A decentralized approach would mean that several authorities appear as providers of security patterns. If we assume that they work together, certain agreements regarding a common interface, similar structures, etc., have to be made. Especially for our ontology-driven approach it is important that different groups work together and exchange knowledge. That way the real benefits can be made available when such subcultures are joined together. In the long run this should be the more suitable approach [20].

We expect, however, a mix of these generic approaches. From presentations of our approach in certain companies as well as discussions at various conferences of the PLoP-series we conclude that most organizations will keep patterns related to internal problems/solutions and only contribute generally applicable security patterns to a public security pattern repository.

Implementation Aspects. As shown in Chapter 3 we have examined several ways of representing ontologies and corresponding tools for the development and application of ontologies. Gathering practical experience with the tools revealed that it is required to use different tools as all of them have different strengths. For example, K-Infinity (see Section 3.4.4) has a very powerful graphical tool for designing ontologies but the inference capabilities are limited. The requirement is, however, that the tools share a common representation such as RDF. As this didn't appear as a straight-forward task (e.g.

considering availability and interoperability), we decided to use an integrated set of tools, namely OntoBroker and related tools. In particular, OntoBroker is shipped with an inference engine which plays an important role in the prototype. As this platform features the export to popular open representations, however, this decision doesn't restrict the applicability of our approach: the prototype is basically independent of the platform as the knowledge base and not a particular API or programming language is the key to our solution.

The prototype itself passed through several iterations. We started with a command-line interface (CLI) version. The client reads the queries from a file, sends them to the inference engine server which in turn operates on the knowledge base. The next stage of extension included again the inference engine, a Web-server containing several Java servlets for interacting with the inference engine, and a browser-based query interface. The queries themselves were integrated within the Web-pages as JavaScript. The user could compose the queries with drop-down menus as well as selection check boxes. Due to the known limitations of this approach the final platform was completely implemented with Java servlets, i.e. it can be accessed with any browser. This should be convenient for users as they are accustomed to browser-based user interfaces. The overall usability of the interface is, however, out of the scope of this book.

For the maintenance of the knowledge base we have used OntoEdit, OntoAnnotate and OntoMat (for generating facts from given pattern documents). Furthermore, we have used the customized tool "Neptune" which has been developed during an accompanying Master Thesis for generating the meta-information for security patterns [17].

In particular, Neptune can be used to annotate security patterns by selecting corresponding entries from an ontology. As proof of concept, we annotated about 20 security patterns. Hereby, we could chose from predefined, hierarchical concept catalogs which cover entries for context, problem, forces, solution and consequences. The tool can also be used to specify the relations between patterns. As proposed in Section 7.5 the underlying ontology has been derived from standards such as the IT Baseline Protection Manual, the Common Criteria and ISO 9126.

9.2.4 Related Work

Bhambhani presented an expert system for suggesting design patterns [22]. The prototype was implemented with Gamma's design patterns [93]. The system is based on if/then rules and offers a question/answer interface, i.e. the user answers a sequence of questions and the expert system suggests the most appropriate design pattern. These questions are classified in several levels. There are questions to select the category of the pattern (i.e. creational, structural or behavioral design patterns) and sub-categories. Other questions are provided in order to determine the intent of a design pattern. Furthermore, there are pattern specific questions which deal with the conditions for applying a pattern. Eventually, there are auxiliary questions which are derived from sub-conditions. Having compiled the questions, thresholds are assigned to each pattern. A threshold determines how many weights or points are required for a certain pattern to be suggested. It is planed to gather statistical data in order to assign higher priorities to patterns which are used more frequently.

We consider the above approach (in contrast to ours) as a traditional expert system, i.e. experts write the rules and regular users apply the system. The current version only considers design patterns, however, the author mentioned that more patterns will be included. A problem could be that at least one additional distinguishing question is needed for each new pattern. This could reduce the applicability if users are not willing to answer several couples of questions before a pattern is suggested eventually. Furthermore, Bhambhani treats patterns in isolation, i.e. one dedicated pattern is suggested and the relations to other patterns aren't considered.

9.3 Enhancing Security Patterns with Meta-information

In this section we show how the theoretical model can be implemented in the selected symbolic representation: the F-Logic syntax. Based on the knowledge base (i.e. the security ontology and the mapping between the concepts and the pattern elements) we can already show some basic applications of our model.

9.3.1 Codifying the Knowlege Base and Inference Rules

In this Section we show by examples how the security pattern meta-information is represented internally. Our knowledge base consists of the security core ontology and additional ontologies derived from community terminology. Besides, we have a "pattern mapping" which assigns elements of the ontologies to the pattern elements. Furthermore, we show how the inference rules are implemented. That way, we codify the premises of our theoretical model and make it usable for requests to the knowledge base.

The native language of OntoBroker is F-Logic which is a powerful ontology representation language. As we provide certain F-Logic examples, a brief introduction to the used language primitives is provided in Appendix D. For the sake of readability we only provide those parts of the listings which are required for understanding the given representation or functionality.

Representing Ontologies. The definitions of the theoretical model can be represented as an ontology. At the top-level this is modeled in F-Logic by expressions as shown in Figure 9.3 on the following page. For example, Countermeasure is a sub-class of SecuritySolution. Furthermore, we can represent attributes of concepts, e.g. a SecuritySolution *protects against* at least one **SecurityProblem**. Note that each concept has to be a sub-class of a default root concept[1].

The relation *protects_against_{ont}* between countermeasures and threats is, for instance, the key relation between the concepts of our security core ontology. This means that a countermeasure protects against one or more threats. Other concepts and the relations between them are represented accordingly, such as the **Attack** *realize* **Threat** relation.

```
Countermeasure :: SecuritySolution.
Threat :: SecurityProblem.
Attack :: SecurityProblem.

SecuritySolution [protectsAgainst =>> SecurityProblem].
Attack [realize =>> Threat].
```

Figure 9.3. Representing concepts and relations.

The next step is to include taxonomies derived from terminologies of certain communities. For example, we implemented that for the threat and safeguard catalogs of the IT Baseline Protection Manual as illustrated in Figure 9.4 on the next page.

As long as such taxonomies show the *protects_against_{ont}* relation, virtually any terminology can be integrated. In fact we expect that any security approach adopts this understanding. As we will show later, it is also possible to combine several terminologies as long as there is no generally accepted "super security ontology". As such, our solution can be easily customized for different user groups. In our example we also provide a natural language description for each instance. This can be either a link to an external source[2] or encoded directly using another attribute.

Pattern Mapping. In Section 8.4 we provided the core definitions for the elements of a security pattern. This can be directly codified in the F-Logic syntax, too. In Figure 9.5 we show the definition of the security context as an element of a security pattern. Note that each entry has again a natural language description which can be either text or a link to an external document.

Basically it is possible to declare the relations explicitly or to identify them according to our definition of the core relations between security patterns. This is illustrated in Figure 9.6. The regular user will, however, work with meta-information which contains the explicit relations, mainly due to

---

[1] For example, **SecurityConcept** is a subclass of **Root** as well as **SecurityPattern**. However, we don't show this in the following listings.

[2] In our example a link to the corresponding threat entry of the IT Baseline Protection Manual is indicated.

```
ForceMajeure::Threat.
OrganisationalShortcomings::Threat.
HumanFailure::Threat.
TechnicalFailure::Threat.
DeliberateActs::Threat.

Theft:DeliberateActs.
Theft[
    description->"http://www.bsi.bund.de/.../t501.htm"
].

DataMediaControl:Countermeasure[
    protectsAgainst->>Theft
].

SafekeepingDataMedia:Countermeasure[
    protectsAgainst->>Theft
].
```

Figure 9.4. Integrating community terminology.

performance reasons: it is "cheaper" to follow explicitly declared relations instead of calculating them first. Basically, any other type of relation can also be annotated that way. We will define the implicit variant later as inference rules which will be used for maintaining security pattern repositories (see Section 9.4.3).

Inference Rules. The inference rules represent the definition of the primary security pattern relations, the definitions for internal and external coverage and the Coverage Theorem. These are going to be used to send sophisticated queries to the inference engine which will derive results that are not explicitly encoded in the security patterns themselves. Beside this more complex rules we can, for example, apply a straight-forward implementation of the *relation* that computes the transitive closure of all security patterns which are required by a specific security pattern. This is shown in figure 9.7.

9.3.2 Basic Applications

Equipped with the knowledge how ontologies and inference rules can be implemented in principle, we are already able to show some basic applications (i.e. we don't even need the inference rules) of our approach: a precondition for further applications is the annotation of security patterns. Furthermore, we show how pattern authors can benefit from our approach when they write new patterns. Finally, we show, how non-pattern sources can basically also be added as facts of the knowledge base.

```
Context [
  description => string;
  hasLayer =>> Layer;
  hasLifeCycle =>> LifeCycle
].

SecurityPattern [
  name => STRING;
  hasContext => Context;
  hasProblem => Problem;
  hasSolution => Solution;
  description => string
].
```

Figure 9.5. Mapping between concepts and patterns.

```
SecurityPattern [
  requires =>> SecurityPattern;
  specialize =>> SecurityPattern
].
```

Figure 9.6. Explicit declaration of pattern relations.

```
FORALL X,Y,Z X:SecurityPattern[requires->>Z]
  <- X[requires->>Y] AND Y[requires->>Z].
```

Figure 9.7. Example for an inference rule.

Annotating Security Patterns. A key premise of our approach is not to touch existing patterns. Particularly we expect that authors will not follow a mandatory, predefined pattern template. However, our approach allows to keep the patterns untouched and to assign corresponding meta-information instead. With tools such as OntoMat and OntoAnnotate new facts can be derived from patterns. With our customized application Neptune, security patterns can be annotated according to the entries in the knowledge base. That way, new instances (especially new security pattern nodes of the overall repository) are added to the knowledge base. Usually, the author opens a given pattern document (e.g. a HTML-page), can browse through it, selects the corresponding concepts and adds these facts by using, for instance, drag & drop mechanisms. Some tools also allow to export the resulting facts in a separate file or to write them directly into the source document. Certainly, it is also possible (and convenient) to edit this information manually. Examples for such meta-information can be found in Appendix B.

Supporting Pattern Authors. The knowledge base allows also to support pattern authors during writing patterns. We proposed the following approach: the author can to refer to catalogs containing predefined concepts which describe context (e.g. layer and life-cycle), problem statements (i.e. threats and attacks), forces as well as the solution and the consequences. As proof-of-concept we published some example patterns [200] and other authors found this approach useful (e.g. Lehtonen and Pärssinen [147, 204]). That way, authors can be sure that their pattern contains the most important elements. As the ontology relates the concepts to each other, a certain level of completeness can be achieved more easily. We can imagine to implement this function as a dedicated authoring tool. In fact, the security pattern search engine already contains a functionality that allows to browse context and problem entries of the ontology. This can already be a sufficient support as the author gets inspired and can basically check whether he missed essential parts.

Integrating Non-Pattern Resources. Another basic application of the theoretical model is to annotate non-pattern information resources which fit in the defined structure. We examined this approach for security improvement artifacts as discussed in Section 5.6.2. Recall that each block usually contains countermeasures against threats which occur in certain "modules". However, the lists of threats and security objectives as well as the corresponding countermeasures cover not only a single aspect. In contrast, patterns have one context, one problem, one solution, i.e. they are more focused. Covering an overall problem domain is realized with a set of related patterns. That way, the relationship between problems and solutions, the dependencies between problems and the consequences of applying certain countermeasure is represented in a more comprehensive way.

Annotating non-pattern resources makes this advantage accessible for the user. Besides, such meta-information helps to maintain the consistency of such non-pattern resources. Finally, it is always useful to provide linkage from patterns to external resources (e.g. by hyper-links). That way known-uses of the pattern and specific implementation aspects can be considered more easily. A practical aspect is that copyright issues have not to be taken into account, e.g. we provide hyper-links to the original sources. In fact, we compose such external knowledge in a different way and generate additional, new information. For example, we applied this approach by mining patterns from the IT Baseline Protection Manual, the CERT Security Improvement Modules and related sources [207].

9.4 Advanced Techniques

In this section we present selected advanced applications which show how security patterns can support security engineering. First, we show how the search and retrieval capabilities for security patterns can be improved. Then we discuss how security patterns can be used in order to consider the side-effects of the application of a solution appropriately. Finally, we outline some ways how an overall collection of security patterns can be maintained more efficiently.

9.4.1 Improvement of Search and Retrieval Capabilities

With our security pattern search engine the search and retrieval capabilities for security patterns can be improved significantly. As selected examples we discuss how a pattern hierarchy can be browsed and how conflicting or respectively alternative and duplicate patterns can be detected.

Browsing the Pattern Hierarchy. As we have annotated (or can detect) the relations between security patterns, we can browse the pattern hierarchy more efficiently. Without meta-information it would be required to read each pattern, look at the relationships and search the related patterns (particularly if the relations refer to external documents). Furthermore, our search engine can deliver the transitive closure of related patterns which shows, for example, *all* required patterns as illustrated in Figure 9.8 (thereby `pattern` is the identifier for a particular instance of a security pattern). This is a clear advantage as the user immediately knows what else has to be done when implementing a solution. Accordingly, it is also possible to find more general or more special security patterns. That way, the user can browse the overall pattern collection more conveniently than with conventional keyword-based searches.

```
FORALL X,URL <- pattern:SecurityPattern[requires->>X]
               AND X[description->URL].
```

Figure 9.8. Finding and refering to all required security patterns.

The inference engine returns an array where each row represents a security pattern and each column contains the value of the requested variables (`X` and `URL` in our example). This array can be processed further. For example, we displayed the result as a table on a web-page. Furthermore, we are able to show the resulting set of patterns graphically. From here, further requests can be submitted.

Detecting Conflicts, Alternatives and Duplicates. In Section 8.5 we defined the *specializes*$_{pat}$ relation between security patterns. A special case of this definition can be interpreted as a conflict between two patterns (another primary pattern relation according to Noble's definition [165]). A conflict between two patterns occurs when both context and problem are identical and the solution is different. This can be called either a conflict or an alternative

- its up to the user to decide this in the end. The corresponding query which returns an array of all conflicting patterns can be implemented as shown in Figure 9.9. Similarly, identical patterns can be detected. In that case the solution is identical, too.

```
FORALL X,Y,CONTEXT,PROBLEM,SX,SY
   <- X:SecurityPattern AND Y:SecurityPattern
      AND X[hasContext->CONTEXT]
      AND Y[hasContext->CONTEXT]
      AND X[hasProblem->PROBLEM]
      AND Y[hasProblem->PROBLEM]
      AND X[hasSolution->SX]
      AND Y[hasSolution->SY].
```

Figure 9.9. Detecting conflicting and alternative patterns.

That way, regular users can look for alternative or alias patterns. Furthermore, this type of query is very useful for pattern authors who submit a new pattern. If they see that there is a conflict they can try to make context and problem statements more distinguishing. If they detect identical patterns, one of the patterns can either be replaced, the two patterns can be merged or one of them can be deleted.

9.4.2 Considering Side-Effects

In Section 4.3 we found out that people tend to a repair-service behavior and to ad-hoc solutions in complex situations. Applying our theoretical model we can use security patterns to consider side-effects appropriately and to solve problems more professionally. We show this by two examples, namely the propagation of errors and the qualitative comparison of security patterns.

Propagation of Errors. Considering possible side effects of the application of a solution is important, especially if such side-effects would lower the overall security level or - even worse - breach the security of an asset (see Section 4.3). Thus, we envisioned that security patterns can be used to determine the propagation of errors [208, 207]. The basic idea are the worst case assumption that errors basically propagate in two directions. First, errors in the more general system usually propagate to the specialized systems. Second, errors of a system can have an impact on systems which depend on the broken one (i.e. they require it).

We implemented such a functionality referring to the relations between security patterns. If we want to find out how an error propagates along the $specializes_{pat}$ relation we have to calculate the transitive closure of all security patterns which specialize the "broken" security patterns. In fact, this means that the actual implementation of the pattern is broken. This can have several reasons, e.g. a new bug is discovered and the assumptions for applying the pattern do not hold anymore. That way, time-dependencies can also be considered, i.e. as soon as the assumptions of a pattern don't hold any longer, the user can determine the impact on other patterns.

If we want to determine how errors propagate from a pattern which is required by others, we have to follow the reverse direction of the $requires_{pat}$ relation and calculate the transitive closure again. Basically, the result can be a graphical representation where all affected security patterns are highlighted (e.g. colored red).

Users have now the possibility to conduct what-if experiments and see what would happen in case of a failure. Another scenario could be to integrate our system into a real-time alerting system: in case of a failure one would immediately know what other systems could be compromised. This would improve both the incident handling and recovering capabilities of an organization.

Qualitative Comparison. The previous applications of security patterns are a result from a security point of view, i.e. patterns are used to establish and maintain a state of security. However, we can also consider more pattern-related aspects. An interesting aspect of considering side-effects is to examine the impact of the application of two related security patterns regarding a particular property. As described in Section 7.4.3 the forces of a pattern can describe such desired properties. For example, one could say that users prefer a usable (i.e. usability) application over a fast one (i.e. performance).

As a solution solves these forces it has an impact on these properties, i.e. each solution has certain consequences. Thus, it would be nice to find out what happens if two subsequent patterns are applied. Is the overall result faster, slower or is there no significant change? In order to implement such a functionality it is sufficient to look at the values of properties qualitatively. According to the principles of qualitative reasoning the actual values can be abstracted as symbolic values, e.g. *negative, zero* and *positive* [28]. Then we can specify the qualitative trend when two of these values are added, e.g. *positive + zero = positive.*

With this approach it is possible to make statements about the *quality* of a particular solution. Implementing this functionality we extended the pattern mapping (without changing existing relations) and added forces and consequences accordingly. Then we could put together a corresponding query according to the following steps: first, we determined a set of neighboring patterns, for example, by looking for a required pattern (we assume that these are applied in a sequence). Second, we determined the values of a specific force in each pattern. This and the resulting trends were defined as inference rules. Finally, we could ask which of these combinations have a positive (or negative) trend. The extension of the pattern mapping, an example inference rule and the query are shown in Figure 9.10.

```
Trend(negative,zero,positive).

Consequence[
    resolveForce=>Force;
    hasValue=>Trend.
].

FORALL RESULT,FORCE,CX,CY,X,Y X[hasTrend->positive]
    <- EXISTS Y
        X[requires->>Y] AND
        X[hasConsequence->>CX] AND
        Y[hasConsequence->>CY] AND
        CX[resolveForce->FORCE] AND
        CY[resolveForce->FORCE] AND
        CX[hasValue->positive] AND
        CY[hasValue->zero].

FORALL X,Y,FORCE,TREND
    <- X[hasTrend->TREND;
        requires->>Y;
        hasForce->>FORCE
        ].
```

Figure 9.10. Qualitative comparison.

By nature, such a qualitative reasoning is a gross abstraction of reality, i.e. the results have to evaluated with certain care. However, the determination of trends is often sufficient or the only way to reason about the consequences of the application of a pattern as it is difficult to determine the exact numerical values of a property and to apply them to models of reality. In fact, the qualitative comparison approach reflects the pattern paradigm which is usually not at such a numerical level. Users can take advantage of this function as they can quickly decide whether a particular combination meets their demands or not.

9.4.3 Maintaining Security Pattern Repositories

So far we have relied on explicitly drawn relations between security patterns. However, it is possible to detect the primary relations by inferring them from rules which correspond to our definitions. Furthermore, we can conduct certain sanity checks by applying the Coverage Theorem. Furthermore, it is possible to analyze the overall security pattern collection as well as the user behavior in order to assign different priorities to security patterns. All of these applications are useful for the maintenance of a security pattern collection and are discussed in the following.

Detecting Relations between Patterns. We defined two primary relations between security patterns in Section 8.5. Based on these definitions we can express corresponding inference rules. For example, a part of the definition of the *specializes_{pat}* relation, namely the specialization of the context, is shown in Figure 9.11. The remaining definition for the specialization of the problem can be codified accordingly. The inference engine will then consider both rules while evaluating requests. The query itself remains basically the same, i.e. we are looking for a pattern X which specializes a pattern Y. Note that we have to distinguish between the *specializes_{pat}* between security patterns and the *specializes_{ont}* relations between security concepts.

```
FORALL X,Y X[spezialize->>Y] <->
  (X:SecurityPattern[hasContext->CX] AND
   Y:SecurityPattern[hasContext->CX])
      OR
  (Y:SecurityPattern[hasContext->CY] AND
   CY[spezializeONT->CX]).
```

Figure 9.11. Detecting relations between security patterns.

The pattern authors or the maintainer of a security pattern repository clearly benefit from this functionality. Assuming that the patterns are annotated appropriately the search engine can automatically detect what patterns are related. Note that it is also possible to detect a cycle, e.g. when a security pattern requires itself transitively. Furthermore, the functionality can be extended easily by the ontology expert if there will be more relations.

Conducting Sanity Checks. The Coverage Theorem says that a set of security patterns implies a state of security if the patterns are covered, i.e. there is a countermeasure against each threat. This is a condition which should always be true (an axiom), i.e. we implemented it as an inference rule which is considered for each request. If we negate the rule body and include it in a query the result will be the set of security patterns which are not "covered". This is shown in Figure 9.12. As we have proven the theorem we can be sure that the result of queries will be meaningful.

```
FORALL X,PX,Y <-
   NOT (X:SecurityPattern[hasProblem->PX] AND
   Y:Countermeasure[protectsAgainst->>PX]).
```

Figure 9.12. Determine the coverage of security patterns.

Such sanity checks are a very powerful tool for both pattern authors and users. The authors can use it in order to ensure that a new pattern is in fact covered. Pattern users can ask whether a set of selected patterns is covered, i.e. whether the planned system will be secure assuming that the overall security pattern system contains all relevant patterns of the problem domain.

9.5 Summary and Conclusions

In this chapter we have shown how security patterns can be used for security engineering. Hereby, we have always referred to our theoretical model for security patterns. In particular, the implementation of selected new applications of security patterns serves as a proof of concept.

9.5.1 Summary

The security pattern search engine provides meaningful answers to the competence questions (see Section 6.3). With the prototype we have been in the position to show several new applications of security patterns which would not be possible without our theoretical model.

First of all, we have clarified the relationship between our security pattern search engine and expert systems. As the tool has all components of an expert system it can be counted among them. However, we prefer the term knowledge-based system as the practical focus of our approach is not on the rules (which are fixed) but on the maintenance of the knowledge base. Based on that we have discussed selected use cases. As actors we consider experts, pattern authors and regular user. That way, we can implement the search engine with a focal point on the management and the application of security knowledge. Regarding the prototype we made certain conceptual decisions. Namely, we have decided to rely on open and free technologies as far as possible in order to achieve flexibility and extendibility. Furthermore, we built a browser-based user interface in order to achieve a certain level of familiarity. In particular, we have implemented a traditional three-tier architecture consisting of the browser interface, a web-server with servlets and the inference engine which also contains the knowledge base. Beside certain third-party annotation tools we also have implemented the customized tool Neptune which can be used to annotate security patterns. As far as we know there is only one other contribution regarding an expert system in relationship with patterns. However, the intention of this work is to propose certain design patterns based on a kind of decision trees. Our ontology-driven approach is different as it is based on inference rules, relies on a security ontology and takes advantage of the syntactial structure of security patterns. Thus, our approach is a unique contribution.

Equipped with the prototype of the search engine and our theoretical model we have shown how security patterns can be enhanced with meta-information. Hereby, the first step is to codify the knowledge base, the inference rules and the queries. We have mapped key security concepts to the elements of patterns. The ontology as well as the inference rules have been implemented in a declarative way. With this approach we have already been in the position to show some basic applications of our theoretical model. The annotation of security patterns is the requirement for further applications. For example, we can support pattern authors during writing patterns as we can offer them a library of key pattern elements. Another example is the integration of non-pattern sources into the pattern structure. That way, the relation between problems and solutions can be made explicit and accessible for users.

The theoretical model also enables more advanced techniques. A major limitation of patterns today is that they are distributed all around the world and that keyword-based search is often the only way to find a particular pattern. Using the relations between patterns we can, for instance, browse the pattern hierarchy and find all related patterns. Another application is the detection of conflicts, alternatives and duplicates which is useful for both pattern authors and users. Furthermore, we can now use security patterns in order to consider side-effects of the implementation of a security solution. In particular, we have been able to show how errors propagate along the relations between patterns through the overall graph of patterns. Another interesting application is the qualitative comparison of related patterns considering the resolution of a particular force. We have extended the pattern mapping accordingly and could determine the consequences of the application of security patterns. That way, statements about the quality of the state of security achieved with patterns can be made. More sophisticated functionalities are the automatic detection of the relations between patterns according to our definitions. Furthermore, we have been enabled conduct sanity checks referring to the Coverage Theorem.

The prototype of our security pattern search engine has been presented at the CeBIT exhibition in March 2003.

9.5.2 Conclusions

In summary we have implemented selected use cases and competence questions. This serves as a proof for the feasibility of a search engine for security patterns which makes the added values of security patterns usable. Furthermore, we have implemented more queries which correspond to the identified competence questions in several accompanying master theses [17, 97].

As we have outlined before, the pattern mapping can be extended in order to consider the more pattern-specific aspects. For example, we can imagine more (i.e. secondary) types of relations between patterns. We can also imagine to extend the theoretical model, especially regarding the qualitative comparison of patterns.

Concretely, the next steps are to work on a more customized search engine for day-to-day usage. For example, this means to design a more task-specific interface which can be integrated into the development work-flow. Another important aspect is a security model for the search engine itself (e.g. authentication and access control). Based on that it would be nice to have additional supplementary services such as a chat system for online writer's workshops or a rating system in order to determine how mature a pattern is. Furthermore, working sequences of security patterns could be provided in order to show how certain patterns should be applied.

Expecting that the search engine will have a certain user community, it makes sense to analyze both the knowledge base and the dynamic user behavior. For example, we could count the relations that point to a particular pattern and assign a higher priority to patterns which are required frequently by other patterns. Similarly, usage profiles can be used to determine weights for specific patterns. Such data allows also a feedback to the pattern's author as he sees how often the given problem really occurs.

In the long run our pattern-based approach can be integrated with other security improvement concepts. As we rely on a security ontology we can basically integrate any information source which follows our information model of the security domain. For example, we suggest to apply filters to security mailing lists which scan the text and assign it to the corresponding security patterns. Similarly, entries of vulnerability databases can be clustered. Then the patterns can be seen as a means for structuring the overall problem domain. Beside such indexing approaches [228] it is also possible to integrate new facts automatically [77, 78].

Other interfaces can be built for risk analysis and attack modeling tools. Hereby, the interface for risk analysis is bi-directional. A set of estimated risk values assigned to certain assets serves as an input for selecting the right security patterns. By nature, the application of such patterns should increase the security level and decrease the risk. That way, a feedback loop for a security engineering process can be implemented. Another approach for selecting security patterns would be to treat attack trees as input for the security pattern search engine. In fact, such sub-trees are already codified in the ontology.

The question remains whether the above results will be accepted and applied by a user community. However, this chapter shows the feasibility of implementing a security pattern search engine which makes the added-values of security patterns as a security improvement approach usable.

10. Summary and Outlook

Complexity is the worst enemy
of security.

BRUCE SCHNEIER

There's no other way to handle
the complexity than by breaking
it up into manageable pieces.

BRUCE SCHNEIER

The trustworthiness of IT systems remains an important prerequisite for the success of today's and future business in the digital world. As one of the challenges we identified to establish an acceptable security level. Hereby, we identified recurring and well-known errors as a major reason for the steadily increasing number of security incidents. Furthermore, we identified patterns as a suitable approach for capturing expert knowledge and make it available to novices. In principle it should be possible to avoid known errors and to apply proven countermeasures on them. That way, protection against known threats can be achieved which is by definition a state of security.

Security patterns are an evolving sub-discipline within the pattern community. As put by Bruce Schneier they are a way to break up the problem domain into smaller pieces and making the complexity of IT systems and the environment manageable. Furthermore, people begin to apply security patterns today. In this book we clarify the key concepts of security patterns, define syntax and semantics of them and show new applications. In order to improve the unsatisfying security level we have to close a gap between theory and the code of security practice. We also have to close a gap in the security knowledge process and make proven solutions available in a suitable way. That way, we are able to close the knowledge feedback loop. We consider this book as a contribution to this problem.

In the following we summarize the results and findings of the chapters containing the specific contributions of this book in more detail.

M. Schumacher: Security Engineering with Patterns, LNCS 2754, pp. 161-166, 2003.
© Springer-Verlag Berlin Heidelberg 2003

Chapter 5: Security Improvement Artifacts. In Chapter 5 we have examined selected security approaches and techniques which are commonly used to improve security according to the experiences of the author. Hereby, the focus was on a comparison based on criteria which consider the human factor: how can non-security experts manage security appropriately?

We have drawn the following conclusions: especially the approaches at earlier phases of a systems development cycle are not suitable for novices. This is not convenient as errors in the earlier phases are hard to handle later – if at all. Another finding was that such approaches are basically suitable for tool support if they show a certain degree of structure. As such, they are also often suitable for novices. A major drawback is, however, that many approaches don't consider side-effects and time-dependencies appropriately. That way a false sense of security can be perceived. Based on these results we have been in the position to identify the added values of a pattern-based security approach:

They are suitable for novices and can basically be used at all phases of a system's life-cycle. In principle they can also be included in tools and help to consider side-effects. However, security patterns have features which cannot be used efficiently. On the one hand there are no search and retrieval capabilities which go beyond keyword-based search. On the other hand there is no theoretical model for defining the syntax of such patterns which would allow to take advantage of the added-values of security patterns. Hereby, an important boundary condition for a solution is that patterns should remain prose! Otherwise they would be no longer patterns and not accepted by the user community.

Chapter 6: Security Core Ontology. In Chapter 6 we have shown how we developed a security core ontology based on a collaborative approach for ontology design. On the one hand we have defined the key security concepts as used throughout the document. On the other hand this ontology is a major building block for defining the syntax of security patterns.

Designing the ontology has revealed that a collaborative approach is suitable as it helps to identify blind spots and to eliminate ambiguities. The resulting ontology is small and consists of pragmatic definitions. It contains only the core concepts which we identified by gathering competence questions, i.e. what task should the user be able to conduct with this ontology? However, it is possible to extend the ontology and to integrate specific community terminology assuming that the understanding of security is identical.

Chapter 7: Foundations of Security Patterns. In Chapter 7 we have given an overview over the history of security patterns. Since their introduction in 1997 a couple of single patterns and pattern languages dealing with security have been published. Then we have introduced the structure of security patterns and their distinguishing features. Our security pattern template is compliant to a common understanding of security and has served as a model for subsequent security pattern contributions.

The key premise of the template is that the problem statement of security patterns deals with threats and attacks whereas the solution should provide corresponding countermeasures. We also have discussed security-related forces and how they are resolved applying a particular pattern. We have concluded that security has always an impact on other requirements and a solution has to balance such forces. Furthermore, we have briefly introduced a simple, extensible model for organizing security patterns.

Finally, have identified two basic approaches for mining security patterns: pattern authors can either look at "solutions" which failed or consider proven approaches which are usually provided in security standards. Beside identifying these approaches, we have also classified relevant sources for pattern mining and discussed practical issues of using our mining approach. Namely, it is necessary to consider more than one source as a single source doesn't contain all elements required for describing pattern.

Giving a thorough introduction to security patterns we have concluded that a set of security patterns is more helpful and specific than the sources for mining patterns: security patterns are more clearly structured and provide explicit linkage to other security patterns. Furthermore, they explicitly state the problem (thus they are suitable for novices which don't know the solution but only the problem), they specify the context (i.e. assumptions and preconditions which describe the situation in which the problem occurs), and they show how a solution changes the context (i.e. the application of a pattern has consequences the user should know).

Future contributions will show how our approach for mining security patterns will be adopted by both the security and the pattern community. Besides, it remains for future work to identify other approaches for mining security patterns and making the overall landscape of security patterns as complete as possible.

Chapter 8: Theoretical Model. Chapter 8 is a central contribution of this book. First, we have specified the core elements of security patterns. Hereby, we have referred to the security core ontology introduced before. Then, we also modeled the primary relations between security patterns, namely *specializes* and *requires.* Based on that we have defined the coverage of security patterns. This local criteria basically says that there has to be at least one countermeasure which protects against each threat occuring in the problem statements of patterns. Finally, we have provided a proof that the coverage of an overall security pattern system implies the security of the corresponding assets according to the given definitions.

In summary, we have developed a theoretical model for the syntax of security patterns (based on the semantics of security patterns introduced before). That way, the solutions and in particular the problems (which are more difficult to explain for a domain expert than the solutions) can be specified more precisely. With a set of intuitive assumptions, we have been able to implement the preconditions for using the added values of security patterns.

With our model, it is now possible to use patterns as means of security improvement. In particular, they show all properties we have introduced in Chapter 5: the effort for using them is reduced as we are enabled to look up security patterns based on pattern-specific queries. In particular, we added more structure to the patterns. This is an important prerequisite for achieving tool support. Based on that, we can also consider side-effects and time-dependcies of the problem domain captures with security patterns. Hereby, we have met the boundary condition to keep the pattern documents themselves untouched and to process the corresponding meta-information instead.

An notable conclusion is that security patterns can also be used a complementary approach for some of the security improvement artifacts we have classified before. We show this by the following examples:

As we have shown in Section 7.5, security patterns are more specific than evaluation criteria and security management standards which don't contain all relevant elements for solving security problems. Security patterns provide linkage to context, problem, solution and related patterns and are therefore more complete than such standards. Security patterns can also be used as a means of describing a security policy in a structured way. The patterns help to address all relevant issues and - even more important - help to keep a policy up-to-date.

Security patterns can also be combined with security improvement artifacts for the analysis phase of the security engineering process. For example, goal trees represent a part of the problem ontology and can be either used to annotate security patterns or to select the relevant ones. Similarly, an interface to risk analysis and prioritization approaches can help to identify the solutions for specific problems efficiently. As input we consider a prioritized list of risks. A risk is derived from the value of specific assets (covered by the context of patterns) and corresponding threats/attacks (contained in the problem statement of patterns). As ouput we expect a set of relevant patterns. As these are related to other patterns, dependencies to other threats/attacks can be considered, too.

Regarding architecture and design of a system, patterns are a natural way of complementing modeling techniques and formal methods. The former are part of specifying solutions of patterns (e.g. UML sequence charts, class diagrams, use cases, etc.). The latter can be integrated if more formal attributes are assigned to specific elements of patterns. For example, there are patterns dealing with security models or cryptographic solutions. Beside showing how a proven solution works we can even prove that a particular solution is correct.

Secure programming guidelines, security building blocks, and best security practices can benefit from the additional structure that patterns provide.

As another input for security patterns we see testing approaches based on vulnerability databases and runtime tests. Such examinations help to validate whether the assumptions captured in security patterns are still valid. If not, we are able to simulate how a "broken" pattern would affect other patterns.

The question remains whether our formalization approach is applicable for other pattern domains and we think that it cannot be answered today. However, we can derive a methodology for developing such models. The first step is to identify a set of core concepts and to find a few important relations between them. That way, the core semantics of a domain can be captured. The next step is to assign these concepts to corresponding pattern elements. Then one has to reason how the ontology semantics can be used to specify the pattern semantics. That way it could be possible to build other models for more pattern domains.

Chapter 9: New Applications. In this chapter we have described our prototype for a security patterns search engine. We have shown that it is possible to implement the theoretical model of security patterns. Selected new applications of security patterns proved that they are a suitable tool for security engineering. The prototype also proves that our approach relies on a stable and sound standing methodology which leads to a demonstrable improvement of security.

It is left for future work to annotate enough patterns and to reach a sufficient level of the coverage of the pattern system. Hereby, the person who annotates the patterns (e.g. the author) has to take care to use the theoretical model correctly. Besides, the limitations of our search engine lies in the quality of the security ontology and its extensions (and in particular the community terminology that extends it) as well as the quality of the security patterns and the annotations.

Another question is whether security patterns lead to a false sense of security. This highly depends on the completeness of a security pattern systems. If relevant problems are not contained, the user would falsely believe to be secure. However, the community processes and the suggested approaches for mining security patterns should prevent this. During shepherding and writer's workshops a group of experienced software people have a critical look on the pattern candidates. This helps to ensure that both the structure and the content of patterns are correct. Besides, mining patterns from standards helps to draw an overall landscape of security patterns and to identify blind spots. That way, security pattern systems can even be used if they are not complete: knowing the landscape, the author can provide hints what else has to be considered and how the user can get further information.

In summary, new applications of security patterns are only possible if our definitions and rules are applied. The implemented sanity checks can help here to detect ambiguities, cycles, or other blind spots within the security pattern system. As the theoretical model is, however, based on an intuitive

understanding of security concepts and patterns, we expect a high value for
practical usage.

A. Sources for Mining Security Patterns

Introduction

The intention of this Appendix is to introduce some information sources which were observed while looking for representative case studies as examined in Chapter 4. Alternatively, we could enumerate representative incidents which occurred recently. However, Bruce Schneier motivated his book "Secrets & Lies" that way keeping logs of security events from different sources [194]. The introduction of his books covers a time period from seven days (in March 2000) and contains only the "highlights" (about 16 announcements with news character, 13 severe vulnerabilities and 65 defaced Web sites). He came to the conclusion that "the first seven days of March 2000 were not exceptional." Furthermore, he presumed that the situation will get worse. In fact, he was right - there is no week without alarming security news. Therefore, we abandoned the idea of keeping similar logs in order to motivate the hypothesis in Chapter 4. Instead we selected two representative case studies and analyzed them thoroughly. We also decided to introduce some interesting information sources. Once more this underlines several statements we made before (e.g. in Section 7.5.2): first, it is very time consuming to observe *all* relevant source. Second, a published security incident is usually very embarrassing for the victim, maybe the loss of reputation can never be regained. This holds especially when errors are tolerated or security aspects are ignored in a negligent way.

BugTraq

BugTraq is one of the most respected security mailing-lists with over 27.000 subscribers. It is hosted at SecurityFocus, a company which was taken over by Symantec in July 2002. Fortunately, this acquisition seems to have no effect on the overall high quality of BugTraq. According to the Web site the objectives of BugTraq are the following [211]:

> "Bugtraq is a full disclosure moderated mailing list for the detailed discussion and announcement of computer security vulnerabilities: what they are, how to exploit them, and how to fix them."

M. Schumacher: Security Engineering with Patterns, LNCS 2754, pp. 167-169, 2003.
© Springer-Verlag Berlin Heidelberg 2003

The publication of the following vulnerability is typical for BugTraq. A severe bug (or feature) was uncovered and a group of subscribers identified almost all affected systems and more related "hidden features".

Accesspoints disclose WEP Keys, Password and MAC Filter. A company who develops Wireless Access Points for OEM customers had obviously forgotten a testing routine in the firmware of the system's chip. Monitoring the traffic of such a system revealed the security problem: when a broadcast packet was sent to UDP port 27155 containing the string `gstsearch` the access point returned the WEP keys, the MAC filters and the adminstrator password. This worked both on the WLAN and the LAN side of a network. Another string of this type even allowed to set the above values.

Findings. One can call it Security by Obscurity or just a forgotten testing routine. In any case, such a problem should *never* occur as it subverts any security precautions taken by the owner of the affected systems. Even worse, those people think that they are secure but they aren't! This is one of the benefits of BugTraq - but only if you are subscribed and read the relevant messages. As SecurityFocus also operates a corresponding vulnerability database it is possible to look for such vulnerabilities in a well-directed way. Nevertheless, you have to know all your systems and have to monitor such information sources regularly.

The Register

The Register is owned and operated by a British publishing company and offers any kind of IT-related news including a dedicated section for security news. They publish e-mails from subscribers, press releases and articles from third-parties. Furthermore, subscribers can send comments to the articles (either directly to the author or to The Register). A slogan at the Web site says that The Register is "the biting the hand that feeds IT." This indicates that news which are published at The Register are not very pleasant for the company concerned. Often, the articles are cynical and/or ironical pointing with fingers at the embarrassing details of a security incident. We consider the following article as typical for The Register.

Recording Industry Association of America website defaced. The RIAA believes that the success of P2P platforms is the reason for a steadily increasing loss of sales. Thus it works against any kind of music piracy. In September 2002 the Web site of Recording Industry Association of America (RIAA) was defaced two times. Thus it is very embarrassing, that the attackers were able to install pirate music files on the site for download. The reason was that they did not care for even an elementary security level of the own Web site: the `robots.txt` file which is meant to block web crawlers away from certain folders contained reference to a administration module of the Web server. The attacker could simply to follow this link and could (mis)use the administration module as is wasn't protected with a password. Furthermore, there was no filter configured which could have prevented the upload of mp3 files. You can find the original article as a humorous dialog between Dr. Watson and Mr. Sherlock Holmes at `http://www.theregister.co.uk/content/archive/27230.html`.

Findings. Again, this article shows that security is very important - not only for protecting intellectual and physical properties but also the reputation of the own company. This is even more important if an organization fights against a crime and the own platform is misused for committing exactly an offense of this kind. This time it was no hidden feature or a programming fault - it was wrong (or no) configuration and the basic security features which are shipped with any Web server were not used appropriately.

Slashdot.org

Since 1997 the Web site Slashdot is online and provides "news for nerds" and "staff that matters". Slashdot is operated by the Open Source Developer Network (OSDN) and offers several million pages to several hundred thousand readers. In an editorial Slashdot is decribed as an "omelette" which contains many components: Linux-related news, technical stories, scientific discoveries, toys, book reviews and many more (read the full editorial "The Omelette" here: `http://slashdot.org/faq/editorial.shtml`.). "By mixing and matching these things each and every day, we bring you what I call Slashdot." That means that Slashdot basically publish anything. Furthermore, readers can submit feedback. This is important as Slashdot doesn't check the accuracy of published stories. The following example shows how this works.

Buggy Bugging Backfires On German Police. A reader submitted that the BBC published an accident happened to the German police. They were caught when they bugged cellular phones as the suspect found an unknown and inaccessible voicemail number in their bills. In fact, this number was used in order to record the calls. According to Telecommunications authorities about 20.000 were tapped to that time. You can find the original posting here: `http://yro.slashdot.org/article.pl?sid=02/11/06/1912232&mode=thread&tid=158`.

Findings. This clearly represents the character of Slashdot as the news (staff that matters) refer to an external source. As so many people are subscribed or read the Web site day-by-day, such news spread very quickly. The above story shows that even state-run facilities make errors which should never occur.

B. Example Security Patterns and Annotations

Introduction

In this Chapter we present two examples for security patterns which have initially been presented at EuroPLoP 2002 [200]. In contrast to the original paper, we present a few patterns here in an often-used pattern form which is similar to Alexander's original template: Each pattern is divided into three parts which are separated by three diamond symbols (◊◊◊). Hereby, name and context create the *introductory part*, problem statement, forces and solution build the *central part* and the references to other patterns present the *closing part*.

Each pattern begins with a name (i.e.the heading of the section). The next few sentences are in a "you" form. They describe a context in which you may or may not find yourself. If you don't find yourself in such a context, the pattern probably isn't relevant for you. Then we provide a brief description of the problem in bold face (highlighting core elements of the pattern instead of giving them separate headings increases the readability). Afterwards, a number of forces that must be considered are discussed (now with a regular font face). The next section begins with a bold face "Therefore" and contains the core of the solution. This may be followed by additional information about the pattern, how the forces are resolved and how to use or implement the pattern. Finally, we include references to related patterns.

We followed the convention that each pattern should start at a new page. That way, it can be identified more easily. After the presentation of the pattern examples, we show how they could be annotated according to our theoretical model. The original patterns submitted to EuroPLoP were more structured and less prose (as we wanted to prove our point that security standards can be used for pattern mining). Thus, they were not as readable as the rewritten pattern in this chapter. With our approach we can reach both goals. The patterns remain prose and are still readable as we followed a template with limited structure. However, as we can annotate the patterns accordingly, we define both syntax and semantics of the patterns more precisely and in a machine-readable form. That way we can show how the added values of the patterns are now available for improved search and retrieval.

M. Schumacher: Security Engineering with Patterns, LNCS 2754, pp. 171-178, 2003.
© Springer-Verlag Berlin Heidelberg 2003

Handling Cookies

You are planning to access a third-party Web-site in order to conduct some sort of business. The site you want to access is using Cookies in order to store and retrieve information about you.

◇◇◇

Enabling cookies affects the privacy and especially the anonymity of users. Since the introduction of the cookie technology the possibilities for such a misuse have been discussed over and over again.

To protect the identity of users some rules have been prescribed. First, a cookie can only be read from the server that created it. Second, only information provided either by the client or by the server can be exchanged with the cookie mechanism.

However, this rules can be subverted if several Web content providers work together. For example, Web service providers track users visiting their pages. They can do user profiling which ignores privacy concerns of many users. Furthermore, user data gathered at several sites can be combined and/or sold to other companies. The most prominent examples are advertisement companies such as Doubleclick which place banners at a large number of Web sites and so are able to collect a huge amount of user data. Besides, HTML-based E-Mail messages can be used to set a cookie with user related information and personalize cookies that way.

The following forces should be considered: service providers and other users should be unable to determine the identity of a user bound to a HTTP request. Besides, a service should be provided without soliciting any reference to the real user name. Furthermore, a user should be able to make multiple HTTP requests to Web resource or services without others being able to link these uses together. Moreover, many Websites do not offer access if cookies are not accepted by the browser. Finally, a user might not want to buy, install and configure additional software.

Therefore, don't trust the service providers and restrict the usage of cookies on the client side. That way you can control what will happen to private information. It could happen, that you cannot use some sites any longer.

There are several strategies to implement this solution. Note that each alternative resolves the forces in different ways:

1. In almost all Web browsers cookies can be enabled case-by-case (e.g. turn on the "Warn me before accepting a cookie." option in Netscape). Then

the user has to decide whether he trusts the WWW service provider or not with every request. Typically it is possible to accept a cookie only for the current session or to accept a cookie from a given server forever (i.e. as long as the cookies are not deleted). The consquence is that this approach slightly decreases the usability of Web applications. When you visit sites that make heavy use of cookies you'll have to make many case-by-case decisions. On the other hand this is often only a one-time effort if you store your decisions. Furthermore anonymity cannot be guaranteed if the user's assessment of a Website turns out to be wrong, i.e. the service provider was not trustworthy and created/sold profile information. When you decide to reject a cookie some sites could not be used.

2. Another option is to delete cookies periodically, e.g. at every start-up of the operating system. That way a service provider has no chance to trace the user's requests. Tools such as Opera or Junkbuster allow to configure such a cookie management. Hereby, the comfort of browsing is more decreased than with case-by-case enabling of cookies. As the cookies are deleted, web applications that rely on cookies cannot be used appropriately. On the other hand this solution protects against misuse of cookies as it is not possible for a service provider to trace the user's behavior across several sessions.

3. The most consequent way to handle cookies is to disable cookies at all. This solution provides the highest degree of protection against misuse. However, you cannot access any site that requires cookies to be enabled.

This pattern has several relations to other security patterns. For example, a SECURE ACCESS LAYER should be used in order to protect authentic-ity and confidentiality of exchanged information, too. Besides, a SECURITY PROVIDER could be used in order to integrate information providers which are a AUTHORATIVE SOURCE OF DATA securely.

Pseudonymous E-Mail

You use E-Mail as means of online communications which have become a day-to-day tool for almost all Internet users. You want to use email services anonymously.

How can you use an email service without revealing the own identity?

There are certain circumstances where you cannot afford to send E-Mails using your real identity. For example, this includes the following scenarios:

− Free speech in countries with oppressive governments.
− Embarrassment, harassment, or loss of job due to sensitive topics such as advice on alcohol addiction.
− Prevention of unforeseen ramifications of email messages.
− The recipients should not be biased by identity of the sender.
− ...

Despite the desire for anonymity users may be required to authenticate to the email service, e.g. to receive answers to email messages later.

In particular, the following forces should be considered: offering individual or personalized services requires authentication or registration. However, people want to use services anonymously. On the other hand, people may want to be recognized by the service or other users or to receive private messages, e.g. on a message board.

Therefore, send your E-Mails from a pseudonym server. The usage of pseudonyms are an established approach for communication without revealing the user's identify.

The user sends an email to the pseudonym server which replaces the sender's address with the pseudonym. Answers are sent back to the pseudonym address which will then be replaced with the original address. It is basically possible to cascade such servers in order to increase the efforts for exposing the message path.

An example is `nym.alias.net` which is an email pseudonym server that allows to create an email pseudonym without revealing the user's identity. Such a pseudonym "appears as an ordinary email address to the rest of the world" [151].

However, the usage of a pseudonym server could lead to some new problems. For example, the strength of the pseudonym depends on the security of the pseudonym server. If an attacker can gain access to the system he can reveal the user's identities. Besides, there are certain known attacks such as flooding or mail bombs that can decrease the performance of the pseudonym server or interrupt its overall operation. Moreover, pseudonym E-Mail servers can be used to send offensive messages or spam mails to people who don't want to receive it. Even worse, pseudonym servers can be misused by criminals e.g. for child pornography or other illegal activities. Finally, it could happen that the users configure their message chains in such a way that a loop occurs, i.e. somewhere the replaced E-Mail points back to the initial pseudonym.

This pattern requires some other security patterns. For example, you should be sure that the providers use a HARDENED HOST. Besides, INTRUSION DE-TECTION would help to detect misuse of the server at protocol level. In combination with a properly configured FIREWALL this could help to prevent and stop attacks. In order to prevent crimes, it is necessary to activate the AU-DITING facilities of the server. In case of a crime a DISCLOSURE TO LEGAL AUTHORITIES might be necessary. This should, however, be described in the terms of use of such a server.

Example Annotation

In the following we introduce the corresponding annotations for the pattern HANDLING COOKIES that we presented before. Step by step we discuss some parts of this meta-information and show how it can be used by our implementation of a security pattern search engine. The examples below are not complete but illustrate once more the idea of keeping the patterns as they are (e.g. prose) and representing syntax and semantics (i.e. making them computer-processable) separately. By that way, non-pattern sources can be integrated into a pattern repository, too.

Pattern Structure

```
handlingCookies:SecurityPattern[
  name -> "Handling Cookies";
  hasContext -> context_10;
  hasProblem -> problem_10;
  hasSolution -> solution_10;
  description -> "http://www.securitypatterns.org/"
].
```

This part contains the top-level information: the name, a link to the original pattern document and some more references to other ontology nodes. The internal identifiers such as handlingCookies or problem_10 are automatically assigned by our pattern annotation tool Neptune. For a meaningful human interpretation we always provide a short natural language description.

Context

```
context_10:Context[
  description -> "Access of a third-party Web-site
                  which uses cookies";
  hasLayer ->> www;
  hasLifeCycle ->> usage;
  hasLifeCycle ->> operation
].
```

This part shows how the context of the pattern is composed. Again, it contains a description as well as references to instances of layers and life-cycle phases (these instances contain again a description). Now we are able to classify the pattern according its context entries. Furthermore, we can already use this information to ask specific questions such as "Show me all usage-related patterns in the context of the World Wide Web."

Problem

```
problem_10:Problem[
  description -> "The privacy and the anonymity of
                  users are at stake.";
  hasThreat ->> threat_2;
  hasThreat ->> threat_11;
  ...
  hasForce ->> commoncriteria_unl_1;
  hasForce ->> usability_2;
  ...
].

threat_2:SecurityProblem[
  description -> "Personalization."
].

threat_11:SecurityProblem[
  description -> "Profiling of users."
].

cc_fpr_unl_1:Force[
  description -> "A user should be able to make
                  multiple requests to resource
                  or service without others being
                  able to link these."
].

iso_usability_2:Force[
  description -> "Users don't want to buy, install
                  and configure additional software."
].
```

The problem statement is built accordingly. Moreover, we assigned several threats to the pattern. Note that these could also be taken from external sources such as the threat catalogs of the IT Baseline Protection Manual. In fact, we relied on the Common Criteria (e.g. the force cc

_fpr_unl_1 corresponds to the security requirement "Unlinkability" of the class "Privacy") and ISO 9126 in order to assign appropriate forces to this and other patterns. This also underlines, that such standards are useful for mining patterns. Besides, a corresponding tool (such as Neptune or any ontology browser which supports F-Logic or RDF) can be used to support authors during writing patterns as they can browse the different ontology entries.

Solution

```
solution_10:Solution[
  description -> "Restrict the usage of cookies.";
  hasCountermeasure ->> c1;
  hasCountermeasure ->> c2;
  hasCountermeasure ->> c3;
].

c1:SecuritySolution[
  description ->> "Enable cookies case-by-case.";
  protectsAgainst ->> threat_11;
  protectsAgainst ->> threat_2
].
```

The solution is also more a part of the security ontology (and not necessarily the higher-level security pattern ontology). The ontology contains a mapping between countermeasures which protect against certain threats and/or attacks. Again, this can be derived from security standards (e.g. the IT Baseline Protection Manual contains a table which contains such relations).

Relations

```
handlingCookies[
  requires ->> secureAccessLayer;
  requires ->> securityProvider;
  requires ->> authorativeSourceOfData;
].
```

Finally, we provide links to related patterns which can have links to further patterns (provided from different authors, located at different sources). That way, we can browse the pattern hierarchy efficiently, conduct what-if experiments, etc.

C. Ontology Development

Introduction

In this appendix we provide additional material regarding the development of the security core ontology in Chapter 6. In particular, we present the competence question which were used to define the task of the ontology. Hereby, we show how we implemented some of these questions within our security pattern search engine (see also Chapter 9). Furthermore, we briefly present the results of the two feedback rounds which once more justify the overall approach of designing an ontology collaboratively with a small group of participants.

Competence Questions

In this section we provide a list of generalized competence questions. They were collected through a couple of interviews with several security experts after giving a brief introduction to security patterns. The purpose of these questions were to determine the tasks one should be able to perform with the resulting ontology. Thus, we show for each question how we actually implemented (or how could we implement) corresponding queries. The numbering of the questions is only given for reference purposes rather than indicating an order. Usually, the result of a request to the knowledge base is a single pattern or a set of patterns which matches the query and as well as the current inference rules.

1. Assume an attack X.
   a) What is problem?
   b) What protects against X?
   We implemented this scenario. The user can select an attack and the search engine looks for all security patterns which address this attack. That way, both questions at once can be answered as the pattern contains the corresponding problem description as well as the solution.
2. Assume a problem X.
   a) What solutions are available?
   b) Are there dependencies to other problems?

M. Schumacher: Security Engineering with Patterns, LNCS 2754, pp. 179-184, 2003.
© Springer-Verlag Berlin Heidelberg 2003

This is also implemented. The user can either select a threat (which is part of the problem) or the corresponding security pattern directly. The search engine can then look for alternative solutions and it can calculate the transitive closure of all required security patterns.

3. Assume a solution X.
   a) What are the side-effects?
   b) Are there more general corresponding problems?
   c) Are there more special corresponding problems?
   d) Are there dependencies to other solutions?
   e) Show examples for X.
   f) How can the solution be implemented?

Again, it makes sense to select a security pattern first. We implemented the propagation of errors as well as a qualitative comparison of security patterns. This are examples for a determination of side-effects. As we also can browse the pattern hierarchy, we can easily identify more special, more general and depending security patterns. If the pattern contains examples and/or implementation details, they can be displayed, too (however, we didn't implement this in the current prototype). In fact, we have implemented a function that shows all annotations in a configurable view.

4. Assume a context X and a solution Z.
   a) Am I (still) vulnerable?
   b) Is there a solution missing?
   c) What side-effects has the solution?

This function was not implemented but it is possible to do so. Basically, the use could select a set of security patterns he implemented. Then the system can calculate the missing (=required) set of security patterns. It can also show which parts of the problem (i.e. attacks and/or threats) are not yet addressed. Moreover, we can calculate certain side-effects.

5. Assume a topic X or a context X.
   a) What information is available?

This is a basic search function. Given a certain context the search engine returns all matching security patterns and the user can inform himself. It is possible to filter the list of security patterns for most of the other queries according to a set of context entries. Again, the user can display information selectively.

6. Assume a solution X.
   a) Is there another solution which is faster, cheaper, etc.?

7. Assume a solution is implemented.
   a) Is it still secure? or: Is there a new problem?
   b) How would an error propagate?

This is not implemented but an envisioned use case. It would mean that we integrate other information sources (e.g. vulnerability databases) to the pattern search engine. Assuming that such information can be indexed with ontology entries automatically, we could find out whether a particular implementation of a security pattern is still secure. The propagation of possible errors is implemented.

8. Show different levels of detail for each pattern for ...
   a) administrator's
   b) regular users
   c) knowledge-engineers
   d) novices

This is not fully implemented as we can only select different views manually. However, the meta-information can be used to achieve such a function easily.

Evaluation Results

In this Section we present the results of the two feedback rounds for the design of the security core ontology as presented in Chapter 6. The goal was to identify blind spots, ambiguities, and inconsistencies by asking selected set of participants. The overall evaluation which also shows the relative frequency distribution of the participant's ratings as well as the answers in detail are available as technical report [202].

We have captured the opinions of the participants with a simple Likert-scale schema, i.e. the participants can rate each item as *strong agree, agree, undecided, disagree* or *strong disagree*. Besides, we have asked for additional free-form responses. Especially if a participant has been dissatisfied with a specific definition we have asked how the definition can be improved or if an alternative definition can be provided.

Results of the 1st Feedback Round

In this section we show the consequences which arised out of the feedback of the participants. Besides, we briefly discuss the feedback for the relations between the concepts. Finally, we summarize the feedback of the 1st round.

Improving the Concept Definitions. In this paragraph we show how we improved each concept definition. Hereby, we show the original definition and the conclusion we have taken after evaluating the feedback of the participants. Note, that the intention was to identify ambiguities and blind spots in the ontology. It was not the intention to come to an ontology that is accepted by all participants (which is basically impossible, even by the rather small group of participants.

Asset: Assets are information or resources exposed to threats. Examples are documents, applications, and networks.

Some participants wanted to restrict the definition to the software area whereas other wanted a broader scope. We decided to include the aspect that an asset is something that is required for someone (a organization or person) doing his business as the core of the definition. In fact, it doesn't matter, if an asset is threatened or not - it's still an asset.

Owner: The owner of an asset is responsible for its security. He defines security objectives, requirements, and the countermeasures.

This definition was obviously too far from reality. It is clear that someone must care for security, but this is not necessarily the owner. As this term is indeed misleading, we used the term Stakeholder instead. This should express that there is someone (organization or person) who puts some value in an asset.

Security Objectives: The primary security objectives are confidentiality, integrity and authenticity.

It seems to be non trivial to find out what "qualities" are security objectives. Instead of extending the given list, we decided therefore to define security objectives as a statement of intent to counter certain threats and to meet certain security requirements (whatever these are).

Threat: A potential for the violation of security which exists when there is a circumstance, capability, action, or event that could breach security or cause harm.

This definition seemed to depend on too many other concepts. In order to make it less confusing we decided to define it simply as a potential for a security breach of an asset.

Attack: An intelligent act that is a deliberate attempt to evade security services and violate the security policy of a system. Attacks are a threat to assets.

Again we clarified the definition making it more specific. We adapted the suggestion that an attack doesn't necessarily to be intelligent. However, we still think that it is a deliberate act (in opposite to human errors/accidents - these are just other ways to realize a threat).

Attacker: Attacker carry out certain actions in order to misuse a assets.

It seems to be sufficient to define the attacker as someone/something who carries out the attack. We can still extend the ontology if we want to consider further attributes of an attacker (motivation, skills, location, equipment, etc.).

Requirement: A requirement is a quality an asset must have in order to be valuable for its owner. Requirements can be contradicting, e.g. usability and security.

This definition was not accepted. Therefore, we decided to skip it (especially as we don't necessarily need it for the current theoretical model).

Vulnerability: An asset is vulnerable if it is weakly protected or without any protection against misuse. If vulnerabilities are exploited, the security of an asset is jeopardized.

Again we brought this definition more in line to the other definitions. In order to avoid the "relativity" discussion of vulnerabilities, we define it - as suggested - as flaw or weakness that could be exploited in order to misuse an asset.

Countermeasure: A countermeasure is an action taken by the owner of assets in order to weaken the effect of an attack or to make it harmless.

Again the *owner* discussion came up. As we changed this definition we also adapted the definition for countermeasure as an action taken in order to protect an asset against a particular threat.

Risk: The risk is the expected loss that is derived from the probabilities for a particular attack that exploits a certain vulnerability and leads to a specific damage.

As we had a balanced view here, we only tried to clarify this definition a little bit. It seems to be acceptable that risk depends on the likelihood for the occurrence of a threat as well as the expected loss.

Relations between Concepts. The participants were also asked to rate small graphs which show some relations between the concepts introduced before. These relations were accepted assuming the definitions given before. Most comments were similar to the ones given by the definitions of the comments. The overall idea of drawing such graphs was found to be useful. Therefore, we adapted the graphs according to the comments and presented the new version in round 2.

Summary. The first round was very helpful. It helped to make the definitions more precise and to identify misleading definitions. We changed the concept Owner to Stakeholder which better reflects the real situation. Furthermore, we deleted the term Requirement from the ontology as we don't need it currently. Comments considering missing concepts were not taken into account as we want to keep the ontology small. It should only contain core concepts, details can be added/integrated later. Furthermore, we didn't consider remarks without suggestions for improvements.

Results of the 2nd Feedback Round

During the second feedback round only 10 participants provided some input. As we found out, this was not lack of interest but unfortunately a lack of time. However, the results still helped to get the definitions more precisely.

Improving the Concept Definitions. Some participants remarked that the definitions are a definite improvement over last time. In particular they were logically more consistent than before. This corresponds to the predominant *agree* and *strongly agree* ratings of the concept definitions.

Relations between Concepts. Again, the participants were asked to rate small graphs which show some relations between the concepts introduced before. This time, we presented screen shots taken from a visualization of the concepts and relations between them. As the tool had not shown the meaning of the arrows between the concepts, some participants suggested to add labels again to each edge of these graphs. Thus, we returned to manually drawn figures for illustrating the relations.

Summary. The evaluation revealed that no more major changes of the ontology were necessary. Most participants accepted the definitions and made only minor suggestions for improvements. As a trend we could determine that most participants prefer short, rather abstract definitions (instead of long definitions which might be ambiguous).

Our experience with the collaborative approach to ontology design was good: even a small group of people can help you to improve an ontology significantly. A face-to-face workshop might be, however, even more efficient as you get immediate response interacting with the participants directly. On the other hand you might not have so much time for evaluation and the participants might be biased by other participants.

D. F-Logic Primer

Introduction

As discussed in Section 3.4.3, F-Logic is a knowledge representation language based on first-order predicate calculus and frames. F-Logic is a deductive, object-oriented database language. In this appenix we introduce only a subset of F-Logic as our approach should be independent of the representation language and its special features. For example, we did make no use of built-in features such as string handling, type conversion, method overloading or access to databases. More detailled introductions to F-Logic are available [133, 96]. This chapter is organized as follows: first of all we briefly introduce the syntax of F-Logic based on the basic alphabet of the language. Then we briefly show how classes and their signatures are described. Besides, we describe how facts of an ontology can be represented with objects. Finally, we outline how inferencing rules and queries are written in F-Logic .

Syntax

Formally, the alphabet of F-Logic contains a set of object constructors ($\mathcal{F}$), a set of variables ($\mathcal{V}$), auxiliary symbols (e.g. '(', ')', [,], $\rightarrow$, $\Rightarrow$, etc.) as well as logical connectives and quantifiers ($\land$, $\lor$, $\neg$, $\leftarrow$, $\forall$, $\exists$)[1]. Any information about classes and objects is expressed by so called F-atoms. This is illustrated by the following example that shows how information about an object *nadja* can be written with F-atoms:

```
nadja:woman.
nadja[age->6].
nadja[name->"Nadja"].
nadja[friend->>johanna].
```

In this case, the objects has an attribute *name* with the value "Nadja" and an attribute *age* with the value '6'. Besides, the object has an attribute *friend*

---

[1] Presenting the F-Logic examples we use a textual representation of the mathematical symbols (e.g. => instead of $\Rightarrow$) as the statements are taken from executable code.

M. Schumacher: Security Engineering with Patterns, LNCS 2754, pp. 185-188, 2003.
© Springer-Verlag Berlin Heidelberg 2003

which refers to another object *johanna*. Furthermore, *nadja* is of the class *woman*. Note that the terms *attribute* and *method* are used synonymously. In practice it is usual to collect several F-atoms in a so called F-molecule. The same information as given above can be represented as a F-molecule as follows:

```
nadja:person[
    age->6;
    name->"Nadja";
    friend->>johanna
].
```

It is also possible to denote objects with predicate symbols in the same way as in predicate logic[2]. Such P-atoms can be used equivalently to F-atoms:

```
age(nadja,6).
name(nadja,"Nadja").
friend(nadja,johanna).
```

Note that the double-headed arrows `->>` and `=>>` are used for set-valued attributes. Besides, the single-headed arrows `->` and `=>` are used for scalar attributes. Furthermore, the double-shafted arrows `=>` and `=>>` specify types of an attribute and the single-shafted arrows `->` and `->>` the values of an attribute. Furthermore, every F-Logic expression ends with dot.

Class Signatures

With so called is_a F-atoms, the class membership of an object can be denoted, whereas subclass-F-atoms denote a subclass relation. In F-Logic ':' is used for specifying class membership and '::' is used for representing the subclass relation. This is illustrated by the following example:

```
james:man.
john:man.
sarah:woman.
man::person.
woman::person.
```

In the example, *james* and *john* belong to the class *man* and *sarah* belongs to the class *woman*. The two latter F-atoms denote that *man* and *woman* are subclasses of *person*.

The subclass relation specifies a partial order on the set of classes. Thus, the class hierarchy corresponds to a directed acyclic graph.

---

[2] In order to preserve the compatibility with predecessors of F-Logic .

In order to express the methods for objects of a particular class, signatures are added to the class definition. The signatures declare the method and specify the type of parameters and results[3]. It is possible to define scalar or set-valued methods as shown in the following example:

```
person[
    name=>string;
    friend=>>person;
    age=>integer
].
```

For example, the above class definition says that the class person has a scalar method *name* which returns a value of the built-in type *string*. The method *friend* returns one or more objects of the type *person*.

Defining Facts with Objects

As usual the objects populate the database which is represented by F-Logic statements. Hereby, the objects must comply with the signatures defined in the corresponding classes, i.e. the arity and types of the return values of methods must match. The objects are used to define the facts of an ontology. This was illustrated by the first example of this chapter. Recall that the object *nadja* instantiates the class *woman*.

Inferencing with Rules and Queries

Rules can be used to derive new information from a set of objects (or facts): if the conditions of a rule are true, the conclusion is also true. Hereby, the condition is called the head of a rule and the conclusions is called the body of a rule.

The rule body consists of F-molecules which can be logically connected. Variables in the rule body can be quantified universally or existentially. The rule head consists of a comma-separated list of the occurring variables (each variable has also to occur in a F-molecule or F-atom in the body) and F-molecules which specify the conclusion. The head of a rule is separated from the body by the symbol <-. Assuming a set of objects which define the friend for persons. Then, the following rule computes the transitive closure of all friends of a given object and defines a new method *clique*:

```
FORALL X,Y,Z X[clique->>Z]
    <- X[friend->>Y] AND Y[friend->>Z].
```

---

[3] We don't use methods with parameters as is is difficult to translate this feature in other representation languages.

Now we can send query request to the database which consists of facts and rules. A query can be called a rule without a head. The following rule would, for instance, ask for the *clique* of the object *nadja*:

```
FORALL X <- nadja[clique->>X].
```

The result will be all variable bindings which represent an instance of the rule body. Assuming that the object *johanna* has also a friend *lisa* the following variable binding would be returned:

```
X = johanna
X = lisa
```

Together with the rules, new information can be derived from the knowledge base. In this case we know who the members the *clique* of *nadja* are.

E. Gaining Security Expertise

Introduction

Security patterns capture knowledge of security experts. Security patterns contain solutions for recurring security problems. Besides, they don't exist in isolation and show relations to other security patterns. Thus, it requires a certain degree of expertise to understand the nature of security patterns, to define syntax and semantics of them and to contribute to an overall security pattern system. In this chapter we show different ways the author followed in order to gain security know-how and practical skills. Hereby, the education of students played an important role. In particular, he planed, organized and carried out the security workshop *Hacker Contest* and supervised a couple of security-related *Master Theses*. Furthermore, he worked in certain *research projects* analyzing, developing and implementing security solutions. These efforts are briefly introduced in the following.

Educational Work

Since 1998, the author has been in a position to conduct certain experiments heading toward new security approaches. In particular, he planned, organized and carried out the security workshop Hacker Contest. Besides, he planned and supervised a couple of security-related master theses from which he could extract important input for this thesis.

Hacker Contest

The security workshop Hacker Contest is part of the curriculum at the Department of Computer Science at Darmstadt University of Technology since 1999. Moreover, a condensed version of the workshop is offered as advanced vocational training for IT professionals since 2002.

The overall goal of this workshop is to understand security problems from the attacker's point of view. The participants get familiar with the motives and techniques of attackers. As they know the "enemy" they should be able to protect their own systems more efficiently. Another aspect was to consider

M. Schumacher: Security Engineering with Patterns, LNCS 2754, pp. 189-194, 2003.
© Springer-Verlag Berlin Heidelberg 2003

side-effects of security solutions (e.g. the impact on performance or the introduction of new problems) and to be aware of the residual risk (e.g. a packet filter firewall doesn't protect against malicious code). The topics cover different areas of computer science such as operating systems, networks, forensic analysis, intrusion detection, firewalls, PKI, Web-server, Denial of Service attacks, development and implementation of a virtual Honeynet, wireless networks and many more.

We also consider the Hacker Contest as an experiment in order to understand why we have to face so many security incidents today. Our hypothesis was that the increasing complexity of IT systems and applications, lack of time as well as a lack of security know-how and awareness are main reasons for security problems. This hypothesis was confirmed by both participating students and IT professionals. This was an important motive for examining security patterns as means of conveying knowledge in a structured way.

The results of the Hacker Contest are published in a journal and an accompanying book [206, 207]. Besides, several newspapers and magazines reported about the Hacker Contest. For instance, the author of a computer magazine refers to the Hacker Contest as a remarkable model for computer science education [149]. Furthermore, the Humboldt-University Berlin and the Otto-von-Guericke University Magdeburg adopted the concept of the Hacker Contest.

Supervised Related Master Theses

During the way toward this thesis, the author supervised several related master theses. Hereby, the goals were of different nature – the results of selected theses are summarized in the following.

Security Improvement Process.. Some theses directly contributed concepts and components which support a *security knowledge feedback loop* as for example discussed in Chapter 3.2. The examination of vulnerability databases which play a central role in the overall security improvement process can be seen as one focal point of the author's research [118]. The results of this work were a survey on recent vulnerability database approaches, an improved design for a vulnerability database as well as a prototype implementation with a graphical administration interface. Later, more sophisticated interfaces with a corresponding security model were developed.

Building up on this, two other components were developed and implemented. First, we worked on a rating scheme for vulnerabilities [171]. A flexible, multi-dimensional and extensible rating scheme could be applied to a snapshot of a given IT system. Another new feature was that relations between vulnerabilities could be considered. In summary, the high-risk vulnerabilities could be identified more easily and fixed first.

The system snapshot was delivered by another component that relied on results of forensic analysis tools and system-specific information utilities

[189]. Together with the vulnerability database and the rating component the user has a powerful tool to monitor the security level of a given system and to derive required actions from that (e.g. applying a patch or updating the software).

Security in Distributed Systems.. Another set of master theses dealt with gathering some general security insights of operating systems and distributed systems.

For example, we analyzed security aspects of the Windows NT operating system [94]. The results were used to analyze the security level of a given system and to give advise how to fix problems. Hereby, we relied on a simple predecessor of the vulnerability database mentioned before.

A focal point of our research was the examination of security in distributed systems. In particular, we did some accompanying work within a research project dealing with CORBA security. Hereby, we analyzed general problems within the CORBA security service. As part of analyzing this service, we implemented a working version of the non-repudiation function and integrated it in an application scenario [30]. We also analyzed typical attacks to CORBA-based systems - even if they use the CORBA security service - and identified suitable countermeasures [76]. In fact, this was the first time we were systematically looking for solutions for known security problems in a specific context.

Security Patterns.. A third series of master theses contributed directly to the knowledge about security patterns. The first work focused both on a general overview of security patterns and, in particular, a set of security patterns for secure payment systems [142]. A couple of security patterns were developed and a prototype of a system built with these patterns was implemented.

The second contribution dealt with security patterns from a knowledge representation and knowledge management point of view [97]. A pattern-based approach was put into perspective with knowledge engineering approaches. Besides, development tools and methodologies were studied and compared. Based on that, a first prototype of a security pattern search engine that was based both on security and pattern ontologies was designed and implemented.

Equipped with a first prototype we could evaluate its strengths and weaknesses in order to improve the concept and the implementation [17]. It turned out that the information model for security patterns was suitable but the user interface could be improved significantly. Furthermore, we integrated facts derived from the IT Baseline Protection Manual which build a base for further pattern entries of an overall security pattern system. The second prototype helped also to prove that the competence questions (see Appendix C) could be answered by the ontology.

Selected Research Projects

Since 1998, the author has been in a position to gain further security experience during some research projects. Hereby, the focal point was on both the examination of existing systems as well as the development of new security solutions. In the following we briefly discuss selected results.

Secure CORBA

The focus of the project Secure CORBA lied on OMG's Common Object Request Broker Architecture (CORBA) as a basis technology for developing distributed systems and on the Security Service specified for it, since this seemed to be the most promising technology in the field.

The followed approach was thereby twofold. At first, a thorough analysis of the specification itself and known implementations thereof was performed, based also on experiences in the broader area of distributed systems security. We identified several problems such as covert channels within the architecture, weaknesses in the authorization model, and incomplete specifications.

At a second, more practical stage, an own, prototypical implementation of CORBA Security was undertaken, with the main objective of gaining as much practical experience as possible and experimenting with possible alternatives to find solutions to the problems encountered. The software was integrated within the open-source CORBA implementation MICO.

As proof of concept this prototype was used to secure an online auctioning system that will make use of all implemented parts of the security service, e.g. authentication and message protection. We could also integrate a limited non-repudiation service. The auctioning application, which was implemented in C++, was accessible through many platforms supported by MICO, such as Tcl/Tk based clients written for Windows or Linux systems. In addition, we integrated mobile devices like the Compaq Ipaq by Wireless LAN at a later stage of the project.

The results of this project were published in a paper [7] and also presented at the CeBIT and LinuxWorld exhibitions in 2001, each time in cooperation with the project's customer T-Systems Nova and the company ObjectSecurity.

Security for Operation Support Systems

The goal of this project was to design and implement a security framework for distributed systems. The specific application scenario were the Operation Support Systems (OSS). Hereby we assumed that such systems should be interconnected across organization boundaries. Security for OSS interconnection was thereby a mandatory requirement covering not only traditional channel-oriented security but also application-oriented security such as user authentication and message-based non-repudiation.

The framework for secure OSS interconnection comprised two new concepts. One concept was a security policy model that employed a classified set of security configurations named Class of Protection (CoP). Using commonly-defined sets of CoPs, security administrators can refine their security policies into flexible and fine-grained security policy rules that map appropriate CoPs to messages. The other concept was a security platform architecture that consists of a Basic Security Service Layer (BSSL) and a Security Policy Manager (SPM). The BSSL was a layer lying between management applications and the communication layer, and it carried out security-related tasks on behalf of the applications. The SPM stored the security policies, managed them, and distributed appropriate CoPs to BSSL. As a result, this framework enables efficient management of security policies and flexible control over both channel-oriented and application-oriented security while keeping security operations transparent to the applications. We also implemented a prototype of the platform on top of CORBA.

During this project the author had the chance to visit Fujitsu Laboratories in Kawasaki, Japan. During his first stay in 2000, his task was to integrate the first BSSL prototype and a simple Demonstrator of an OSS application with the SPM software developed at Fujitsu Laboratories. During his second stay in 2001 he was invited as Visiting Researcher to do research in the field of network management. In particular, he worked on the subject of "security of operations support systems interconnection".

Some results of this project were published at international conferences [156, 169]. Furthermore, some patents were filed in Europe, Japan and USA of which the author contributed in one patent [72].

Developing and Implementing a Security Policy

In 2002, the Darmstadt University of Technology initiated the work on developing and implementing a security policy for the campus. The author participated in the early discussions, identified suitable models (the draft of the policy was taken from the Technical University in Vienna, Austria) and set up a project for the further implementation.

Security Analysis

Other tasks were to analyze security solutions developed and/or implemented by customers. Hereby, we played the role of either an external or an internal attacker.

Taking the external point of view, we assumed to have no internal knowledge and followed typical steps of external attacks. This included the analysis of external information sources (e.g. search engines, newspapers, etc.), the analysis of the target networks and systems, and specific penetration tests. If appropriate, selected attacks were conducted (as inappropriate we usually considered attacks which disturb or interrupt the operation of the target system).

Carrying out internal attacks included the study of specifications and was usually supported by the customer's IT staff. That way, we could simulate the knowledge of an internal attacker. Besides, co-operative attacks with an outsider were possible.

A variant of such an analysis were studies at the level of the specifications of the target systems. Hereby, we tried to identify known weaknesses in the design before the actual system was implemented.

Besides, we offered a catalog of prioritized countermeasures which should be implemented by the customer. This included technical countermeasures but also improvements in the personnel environment, i.e. we offered security awareness training.

These projects were an opportunity for the author to validate his security knowledge, verify some of his working hypotheses (the human factor) and to gather practical experience.

Secure Network Topologies

As member of a project for the central Siemens CIO Information Security Department we worked on the topic of secure network topologies. The task was to identify security solutions on the network level. Solutions for a variety of topics such as securing business partner access, connecting local area networks to the corporate network, or secure office networks were developed.

In order to accomplish a defined and unified approach, a common framework for all identified scenarios was developed. Furthermore, templates for each scenario were provided.

In a certain way, the resulting set of security solutions could be seen as a rudimentary basis for security patterns as they captured the security expert knowledge within the customer's company. The resulting "IS Framework" as well as the manuals for the identified standard scenarios have continuously been improved and are still in use today.

Controlled Uniform Security Concept for eServices

In this project we worked on a reasonable security level for selected eServices and related platforms/infrastructures both in planning, implementation as well as routine operations [190]. For this we developed user tested security models and (attack-)simulators, an electronic security inspector as well as an experienced based security database. The author contributed especially to the latter providing input from his vulnerability database experience. Furthermore, he contributed to the design and the implementation of the electronic security inspector.

References

1. Ralf Ackermann. Firewalls and their Impact on Multimedia Systems. In *Multimedia Computing and Networking 2000, San Jose*, page 284, January 2000. Panel Discussion: Security Firewalls and their Impact on Multimedia Systems.
2. Ralf Ackermann. *Gateways and Components for supplementary IP Telephony Services in heterogeneous Environments*. PhD thesis, Darmstadt University of Technology, 2003.
3. Ralf Ackermann, Markus Schumacher, Utz Roedig, and Ralf Steinmetz. Vulnerabilities and Security Limitations of current IP Telephony Systems. In *Proceedings of the Conference on Communications and Multimedia Security (CMS 2001), Darmstadt*, pages 53–66, May 2001.
4. Ralf Ackermann and Holger Trapp. Angriffe auf NIS-Systeme und Möglichkeiten einer kryptographischen Absicherung. In *3. DFN-CERT Workshop "Sicherheit in vernetzten Systemen", Hamburg*, March 1996.
5. Christopher Alexander. *The Timeless Way of Building*. Oxford University Press, 1979.
6. Christopher Alexander, Sara Ishikawa, Murray Silverstein, Max Jacobson, Ingrid Fiksdahl-King, and Shlomo Angel. *A Pattern Language: Towns - Buildings - Construction*. Oxford University Press, 1977.
7. Ameneh Alireza, Ulrich Lang, Marios Padelis, Rudolf Schreiner, and Markus Schumacher. The Challenges of CORBA Security. In *Proc. of the Workshop "Sicherheit in Mediendaten"*, pages 61–72. Gesellschaft für Informatik, Springer Verlag, 2000. GI Jahrestagung, Berlin.
8. Julia Allen. *The CERT Guide To System and Network Security Practices*. Addison-Wesley, 2001.
9. Edward Amoroso. *Fundamentals of Computer Security Technology*. Prentice Hall, 1994.
10. Ross Anderson. Why Cryptosystems Fail. In *1st ACM Conference on Computer and Communications Security*, pages 215–227. ACM Press, 1993.
11. Ross Anderson. *Security Engineering - A Guide to Building Dependable Distributed Systems*. John Wiley and Sons, 2001.
12. Brad Appleton. Patterns and Software: Essential Concepts and Terminology. *Object Magazine Online*, 3(5), 1997.
13. Arash Baratloo, Timothy Tsai, , and Navjot Singh. Libsafe: Protecting Critical Elements of Stacks. Technical report, Bell Labs, Lucent Technologies, 2000.
14. M. Bartel, J. Boyer, B. Fox, B. LaMacchia, and E. Simon. XML Signature Syntax and Processing Rules, 2002. W3C Recommendation.
15. Kent Beck and Ward Cunningham. Using Pattern Languages for Object-Oriented Programs. Technical Report CR-87-43, Apple Computer, Tektronix, September 1987.
16. D. Bell and L. LaPadula. Secure Computer Systems: Mathmatical Foundations. Technical Report ESD-TR-73-278, The MITRE Corporation, 1973.

17. Ekkehard Bender. Weiterentwicklung einer Suchmaschine für Security Patterns. Master's thesis, Darmstadt University of Technology, 2003.
18. A. Bernaras, I. Laresgoiti, and J. Corera. Building and Reusing Ontologies for Electrical Network Applications. In Proceedings of the European Conference on Artificial Intelligence (ECAI), 1996.
19. Tim Berners-Lee, Dan Brickley, Dan Connolly, Mike Dean, Stefan Decker, Pat Hayes, Jeff Heflin, Jim Hendler, Deb McGuinness, and Lynn Andrea Stein. Reference Description of the DAML+OIL Ontology Markup Language., 2001.
20. Tim Berners-Lee, James Handler, and Ora Lassila. The Semantic Web. Scientific American, 2001.
21. Reinhard Bertram. Mit Sicherheit Schutz vor dem bekannten Feind. In M. Schumacher and R. Steinmetz, editors, *Sicherheit in Netzen und Medienströmen*, Informatik aktuell, pages 94–104. Gesellschaft für Informatik, Springer Verlag, 2000.
22. Hitesh Ramesh Bhambhani. An Expert System for Suggesting Design Patterns - A Methodology and a Prototype. Master's thesis, University of Texas at Arlington, August 2002.
23. Wolfgang Bibel, Steffen Hölldobler, and Torsten Schaub. *Wissensrepräsentation und Inferenz - Eine grundlegende Einführung*. Vieweg, 1993.
24. Jan Borchers, Janet Ip, and Markus Schumacher. The Pattern Editing Toolkit Project. http://www.ito.tu-darmstadt.de/projects/pet/. Accessed: January 2003.
25. Jan Oliver Borchers. *A Pattern Approach to Interaction Design*. PhD thesis, Darmstadt University of Technology, 2000.
26. Christof Bornhövd. *Semantikbeschreibende Metadaten zur Integration heterogener Daten aus dem Internet*. PhD thesis, Darmstadt University of Technology, 2000.
27. Alexandre M. Braga, Cecilia M. F. Rubira, and Ricardo Dahab. Tropyc: A Pattern Language for Cryptographic Software. *PLoP*, 1998.
28. Ivan Bratko. *Prolog Programming for Artificial Intelligence*. Addison-Wesley, 3rd edition, 2000.
29. Tim Bray. What is RDF? http://www.xml.com/pub/a/2001/01/24/rdf.html, January 2001. Accessed: March 2003.
30. Lars Brückner. Beweisbarkeit in verteilten Systemen. Master's thesis, Darmstadt University of Technology, 2000.
31. F. Lee Brown, James DiVietri, Graziella Diaz de Villegas, and Eduardo B. Fernandez. The Authenticator Pattern. In *PLoP*, 1999.
32. William J. Brown, Raphael C. Malveau, William H. Brown, Hays W. McCormick, and Thomas J. Mowbray. *AntiPatterns: Refactoring Software, Architectures, and Projects in Crisis*. John Wiley & Sons, 1998.
33. BSI. IT Baseline Protection Manual. Bundesamt für Sicherheit in der Informationstechnik, Bundesanzeiger, 2002.
34. Johannes Buchmann. *Einführung in die Kryptographie*. Springer-Verlag, 2nd edition, 2001. ISBN 3-540-41283-2.
35. Frank Buschmann, Regine Meunier, Hans Rohnert, Peter Sommerlad, and Michael Stal. *Pattern-Oriented Software Architecture: A System of Patterns*. John Wiley & Sons, 1996.
36. CERT-AU. Australian Computer Emergency Response Team. http://www.auscert.org.au. Accessed: January 2003.
37. CERT/CC. CERT Coordination Center. http://www.cert.org. Accessed: January 2003.
38. CERT/CC. CERT/CC Statistics 1988-2002. http://www.cert.org/stats/cert_stats.html. Accessed: January 2003.

39. CERT/CC. Incident Notes. http://www.cert.org/incident_notes. Accessed: January 2003.
40. CERT/CC. Survivability Research and Analysis. http://www.cert.org/nav/index_purple.html. Accessed: February 2003.
41. CERT/CC. Vulnerability Notes. http://www.cert.org/vul_notes. Accessed: January 2003.
42. CERT/CC. Vulnerability Notes Database. http://www.kb.cert.org/vuls. Accessed: January 2003.
43. B. Chandrasekaran, J.R. Josephson, and V. Richard Benjamins. Ontology of Tasks and Methods. In Proceedings of the 11th Knowledge Acquisition Modeling and Management Workshop (KAW), Banff, Canada, April 1998.
44. D. Brent Chapman and Elizabeth D. Zwicky. *Building Internet Firewalls.* O'Reilly & Associates, Inc., 1995.
45. V. K. Chaudri, A. Farquhar, R. Fikes, P. D. Karp, and J. P. Rice. Open Knowledge Base Connectivity 2.0. Knowledge Systems Laboratory, Stanford University, January 1998.
46. James R. Chiles. *Inviting Disaster : Lessons from the Edge of Technology.* HarperBusiness, 2001.
47. CIAC. Computer Incident Advisory Capability. http://www.ciac.org/ciac/. Accessed: January 2003.
48. Peter Coad. Object-oriented patterns. *Communications of the ACM*, 35(9):152–159, 1992.
49. James O. Coplien. *Advanced C++ Programming Styles and Idioms.* Addison-Wesley, 1991.
50. James O. Coplien and Douglas C. Schmidt, editors. *Pattern Languages of Program Design.* Addison-Wesley, 1995.
51. Oscar Corcho, Mariano Fernández-López, and Asunción Gómez-Pérez. Ontoweb - technical roadmap v1.0. Technical report, Universidad Politécnica de Madrid, 2001. OntoWeb Consortium, Commission of the European Communities, Project IST-2000-29243.
52. Oscar Corcho and Asunción Gómez-Pérez. Evaluating Knowledge Representation and Reasoning Capabilities of Ontology Specification Languages. Proceedings of the ECAI'00 Workshop on Applications of Ontologies and Problem Solving Methods. Berlin. Germany., August 2000.
53. Countermeasures Corporation. The Buddy System. http://www.buddysystem.net/html/product.shtml. Accessed: March 2003.
54. Ward Cunningham. History of patterns. http://c2.com/cgi-bin/wiki?HistoryOfPatterns, October 2001.
55. Curtis E. Dalton and William Kannengeisser. Instant Headache. *Information Security Magazine*, 5(8):32–41, August 2002.
56. N. Damianou, N. Dulay, E. Lupu, and M. Sloman. The Ponder Policy Specification Language. In *POLICY 2001*, Lecture Notes on Computer Science, pages 18–38. Springer Verlag, January 2001.
57. Ferdinand de Saussure. *Course in General Linguistics.* Gerald Duckworth & Co. Ltd., 1983 [1916].
58. Grit Denker. Access Control and Data Integrity for DAML+OIL and DAML-S. Specification and Analysis of Secure Cryptographic Protocols, Dagstuhl Seminar 01391, 2001.
59. Renaud Deraison. The Nessus Security Scanner. http://www.nessus.org. Accessed: March 2003.
60. Anind K. Dey. Understanding and Using Context. *Personal and Ubiquitous Computing, Special issue on Situated Interaction and Ubiquitous Computing*, 5(1), 2001.

61. Anind K. Dey and Gregory D. Abowd. Towards a Better Understanding of Context and Context-Awareness. In *CHI 2000 Workshop on The What, Who, Where, When, and How of Context-Awareness*, April 2000. The Hague, Netherlands.

62. DFN-CERT. Zentrum für sichere Netzdienste. http://www.cert.dfn.de. Accessed: January 2003.

63. Jana Dittmann. *Digitale Wasserzeichen*. Springer-Verlag, 2000. ISBN 3-540-66661-3.

64. John Domingue. Webonto. http://kmi.open.ac.uk/projects/webonto/. Accessed: March 2003.

65. John Domingue. Tadzebao and WebOnto: Discussing, Browsing, and Editing Ontologies on the Web. In Proc. of the 11th Knowledge Acquisition for Knowledge-Based Systems Workshop, April 18th-23rd. Banff, Canada., 1998.

66. John Domingue, Enrico Motta, and Oscar Corcho Garcia. *Knowledge Modelling in WebOnto and OCML. A User Guide. Version 2.4*. The Open University - Knowlege Media Institute (KMI), 1999.

67. Dietrich Dorner. *The Logic of Failure: Recognizing and Avoiding Errors in Complex Situations*. Addison Wesley, 1989.

68. John Durkin. *Expert Systems - Design and Development*. Macmillan Publishing Company, 1994.

69. Claudia Eckert. Matching Security Policies to Application Needs. In *Proc. of the IFIP TC11 11th International Conference on Information Security*, pages 237–254, 1995.

70. Claudia Eckert. Leitlinien zur Klassifikation und Bewertung von Sicherheitsmodellen. In *Fachtagung Sicherheit in Informationssystemen (SIS)*, 1996.

71. Claudia Eckert. *IT-Sicherheit. Konzepte, Verfahren, Protokolle*. Oldenbourg, 2001.

72. Horst Ehmke, Elisabeth Giessler, Rainer Prinoth, Thomas Schroeder, and Markus Schumacher. Basic Security Service Layer. Patent registration – Europe, Japan, USA, 2000.

73. Ben Elsinga and Aaldert Hofmann. Security Paradigm Pattern Language. In *Proc. of the 8th European Conference on Pattern Languages of Programs (EuroPLoP)*, 2003. To appear.

74. Ben Elsinga and Aaldert Hofmann. Security Taxonomy Pattern Language. In *Proc. of the 8th European Conference on Pattern Languages of Programs (EuroPLoP)*, 2003. To appear.

75. Information technology security evaluation criteria. Department of Trade and Industry, London, 1991.

76. Simone Everding. Angriffe auf CORBA-basierte Systeme. Master's thesis, Darmstadt University of Technology, 2001.

77. Andreas Faatz, Cornelia Seeberg, and Ralf Steinmetz. Ontology Enrichment with Texts from the WWW. In *European Conference on Machine Learning - Semantic Web Mining*, 2002.

78. Andreas Faatz and Ralf Steinmetz. Statistical Profiles of Words for Ontology Enrichment. In *Statistical Profiles of Words for Ontology Enrichment (SMPS)*. Springer Verlag, 2002.

79. A. Farquhar, R. Fikes, and J. Rice. The Ontolingua Server: A Tool for Collaborative Ontology Construction. Knowledge Systems Laboratory, Stanford University, September 1996.

80. FedCIRC. The Federal Computer Incident Response Center. http://www.fedcirc.gov. Accessed: January 2003.

81. D. Fensel, I. Horrocks, F. Van Harmelen, S. Decker, M. Erdmann, and M. Klein. OIL in a nutshell. In R. Dieng, editor, *Proceedings of the 12th European Workshop on Knowledge Acquisition, Modeling, and Management (EKAW)*, number 1937 in Lecture Notes in Artificial Intelligence, pages 1–16. Springer-Verlag, 2000.

82. Dieter Fensel, Ian Horrocks, Frank van Harmelen, Deborah L. McGuinness, and Peter F. Patel-Schneider. OIL: An Ontology Infrastructure for the Semantic Web. *IEEE Intelligent Systems*, 16(2), 2001.

83. E. B. Fernandez and J. C. Hawkins. Determining Role Rights from Use Cases. In *ACM Workshop on Role-Based Access Control*, pages 121–125, 1997.

84. Eduardo B. Fernandez. Metadata and Authorization Patterns. Technical report, Florida Atlantic University, 2000.

85. Eduardo B. Fernandez and Rouyi Pan. A Pattern Language for Security Models. Technical report, Florida Atlantic University, 2001. PLoP.

86. Mariano Fernández, Asunción Gómez-Pérez, and Natalia Juristo. METHONTOLOGY: From Ontological Art Towards Ontological Engineering. Workshop on Ontological Engineering. Spring Symposium Series, AAAI. Stanford, California, USA., 1997.

87. Mariano Fernández-López, Asunción Gómez-Pérez, and J. Pazos-Sierra. Building a Chemical Ontology Using METHONTOLOGY and the Ontology Design Environment. *IEEE Intelligent Systems and their applications*, 4(1):37–45, 1999.

88. Robert Filman and Ted Linden. SafeBots: A Paradigm for Software Security Controls. In Proc. of the New Security Paradigms Workshop, UCLA Conference, Lake Arrowhead, California, USA, September 1996.

89. Stephan Fischer, Christoph Rensing, and Utz Roedig. *Open Internet Security*. Springer Verlag, 2000.

90. Stephan Fischer, Achim Steinacker, Reinhard Bertram, and Ralf Steinmetz. *Open Security*. Springer Verlag, March 98. ISBN 3-540646-54-X.

91. Robert Flanders and Eduardo B. Fernandez. Data Filter Architecture Pattern. In *PLoP*, 1999.

92. The Information Security Forum. Standard of Good Practice. http://www.isfsecuritystandard.com, 2000.

93. Erich Gamma, Richard Helm, Ralph Johnson, and John Vlissides. *Design Patterns: Elements of Reusable Object-Oriented Software*. Addison-Wesley, 1995.

94. Ludger Göckel. Sicherheitsaspekte von Windows NT. Master's thesis, Darmstadt University of Technology, 2000.

95. Holger Giese. Safety Critical Computer Systems - Related Areas. Slides of the Safety Critical Computer Systems Course, 2002. University of Paderborn, Department of Computer Science.

96. Ontoprise GmbH. *How to Write F-Logic Programs*, 2002. Version 1.8.

97. Andreas Goerlach. Ontology-based Knowledge Representation with Security Patterns. Master's thesis, Darmstadt University of Technology, 2002.

98. Stephan Grill. A Framework for Comparing and Querying Certification Practice Statements. In M. Schumacher and R. Steinmetz, editors, *Sicherheit in Netzen und Medienströmen*, Informatik aktuell, pages 83–93. Gesellschaft für Informatik, Springer Verlag, 2000.

99. Carsten Griwodz. Video protection by partial content corruption. In *Proceedings of the Workshop Multimedia and Security at ACM Multimedia*, 1998.

100. Carsten Griwodz. *Wide-area True Video-on-Demand by a Decentralized Cache-based Distribution Infrastructure*. PhD thesis, Darmstadt University of Technology, 2000.

101. Carsten Griwodz, Oliver Merkel, Jana Dittmann, and Ralf Steinmetz. Protecting VoD the Easier Way. In *Proc. of ACM Multimedia*, pages 21–28, 1998.

102. M. Grüninger and M. S. Fox. Methodology for the Design and Evaluation of Ontologies. Workshop on Basic Ontological Issues in Knowledge Sharing, 1995. Montreal, Canada.
103. Achim Gärtner, Jörg Kleinz, and Klaus Reichenberger. Intelligent views - k-infinity. http://www.i-views.de/web/produkt.html. Accessed: March 2003.
104. Tom R. Gruber. A Translation Approach to Portable Ontology Specifications. *Knowledge Acquisition*, 5(2):199–220, 1993.
105. Tom R. Gruber. Toward Principles of the Design of Ontologies Used for Knowledge Sharing. International Journal of Human Computer Studies, 1995.
106. Neil B. Harrison. The Language of Shepherding, A Pattern Language for Shepherds and Sheep. In *Proceedings of the 6th Conference on Pattern Languages of Programs (PLoP)*, 1999.
107. Christian Haul, Markus Schumacher, and Michael Hurler. A Survey on Vulnerability Databases. Technical report, Darmstadt University of Technology, October 2000.
108. Viviane Hays, Marc Loutrel, and Eduardo B. Fernandez. The Object Filter and Access Control Framework. In *PLoP*, 2000.
109. Jeff Heflin. Computer Science Department Ontology. http://www.cs.umd.edu/projects/plus/SHOE/onts/cs1.1.html, 2000. Version 1.1.
110. Ronda R. Henning. Use of the Zachman Architecture for Security Engineering. In Proceedings of the 19th National Information Systems Security Conference (NISSC), 1996.
111. Mark Heuser and Eduardo B. Fernandez. RPC Client: A Pattern for the Client-Side Implementation of a Pipelined Request/Response Protocol. In *PLoP*, 1999.
112. David Hilbert. *Die Grundlagen der Mathematik*. Hamburger Mathematische Einzelschriften 5, Teubner, Leipzig, 1928. Reprinted in English translation in van Heijenoort [1967].
113. Matthias Hollick. The Evolution of Mobile IP Towards Security. In *Sicherheit in Netzen und Medienströmen, Tagungsband des GI-Workshops "Sicherheit in Mediendaten"*, pages 38–49. Springer, September 2000. ISBN 3-540-67926-X.
114. Matthias Hollick. Secure Service Centered Networking for Nomadic Usage. In *Proceedings of Communications and Multimedia Security Issues of the New Century, IFIP TC6 / TC11 Joint Working Conference on Communications and Multimedia Security (CMS'01), Darmstadt, Germany*, pages 375–380. Kluwer Academic Publishers Boston/Dordecht/London, May 2001. ISBN 0-7923-7365-0.
115. Clyde W. Holsapple and K. D. Joshi. A collaborative Approach to Ontology Design. *Communications of the ACM*, 45(2):42–47, 2002.
116. Siegfried Hoppe-Graff and Barbara Keller, editors. *Philip G. Zimbardo: Psychologie*. Springer-Verlag, 5th edition, 1992.
117. HRZ. It security policy der tu darmstadt. http://www.tu-darmstadt.de/hrz/security/policy.tud. Accessed: March 2003.
118. Michael Hurler. Sec://House - A Data Warehouse for Software Vulnerabilities. Master's thesis, Darmstadt University of Technology, 2000.
119. Duane Hybertson, Jody Heaney, and Ann Reedy. Conceptual Aspects of Security Patterns. 7th European Conference on Pattern Languages of Programs (EuroPLoP), 2002. Focus Group "Thinking about Security Patterns".
120. Duane Hybertson, Jody Heaney, and Ann Reedy. Strategy for Automated Identification and Authentication. 7th European Conference on Pattern Languages of Programs (EuroPLoP), 2002. Focus Group "Thinking about Security Patterns".

121. ISO/IEC. Common Criteria for Information Technology Security Evaluation Criteria - Part 1: Introduction and general model. ISO/IEC 15408, 1999. Version 2.1.

122. ISO/IEC. Common Criteria for Information Technology Security Evaluation Criteria - Part 2: Security functional requirements. ISO/IEC 15408, 1999. Version 2.1.

123. ISO/IEC. Information Technology - Code of Practice for Information Security Management. ISO/IEC 17799, 2000.

124. ISO/IEC. Software Engineering - Product Quality. International Standard ISO/IEC 9126, 2001.

125. ISX Corporation. *Loom User's Guide for Loom version 1.4*, August 1991.

126. Peter Jackson. *Introduction to Expert Systems*. Addison-Wesley, 3rd edition, 1998.

127. Dean Jones, Trevor Bench-Capon, and Pepijn Visser. Methodologies for Ontology Development. In Proc. IT&KNOWS Conference, XV IFIP World Computer Congress, Budapest, August 1998.

128. Jan Jürjens. UMLsec: Extending UML for Secure Systems Development. 5th International Conference on the Unified Modeling Language (UML), 2002.

129. Thomas Kamps. *Diagram Design. A Constructive Theory*. Springer-Verlag, 1999. ISBN 3-540-65439-9.

130. R. Karp, V. Chaudri, and J. Thomere. XOL: an XML-based Ontology Exchange Language, July 1999.

131. KBSI. The IDEF5 Ontology Description Capture Methdo Overview. Technical report, KBSI Report, Texas, 1994.

132. Norman L. Kerth and Ward Cunningham. Using Patterns to Improve Our Architectural Vision. *IEEE Software*, 14(1):53–59, January 1997.

133. Michael Kifer, Georg Lausen, and James Wu. Logical Foundations of Object-Oriented and Frame-Based Languages. *Journal of the ACM*, 42(4):741–843, 1995.

134. Henry Kim. Predicting how Ontologies for the Semantic Web will evolve. *Communications of the ACM*, 45(2):48–54, 2002.

135. Jan Kümmerle. Instant Messaging. Technical report, Darmstadt University of Technology, 2001. Proc. of the Seminar "Information and Communication".

136. Eric Knight. Computer Vulnerabilities. Technical report, Security-Paradigm.com, 2000.

137. Bernd Kortmann. *Linguistik: Essentials*. Cornelsen Verlag, Berlin, 1999.

138. Klaus-Peter Kossakowski. *Information Technology Incident Response Capabilities*. PhD thesis, University of Hamburg, 2000.

139. Ivan Victor Krsul. *Software Vulnerability Analysis*. PhD thesis, Purdue University, USA, 1998.

140. Thomas Kunkelmann. *Sicherheit in Videodaten*. Vieweg Verlag, 1998. ISBN 3-528-05680-0.

141. Stanford University Knowledge Systems Laboratory. Ontolingua. http://www.ksl.stanford.edu/software/ontolingua/. Accessed: March 2003.

142. Thorsten Lamby. Ein Patternsystem für sichere Zahlungssysteme. Master's thesis, Darmstadt University of Technology, 2001.

143. Leslie Lamport. How to write a proof. *American Mathematical Monthly*, 102(7):600–608, 1995.

144. J.C. Laprie. *Dependability: Basic Concepts and Terminology*. Springer Verlag, 1991.

145. Doug Lea. Patterns-Discussion FAQ. http://gee.cs.oswego.edu/dl/pd-FAQ/pd-FAQ.html. Accessed: January 2003.

146. Doug Lea. Christopher Alexander: An Introduction for Object-Oriented Designers. ACM Software Engineering Notes, January 1994.
147. Sami Lehtonen and Juha Pärssinen. A Pattern Language for Cryptographic Key Management. In *Proc. of the 7th European Conference on Pattern Languages of Programs (EuroPLoP)*, 2002. revised version.
148. D. B. Lenat and R. V. Guha. *Building large knowledge-based systems*. Addison-Wesley Publishing Company, Inc., 1990.
149. Jörn Loviscach. Harte Kost - Perspektiven fürs Informatikstudium. *c't - Magazin für Computertechnik*, 2001(21), 2001. Heise Zeitschriften Verlag.
150. R. MacGregor. Inside the LOOM classifier. *SIGART bulletin*, 2(3):70–76, June 1991.
151. David Mazieres and M. Frans Kaashoek. The Design, Implementation and Operation of an Email Pseudonym Server. 5th ACM Conference on Computer and Communications Security, 1998.
152. John McHugh. Quantitative Measures of Assurance: Prophecy, Process or Pipedream? Technical report, CERT/CC Software Engineering Institute, Carnegie Mellon University, Januar 2001.
153. Gerard Meszaros and Jim Doble. A Pattern Language for Pattern Writing. http://hillside.net/patterns/Writing/patterns.html, 1996.
154. Microsoft. Trustworthy Computing for IT. http://www.microsoft.com/technet/security. Accessed: March 2003.
155. SUN Microsystems. Security Code Guidelines. http://java.sun.com/security/seccodeguide.html. Accessed: January 2003.
156. I. Morikawa, M. Minoura, K. Fukuda, S. Tomoyasu, and Markus Schumacher. Security Platform for OSS Interconnection. In *Proc. of the 4th Asia-Pacific Network Operations and Management Symposium (APNOMS)*, 2000. Nara, Japan.
157. Enrico Motta. *Reusable Components for Knowledge Modelling - Case Studies in Parametric Design Problem Solving*. Frontiers in Artificial Intelligence and Applications. IOS Press, Amsterdam, Netherlands, 1999.
158. Thomas J. Mowbray and Raphael C. Malveau. *CORBA Design Patterns*. John Wiley & Sons, 1997.
159. NCSA. Secure Programming Guidelines. http://archive.ncsa.uiuc.edu/General/Grid/ACES/security/programming/. Accessed: January 2003.
160. Peter G. Neumann. *Computer Related Risks*. ACM Press, 1995.
161. Fernando Das Neves and Alejandra Garrido. *Pattern Languages of Programs III*, chapter Bodyguard (13). Addison- Wesley, 1998.
162. A. Newell and H. A. Simon. *Human Problem Solving*. Prentice-Hall, 1972.
163. Sergei Nirenburg and Victor Raskin. *Ontological Semantics*. forthcoming, 2003. http://crl.nmsu.edu/Staff.pages/Technical/sergei/book/.
164. NIST. ICAT Metabase: A CVE Based Vulnerability Database. http://icat.nist.gov/icat.cfm. Accessed: January 2003.
165. James Noble. Classifying relationships between object-oriented design patterns, 1998. In Australian Software Engineering Conference (ASWEC).
166. N. F. Noy, R. W. Fergerson, and M. A. Musen. The Knowledge Model of Protégé-2000: Combining Interoperability and Flexibility. 2th International Conference on Knowledge Engineering and Knowledge Management (EKAW), Juan-les-Pins, France, 2000.
167. N. F. Noy, M. Sintek, S. Decker, M. Crubézy, R. W. Fergerson, and M. A. Musen. Creating Semantic Web Contents with Protégé-2000. *IEEE Intelligent Systems*, 16(2):60–71, 2001. Formerly titled, "One Size Does Fit All: Acquiring Semantic Web Contents with Protégé-2000.".

168. Natalya F. Noy and Deborah L. McGuiness. A Guide to Creating Your First Ontology. Technical Report SMI-2001-0880, Stanford University, Stanford, California, 2001.

169. Marios Padelis, Markus Schumacher, Marco Voss, and Ikuya Morikawa. Basic Security Service Layer for Secure OSS Interconnection. In *Proc. of the 5th Asia-Pacific Network Operations and Management Symposium (APNOMS)*, 2001. Sydney, Australia.

170. Henry Petroski. *To Engineer Is Human : The Role of Failure in Successful Design.* Vintage Books USA, 1992.

171. Urban Petry. Ein Bewertungsverfahren für Verletzbarkeiten in IT Systemen. Master's thesis, Darmstadt University of Technology, 2001.

172. Charles P. Pfleeger. *Security in Computing.* Prentice-Hall International, 1997.

173. Kevin Poulsen. Hijackers take AIM accounts. http://online. securityfocus.com/news/119, 2000. Security Focus Online.

174. Frank Puppe. *Einführung in Expertensystemen.* Springer-Verlag, 2nd edition, 1991.

175. Jock Rader. A Look at Measures of Computer Security from an Insurance Premium Perspective. Technical report, Raytheon Electronic Systems, April 2001.

176. Marcus J. Ranum. 7 things i've learned - lessons from 15 years on the front lines. *Information Security Magazine*, 2002(7), 2002.

177. Viktor Raskin, Christian F. Hempelmann, Katrina E. Triezenberg, and Sergej Nirenburg. Ontology in Information Security: A Useful Theoretical Foundation and Methodological Tool. In Viktor Raskin and Christian F. Hempelmann, editors, *Proceedings of the New Security Paradigms Workshop, New York.* ACM, 2001.

178. Christoph Rensing, Ralf Ackermann, Utz Roedig, Lars Wolf, and Ralf Steinmetz. Sicherheitsunterstützung für Internet Telefonie. In *DuD-Fachbeiträge Sicherheitsinfrastrukturen*, pages 285–296, March 1999. ISBN 3-528-05709-2.

179. Christoph Rensing, Martin Karsten, and Ralf Steinmetz. Darstellung der Sicherheitsattribute von Kommunikationsbeziehungen mittels UML. In *Enterprise Security*, pages 132–143. Patrick Horster, 2002. ISBN: 3-936052-03-4.

180. Christoph Rensing, Utz Roedig, Ralf Ackermann, and Ralf Steinmetz. A Survey of Requirements and Standardization Efforts for IP-Telephony-Security. In *Proceedings of the Workshop "Sicherheit in Netzen und Medienströmen"*, pages 50–60, September 2000. ISSN 1431-472-X.

181. Eric Rescorla. Security Holes ... Who cares? Technical report, RTFM, Inc., 2002.

182. RFC. Internet Security Glossary. RFC 2828, 2000. The Internet Society.

183. Dirk Riehle, Ward Cunningham, Joe Bergin, Norm Kerth, and Steve Metsker. Password Patterns. In *Proc. of the 7th European Conference on Pattern Languages of Programs (EuroPLoP)*, 2002.

184. Riskwatch. Risk watch 17799. http://www.riskwatch.com/pdfs/rw17799. pdf. Accessed: March 2003.

185. Utz Roedig. *Firewall-Architekturen für Multimedia-Applikationen.* PhD thesis, Darmstadt University of Technology, 2002.

186. Utz Roedig, Ralf Ackermann, and Ralf Steinmetz. IP-Telefonie und Firewalls, Probleme und Lösungen. *Praxis in der Informationsverarbeitung und Kommunikation (PIK)*, 1(24):32–40, January 2001.

187. Sasha Romanosky. Enterprise Security Patterns. In *Proc. of EuroPLoP*, 2002.

188. RUS-CERT. DV-Sicherheit an der Universität Stuttgart. http://cert.uni-stuttgart.de. Accessed: January 2003.

189. Theopoula Sairaki. Automatisierte forensische und präventive Sicherheits-analysen. Master's thesis, Darmstadt University of Technology, 2001.

190. Heinz Sarbinowski. SKe - Durchgängige Sicherheitskonzeption mit dynamis-chen Kontrollmechanismen für eService Prozesse. Fraunhofer-Gesellschaft, 2002.

191. Jürgen Schmidt. Wurm im Kazaa-Netz. http://www.heise.de/newsticker/data/ju-19.05.02-000/, May 2002. Heise Online News.

192. B. Schneier and D. Mudge. Cryptanalysis of Microsoft's Point-to-Point Tun-neling Protocol (PPTP). In *Fifth ACM Conference on Communications and Computer Security*, pages 132–141, March 1998.

193. Bruce Schneier. Attack Trees. *Doctor Dobb's Journal*, pages 21–29, December 1999.

194. Bruce Schneier. *Secrets and Lies - Digital Security in a Networked World.* John Wiley and Sons, 2000.

195. Bruce Schneier. A Cyber UL? Crypto-Gram Newsletter, Januar 2001.

196. Hans-Peter Schnurr, Steffen Staab, Rudi Studer, and York Sure. Ontolo-giebasiertes Wissensmanagement - Ein umfassender Ansatz zur Gestaltung des Knowledge Life Cycle. Unpublished Technical Report, Januar 2001.

197. A. Th. Schreiber, B. J. Wielinga, R. de Hoog, J. M Akkermans, and W. Van de Velde. CommonKADS: A comprehensive Methodology for KBS Develop-ment. *IEEE Expert*, 9(6):28–37, 1994.

198. M. Schumacher, C. Haul, M. Hurler, and A. Buchmann. Data Mining in Schwachstellendatenbanken. In *DFN Report Nr. 90*, Hamburg, Germay, 2000. DFN-CERT.

199. Markus Schumacher. Aktuelles Schlagwort - Security Patterns. *Informatik Spektrum*, 25(3):220–223, June 2002.

200. Markus Schumacher. Security Patterns and Security Standards. In *In Proc. of the 7th European Conference on Pattern Languages of Programs (EuroPLoP)*, 2002.

201. Markus Schumacher. Thinking about Security Patterns. In *Proc. of the 7th European Conference on Pattern Languages of Programs (EuroPLoP)*, 2002. Focus Group Report.

202. Markus Schumacher. Collaborative design of a security core ontology - eval-uation results. Technical report, Darmstadt University of Technology, 2003.

203. Markus Schumacher, Ralf Ackermann, and Ralf Steinmetz. Towards Security at all Phases of a Systems Lifecycle. In *SoftCom 2000 International Conference on Software, Telecommunications and Computer Networks, Split*, pages 11–19, October 2000.

204. Markus Schumacher, Eduardo Fernandez, Duane Hybertson, and Frank Buschmann, editors. *Security Patterns - Integrating Security and Systems En-gineering.* John Wiley and Sons, 2004. To appear.

205. Markus Schumacher and Klaus-Peter Kossakowski. Prioritization of Computer Security Vulnerabilities. Technical report, Darmstadt University of Technology, 2002.

206. Markus Schumacher, Marie-Luise Moschgath, and Utz Rödig. Angewandte In-formationssicherheit: Ein Hacker-Praktikum an Universitäten. *Informatik Spek-trum*, 6(23):202–211, June 2000.

207. Markus Schumacher, Utz Rödig, and Marie-Luise Moschgath. *Hacker Contest - Sicherheitsprobleme, Lösungen, Beispiele.* Xpert.press. Springer Verlag, 2002. ISBN 3-540-41164-X.

208. Markus Schumacher and Utz Roedig. Security Engineering with Patterns. In Proc. of the 8th Conference on Pattern Languages of Programming (PLoP), 2001.

209. Winn Schwartau. *Time Based Security*. Interpact Press, Seminole Florida, 1999.
210. Project Team 5: Security and Trust on the Internet. A Comparative Study of IT Security Criteria. Initiative D21, 2001.
211. SecurityFocus. BugTraq - Frequently Asked Questions. http://online. securityfocus.com/popups/forums/bugtraq/faq.shtml. Accessed: February 2003.
212. SecurityFocus. Bugtraq Mailing List. http://online.securityfocus.com/ archive/. Accessed: January 2003.
213. SecurityFocus. Bugtraq Vulnerability Database. http://www.securityfocus. com/corporate/products/vdb/. Accessed: January 2003.
214. Cornelia Seeberg. *Life Long Learning. Modulare Wissensbasen für elektronische Lernumgebungen*. Springer-Verlag, 2002. ISBN 3-540-43618-9.
215. A. Seffah and H. Javahery. On the Usability of Usability Patterns. CHI Patterns Workshop, 2002. Position Paper.
216. Sarah A. Sheard. Twelve Systems Engineering Roles. Proceedings of INCOSE, 1996.
217. H. Simon. The Structure of ill-structured Problems, 1973. Artificial Intelligence (4).
218. Richard E. Smith. *Internet Cryptography*. Addison Wesley, 1997.
219. J. F. Sowa and John. A. Zachman. Extending and Formalizing the Framework for Information Systems Architecture. *IBM Systems Journal*, 31(3), 1992.
220. Steffen Staab, Hans-Peter Schnurr, Rudi Studer, and York Sure. Knowledge Processes and Ontologies. *IEEE Intelligent Systems*, 16(1), 2001.
221. Achim Steinacker. *Medienbausteine für web-basierte Lernsysteme*. PhD thesis, Darmstadt University of Technology, 2002.
222. Ralf Steinmetz. *Multimedia Technologie*. Springer-Verlag, 2nd edition, 1999.
223. Ralf Steinmetz, Ralf Ackermann, Utz Rödig, Manuel Görtz, and Markus Schumacher. IP-Telefonie: Protokolle, Herausforderungen, Lösungen und kritische Analyse der Sicherheit. *Presentation Series - Arbeitsgemeinschaft des VDE Rhein-Main*, 2002.
224. G. Stone and G. Xie. Network Policy Languages: A Survey and a New Approach. *IEEE Network*, 15(1), January 2001.
225. B. Swartout, P. Ramesh, K. Knight, and T. Russ. Toward Distributed Use of Large-Scale Ontologies. Workshop on Ontological Engineering. Spring Symposium Series, AAAI. Stanford, California, USA, 1997.
226. Internet Security Systems. Vulnerability Assessment. http://www.iss.net/ products_services/enterprise_protection/vulnerabilit%y_assessment/. Accessed: January 2003.
227. Internet Security Systems. X-Force Database. http://xforce.iss.net. Accessed: January 2003.
228. Amalia Todirascu. *Semantic Indexing for Information Retrieval Systems*. PhD thesis, University Louis Pasteur, 2001.
229. Unitel. Alert Mailing List. http://www.unitel.cx/services/alert.html. Accessed: January 2003.
230. M. Uschold and M. Grüninger. Ontologies: Principles, Methods, and Applications. Knowledge Engineering Review Vol. 2, 1996.
231. M. Uschold and M. King. Towards a Methodology for Building Ontologies. Workshop on Basic Ontological Issues in Knowledge Sharing, 1995. Montreal, Canada.
232. John Viega, J.T. Bloch, Tadayoshi Kohno, and Gary McGraw. ITS4 : A Static Vulnerability Scanner for C and C++ Code. Annual Computer Security Applications Conference, 2000.

233. VIGILANTe.   SecureScan   Homepage.   `http://www.vigilante.com/securescan/`. Accessed: 2001.
234. Markus Voelter. Pedagocial patterns project. OOPSLA Workshop: Pattern Refactoring, 2000. Position Paper.
235. Markus Voelter and Joseph Bergin. Results from EuroPLoP '01 BoF Merging Pattern Languages. `http://www.voelter.de`, 2001.
236. W3C. RDF Primer. Working Draft, November 2002.
237. WebODE. Ontology Engineering Platform. `http://delicias.dia.fi.upm.es/webODE/`. Accessed: March 2003.
238. David A. Wheeler. Secure Programming for Linux and Unix HOWTO. `http://www.tldp.org/HOWTO/Secure-Programs-HOWTO/`. Accessed: January 2003, version 3.005.
239. Gio Wiederhold. Interoperation, Mediation, and Ontologies. In *Proc. of the International Symposium on Fifth Generation Computer Systems (FGCS), Workshop on Heterogeneous Cooperative Knowledge-Bases, Tokyo, Japan*, volume W3, pages 33–48, 1994.
240. Jeannette M. Wing. A Symbiotic Relationship between Formal methods and Security. In *Workshops on Computer Security, Fault Tolerance, and Software Assurance: From Needs to Solution*, 1998.
241. Ennet S. Yee. Security Metrology and the Monty Hall Problem. Position paper, University Of California, San Diego, April 2001.
242. Joseph Yoder and Jeffrey Barcalow. Architectural Patterns for Enabling Application Security. *PLoP*, 1997.
243. John A. Zachman. A Framework for Information Systems Architecture. *IBM Systems Journal*, 26(3), 1987.
244. Z. Zdrahal and J. Domingue. The World Wide Design Lab: an Environment for Collaborative Distributed Design. In Proc. of the 11th International Conference on Engineering Design, Tampere, Finland, 1997.
245. ZID. Security Policy der TU Wien. `http://www.zid.tuwien.at/security/policy.php`. Accessed: March 2003.
246. Walter Zimmer. Relationships between Design Patterns. In J. Coplien and D. Schmidt, editors, *Pattern Languages of Program Design*, pages 345–364, 1994.

Index

Lecture Notes in Computer Science

For information about Vols. 1–2674
please contact your bookseller or Springer-Verlag